VEDIC TEXTS:
A Revision

Professor C. G. KASHIKAR

यस्मात्कोशादुदभराम वेदं तस्मिन्नन्तरव दध्म एनम् ।

Out of what receptacle we bore up the Veda,
within that do we set it down !

Atharvaveda XIX.72.1

VEDIC TEXTS:
A Revision

PROF. C.G. KASHIKAR FELICITATION VOLUME

Editors

T.N. DHARMADHIKARI R.S. SHASTRI

N. P. JAIN

Managing Editor

S.S. BAHULKAR

Foreword by

PROF. R.N. DANDEKAR

Bhandarkar Oriental Research Institute, Pune

MOTILAL BANARSIDASS PUBLISHERS

PVT. LTD. • DELHI

First Edition: Delhi, 1990

ISBN: 81-208-0806-1

Also available at:
MOTILAL BANARSIDASS
41 U.A., Bungalow Road, Jawahar Nagar, Delhi 110 007
120 Royapettah High Road, Mylapore, Madras 600 004
24 Race Course Road, Bangalore 560 001
Ashok Rajpath, Patna 800 004
Chowk, Varanasi 221 001

DTP Typesetting by Dnyana Mudra, Jñāna Prabodhini Bhavan,
510 Sadashiv Peth, Pune 411 030

PRINTED IN INDIA
BY JAINENDRA PRAKASH JAIN AT SHRI JAINENDRA PRESS, A-45 NARAINA INDUSTRIAL AREA, PHASE I, NEW DELHI 110 028 AND PUBLISHED BY NARENDRA PRAKASH JAIN FOR MOTILAL BANARSIDASS PUBLISHERS PVT. LTD., BUNGALOW ROAD, JAWAHAR NAGAR, DELHI 110 007

CONTENTS

PART I

PART II

PREFACE

The editors feel extremely delighted to write this Preface to the Felicitation Volume in honour of Prof. C. G. Kashikar, being brought out by the well-known house of indological publishers, M/s. Motilal Banarasidass, Delhi. This Volume is an outcome of the work of preparing critical editions of Vedic texts, being carried out by various scholars in India. It is Pt. Radhey Shyam Shastri, one of the editors of this Volume, who is instrumental in mooting the idea of preparing a specimen volume of the initial portions of the forthcoming critical editions of the Vedic texts and presenting it to Prof. C. G. Kashikar on the occasion of his eightieth birth-anniversary, as a token of the gratitude on the part of the contributors to this volume, who have been much benefited—directly or indirectly—by Prof. Kashikar's profound scholarship in the field of Vedic ritualistic studies. The editors sincerely hope that the present volume will fulfil their twin desire of honouring the scholar of international repute that Prof. Kashikar is and of presenting the specimens of the critical editions to the Vedic scholars from India and abroad for their valuable suggestions, comments and criticism. At the same time, the editors are fully aware of the shortcomings in the present volume due to the limitations of the printing process and constraint of time.

The editors are grateful to Prof. R. N. Dandekar for writing a Foreword to this volume inspite of his busy schedule and heavy pressure of work. Thanks are also due to the scholars who have contributed their articles to this volume. A special mention must be made of Prof. K. S. Arjunwadkar, an erudite Sanskrit scholar himself, who undertook the difficult work of typesetting of the Vedic texts, took keen interest in seeing the publication through and completed the work of typesetting with utmost care. Finally, the editors are thankful to M/s. Motilal Banarasidass who undertook the publication of the present volume and brought it out within a considerably short time.

Editors

SPECIAL NOTE

Since 1987, I have been running a project of preparing the critical editions of some Vedic works with consultation of Dr. C. G. Kashikar.. The editing costs of most of the works presented here are being met with by Shri R. N. Singh, Gauhati and his friends Shri H. K. Gupta, Delhi; Shri R. K. Agrawal, Tinsukia; Shri Dr. G. L Saraf, Gauhati and Shri H. P. Budhia, Calcutta. My sincere thanks are due to all these generous souls.

I am also very much grateful to Shri N. P. Jain of M/s. Motilal Banarsidass, Delhi for taking up the publication of this Felicitation Volume.

Centre of Indian Studies, Radhey Shyam Shastri
Auroville (T. N.)

FOREWORD

Critically edited texts of Sanskrit works are the *sine qua non* of any serious study and research releting to those works. This dictum, it may be added, holds good particularly in respect of Vedic works. That is why many Vedists of the earlier generations regarded the preparation of critical editions as an essential part of their scholarly activities.[1] Such critical editions have all along constituted the soundest foundations of the further research-superstructure. We, therefore, owe it to these revered pioneers to maintain these foundations ever in the best possible repair. This can be achieved by periodic revisions of those editions with the help of fresh manuscript (and allied) material and new research techniques which are steadily becoming available.

The Vedic texts which have been selected for what I hope will be just the first instalment of revision are important from several points of view.

(1) The three Saṁhitās of the *Kṛṣṇa-Yajurveda,* namely, *Taittirīya, Kāṭhaka (Kapiṣṭhala),* and *Maitrāyaṇī,* are more or less closely related to each other, but the Taittirīya school has preserved its entire literature more extensively and in a far better condition. The *Maitrāyaṇī-Saṁhitā,* which is often referred to in the manuscripts as *Maitrāyaṇīya-Mānava-Saṁhitā,* is mostly similar to the *Kāṭhaka-Saṁhitā* from the point of view of contents and the *mantras,* which latter often show readings different from those of the *Taittirīya-Saṁhitā,* but it varies from the *Kāṭhaka-Saṁhitā* in the matter of mythological details and general presentation of the text. The *Maitrāyaṇī-Saṁhitā* has a *padapāṭha* which proves quite helpful in the editing of its text.

(2) The *Gopatha-Brāhmaṇa* is the only work of this genre which belongs to the *Atharvaveda.* It is, indeed, not unlikely that the *Atharvaveda* did not originally have any Brāhmaṇa of its own, but that, in order to substantiate a well-established tradition, a text which was rather artificially constituted came to be later appended to that Veda. The secondary character and the comparatively late

date of the *Gopatha-Brāhmaṇa* become easily manifest. It is suggested that that Brāhmaṇa is just a compilation of portions from a bigger work consisting of 100 chapters which is mentioned in a *Pariśiṣṭa* of the *Atharvaveda*. Naturally, in its present form the *Gopatha-Brāhmaṇa* cannot be regarded as a complete Brāhmaṇa by itself. There are also indications that it has derived much of its material from other Brāhmaṇa-texts like the *Aitareya*, the *Kauṣītaki*, and the *Śatapatha*. All the same the Atharvanic character of the *Gopatha-Brāhmaṇa* becomes fairly evident from its representation of the twofold magic — *śānta* (ātharvaṇa) and *ghora* or *ābhicārika* (āṅgirasa) — and from the *Atharvaveda-mantras* which it quotes.

(3) I have always felt that adequate attention is not usually paid to a critical study of the Āraṇyakas. Out of the three proper Āraṇyaka-texts, namely, the *Aitareya*, the *Śāṅkhāyana*, and the *Taittirīya* (the Āraṇyaka-portions of the *Śukla-Yajurveda* and the *Sāmaveda* are not taken into consideration here), the *Aitareya-Āraṇyaka* possesses special significance. This Āraṇyaka, which can boast of a fairly uniform textual tradition, comprises five books, each of which is called *āraṇyaka*. Its style, which is often elliptical, aptly suits its subject-matter, which is often esoteric. Among the important topics dealt with in the *Aitareya-Āraṇyaka* may be mentioned those relating to Mahāvrata and the Mahānāmnī verses. Luckily, Sāyaṇa has commented upon the whole Āraṇyaka while Śaṅkara and Ānandatīrtha have expounded its upaniṣadic portions.

(4) The Taittirīya school of the *Kṛṣṇa-Yajurveda* is very rich in Śrautasūtras. From among its six available Śrautasūtras, the *Baudhāyana* is presumably the oldest and the most detailed. The *Baudhāyana-Gṛhyasūtra* characterises (Kāṇva) Baudhāyana as pravacanakāra as against Āpastamba who is referred to as sūtrakāra. This would show that Baudhāyana belonged to that category of śrauta teachers who expounded the ritual orally and in fuller detail before it was codified in the form of sūtras. In other words, he represented a stage between the Brāhmaṇas and the Śrautasūtras. Structurally also the *Baudhāyana-Śrautasūtra* stands apart from the other Śrautasūtras. For instance, instead of recording the views, which diverged from it, in different relevant con-

texts, it has put many of them together in the *dvaidhasūtras* (chapters 20-23). Similarly it has collected the *pariśiṣṭa*-like material in the *karmāntasūtras* (chapters 24-26). It may also be noted that the *Baudhāyana* usually quotes the *mantras* or *yajus* in full and not by means of *pratīkas* like the other Taittirīya-Sūtras. All in all, the importance of the *Baudhāyana-Śrautasūtra* as perhaps the most basic Śrauta text is undeniable.

(5) However, it is the *Āpastamba-Śrautasūtra* which seems to have enjoyed — and perhaps even now enjoys — a wider currency than any other Śrautasūtra, particularly in the South. The *Āpastamba-Śrautasūtra* is closely related to the *Bhāradvāja-Śrautasūtra* both in contents and style except that it quotes a larger number of authorities than the *Bhāradvāja-Śrautasūtra*. It also often mentions the views of the Vājasaneyins or the *Vājasaneyaka*, but, curiously enough, many of those views do not occur in the *Śatapatha-Brāhmaṇa* while a few are even inconsistent with that Brāhmaṇa and the *Kātyāyana-Śrautasūtra*.

(6) Among the Śrautasūtras, the *Satyāṣāḍha-(Hiraṇyakeśi-) Śrautasūtra* perhaps stands in the greatest need of revised edition, for, it has not so far received proper attention from editors and translators. This is probably due to the fact that that sūtra has been considered to be rather a superfluity on account of its palpable similarity to the *Āpastamba-Śrautasūtra* — so much so that tradition regards the Hiraṇyakeśins as *āpastambāntargata* — and to a lesser extent to the *Bhāradvāja-Śrautasūtra*.

(7) The *Mānava-Śrautasūtra* is one of the two Śrautasūtras which belong to the Maitrāyaṇī school of the *Kṛṣṇa-Yajurveda*. Though this Sūtra often betrays the style of a Brāhmaṇa, it is, on the whole, clearly distinguishable from a Brāhmaṇa on account of the absence in it of legends and other Brāhmaṇa-peculiarities. It would appear from the colophons in the manuscripts (which, incidentally, are badly preserved) that the *Mānava-Śrautasūtra* had originally consisted of five sections, namely, *prāksoma, agniṣṭoma, iṣṭikalpa, vājapeya,* and *cayana,* these having been transformed into eleven chapters, probably with some additions, at a later stage. Interestingly enough, it is also suggested that the *Āśvalāyana-Śrautasūtra* may be helpful in the understanding of several abstruse passages of the *Mānava-Śrautasūtra*.

(8) The *Kauśika-Sūtra,* which is regarded as one of the five *kalpas* of the *Atharvaveda,* is certainly not a Śrautasūtra; nor can it be regarded as a normal *Gṛhyasūtra* (though it is often regarded as being one). Besides many *gṛhya* rites, it deals (as is but to be expected) profusely and systematically with the Atharvavedic magic. It may, therefore, be called *Atharva-Vidhāna.* The *Kauśika-Sūtra* is, indeed, fortunate in having such valuable expository aids as the Bhāṣya of Dārila and the Paddhati of Keśava.

The scholars to whom the revision of these eight works has been assigned are, as may be seen from the specimens in this Volume, already quite familiar with those respective works. They are also conversant with the necessary *modus operandi.* All this surely augurs well for the success of this important research project.

I cannot conclude this Foreword without heartily applauding the remarkable sense of propriety which the editors of this Volume and their collaborators have exhibited in offering it as a tribute of respectful gratitude — I earnestly hope that I too shall be permitted to join in that tribute — to Professor C. G. Kashikar. Few other scholars in recent times have made such outstanding contribution towards the understanding of the literature and practice of Vedic ritual as he.

Bhandarkar Oriental
Research Institute, Poona — R. N. Dandekar
June 15, 1990.

Footnote

1. For my own enlightenment I have prepared the following list of the first editions of major Vedic works (Saṁhitās, Brāhmaṇas, Āraṇyakas, and Śrautasūtras) :

(1) *Ṛgveda-Saṁhitā* (with Sāyaṇa's Bhāṣya), 6 volumes; edited by Max Müller; London; 1849-1874; (2) *Atharvaveda* (Śaunaka-Saṁhitā); edited by Roth and Whitney; Berlin; 1855; (3) *Kashmirian Atharvaveda* (Paippalāda-Saṁhitā), 3 volumes; edited

by Bloomfield and Garbe; Baltimore; 1901; (4) *Sāmaveda* (Kauthuma); edited by Benfey (with translation); Leipzig; 1848; (5) *Sāmaveda* (Jaiminīya); edited by Caland; Breslau; 1907; (6) *Taittirīya-Saṁhitā, 6* volumes; edited by Röer, Cowell, and others; Calcutta; 1854-1899; (edited by Weber in two volumes; Leipzig; 1871-72); (7) *Kāṭhaka-Saṁhitā,* 4 volumes; edited by von Schroeder; Leipzig; 1900-1912; (8) *Kapiṣṭhala-Kaṭha-Saṁhitā;* edited by Raghu Vira; Lahore; 1932; (9) *Maitrāyaṇī-Saṁhitā,* 2 volumes; edited by von Schroeder; Leipzig; 1881-86; (10) *Vājasaneyi-Saṁhitā* (Mādhyandina and Kāṇva); edited by Weber; Berlin-London; 1852; (11) *Aitareya-Brāhmaṇa* (with translation), 2 volumes; edited by Haug; Bombay; 1863; (12) *Kauṣītaki-(Śāṅkhāyana-)Brāhmaṇa;* edited by Lindner; Jena; 1887; (13) *Pañcaviṁśa-Brāhmaṇa (Tāṇḍya-Mahābrāmaṇa);* edited by Ananda Chandra Vedantavagisha; Calcutta; 1869-1874; (14) *Ṣaḍviṁśa-Brāhmaṇa;* edited by Eelsingh; Utrecht; 1908; (only Prapāṭhaka I, with translation; edited by Klemm; Gutersloh; 1894); (15) *Jaiminīya-Brāhmaṇa;* edited by Raghu Vira and Lokesh Chandra; Nagpur; 1954; (16) *Taittirīya-Brāhmaṇa,* 3 volumes; edited by Rajendralal Mitra; Calcutta; 1855-1870; (17) *Śatapatha-Brāhmaṇa* (Mādhyandina); edited by Weber; Berlin- London; 1855; (18) *Śatapatha-Brāhmaṇa* (Kāṇva); edited by Caland; Lahore; 1926-1939; (19) *Gopatha-Brāhmaṇa;* edited by Gaastra; Leiden; 1919; (20) *Aitareya-Āraṇyaka;* edited by Rajendralal Mitra; Calcutta; 1876; (21) *Śāṅkhāyana-Āraṇyaka;* edited by Sridhar Shastri Pathak; Poona; 1922; (only Books I and II; edited by Friedländer; Berlin; 1900); (22) *Taittirīya-Āraṇyaka;* edited by Rajendralal Mitra; Calcutta; 1871; (23) *Baudhāyana-Śrautasūtra,* 3 volumes; edited by Caland; Calcutta; 1904-1913; (24) *Bhāradvāja-Śrautasūtra,* Parts I-II; edited by Kashikar; Poona; 1964; (only Praśnas I-IX and a few sections of XII; edited by Raghu Vira; Lahore; 1934-1935); (25) *Āpastamba-Śrautasūtra,* 3 volumes; edited by Garbe; Calcutta; 1882-1902; (26) *Satyāṣāḍha-Śrautasūtra,* 10 volumes; edited by Agashe and Marulkar; Poona; 1907-1932; (27) *Vaikhānasa-Śrautasūtra;* edited by Caland; Calcutta; 1941; (28) *Mānava-Śrautasūtra;* edited by van Gelder; New Delhi; 1961; (only Books I-V, 3 fascicules; edited by Knauer; St. Petersburg; 1900-1903); (29) *Vārāha-*

Śrautasūtra; edited by Caland and Raghu Vira; Lahore; 1933; (30) *Kāṭhaka-Śrautasūtra-Saṁkalana;* edited by Surya Kant; Lahore; 1943; (31) *Kātyāyana-Śraūtasūtra;* edited by Weber; Berlin; 1859; (32) *Āśvalāyana-Śrautasūtra;* edited by Ramanarayan Vidyaratna; Calcutta; 1874; (33) *Śāṅkhāyana-Śraūtasūtra,* 4 volumes; edited by Hillebrandt; Calcutta; 1888-1899; (34) *Lāṭyāyana-Śrautasūtra;* edited by Ananda Chandra Vedantavagisha; Calcutta; 1872; (35) *Drāhyāyaṇa-Śrautasūtra,* incomplete, only Vol. I; edited by Reuter; London; 1904; (36) *Vaitāna-sūtra;* edited by Garbe; London; 1878; (37) *Kauśika-sūtra* (Gṛhyasūtra); edited by Bloomfield; New Haven; 1890.

CONTRIBUTORS

1 Mrs. Sucheta Paranjpe,
Research Assistant,
Bhandarkar Oriental Research Institute,
PUNE 411 004

2 Dr. T. N. Dharmadhikari,
Director,
Vaidika Saṁśodhana Maṇḍala,
T. M. V. Colony, Gultekdi,
PUNE 411 037

3 Dr. Hukam Chand Patyal,
Assistant Editor,
Sanskrit Dictionary Department,
Deccan College,
PUNE 411 006

4 Acharya Munishwar Deo,
Reader,
V. V. I. S. I. S. of Punjab University,
Sadhu Ashram,
HOSHIARPUR 146 001

5 Acharya Vijay Pal,
Principal,
Panini Mahavidyalaya,
Ramlal Kapur Trust,
BAHALGARH, Dist. Sonepat, (Haryana) 131 021

6 Pt. Radhey Shyam Shastri,
In-charge of Sanskrit,
Centre of Indian Studies,
Bharat Niwas,
AUROVILLE (Tamilnadu) 605 101

7 Dr. P. D. Navathe,
Curator,
Bhandarkar Oriental Research Institute,
PUNE 411 004

8 Prof. C. G. Kashikar,
Hon. Professor,
Balamukunda Sanskrit Mahavidyalaya,
Tilak Maharashtra Vidyapeeth,
1242 Sadashiv Peth,
PUNE 411 030

9 Dr. S. S. Bahulkar,
Reader and Principal,
Balamukunda Sanskrit Mahavidyalaya,
Tilak Maharashtra Vidyapeeth,
1242 Sadashiv Peth,
PUNE 411 030

PART I

PROF. C. G. KASHIKAR : A PROFILE

By
Sucheta Paranjpe

"एतद्वै यज्ञस्य समृद्धं, यद्रूपसमृद्धं, यत्कर्म क्रियमाणम्...." We were listening intently. The whole class was spell-bound by this totally new topic—Vedic Ritual—which was included in our post-graduation course. The teacher was nothing short of a mine of knowledge. He spoke with such ease, fluency and authority that we didn't even want to take class notes. We were all ears for him. Here was something new—something unexplored and at the same time, very interesting. There and then I made up my mind to study this subject in details—and, if luck permits, then, under the guidance of this teacher.

His name, I found out later, was Dr. C. G. Kashikar.

He almost initiated me into the vast field of Vedic ritual in his very first lecture. An apparently dry and drab subject was made so simple and attractive by him that after the class, Sanskrit students were often heard discussing—over a steaming cup of coffee in the University Cafeteria—the formulas to be recited while pulverizing the flour to prepare an eleven-potsherd 'puroḍāśa'!

How did he get interested in this subject?

"Do you come from a Vedic family, sir?"

"Yes, my forefathers belonged to a family of Vaidikas." he reminisced about the glorious past. His forefathers were senior astrologers in the old Kolhapur State. "My ancestor in the fifth or sixth generation approached the Chhatrapati of Satara with a request for patronage towards the maintenance of Śrauta Agnihotra. The request was granted and the family shifted to Satara. The Kashikar Wada in Satara still has a room meant for Agnihotra. ......though the practice of offering Agnihotra is long cut off," he said.

Born in a family of such heritage, Sanskrit was, naturally,

his first love. After a year in the New English School, Satara, he switched over to the Rāṣṭrīya Śālā in 1921. He was one of the first twelve students to join it. At the age of 15, he passed his 'pravesh' examination equivalent to the matriculation

Having made up his mind to pursue Sanskrit, he joined the Tilak Mahavidyalaya, a college then affiliated to the Tilak Maharashtra Vidyapeeth, Pune and passed his Visharad, i. e. B. A., in 1929. He joined TMV in 1932 in the capacity of an Assistant Registrar. His association with TMV has grown and matured ever since. Simultaneously, he completed his Parangat (M. A.) as well. In fact he is the first Parangat of TMV. His thesis for this degree so impressed the examiners that they recommended it for publication. The very next year, it was printed in a book-form, titled, "Ṛgvedakālīna Sāṁskṛtika Itihāsa."

This was just the beginning of the great work in the field of research and publication that was to start from now on.

He joined Vaidika Saṁśodhana Maṇḍala in 1933. He was the editor of the Ṛgveda Saṁhitā with Sāyaṇa's Bhāṣya. It was then that the idea of bringing out the Śrautakośa occurred to him. Originally, its scope was limited; it would just be a dictionary of sacrificial terms. Śrautācārya Dhundiraj Shastri Bapat, Shri. Dikshit, Shri Nene, Shri Datar—all these stalwarts from the field of ritual were working with Prof. Kashikar. In fact, it was Dhundiraj Shastri Bapat who introduced and initiated him to Vedic Ritual. While working on this project, Prof. Kashikar read and studied and analysed almost all the available Brāhmaṇas and the Śrauta-sūtras. In this extensive study, he came across Bhāradvāja Śrauta-sūtra. While studying it, he realised that there were many a lacunae in this text. During daytime, he worked in the Vaidika Saṁśodhana Maṇḍala, came back home tired and exhausted; but rest he would not. He burnt the oil in the lamp and studied Bhāradvāja Śrauta-sūtra by night.

" I read and wrote and compared notes and wrote them again," he said. " I sat in the chair for hours on end, till finally , I got back-ache! My fingers went limp by constantly holding a pen. But of course, I had to work hard and do my best. I just could not sleep peacefully before the work was complete."

And then, the work was complete, the thesis ready for submission. However, some technical problems arose and he could not submit it for the Ph.D.

But in 1966, the University of Poona honoured him with a D. Litt. for this very thesis. This, perhaps, was the peak of his academic career.

At the same time, his research activities went on at a galloping pace. He published many research papers and articles. He also collected more than a hundred rare manuscripts on ritual from remote corners of Maharashtra, edited and published a few. He wrote many books on Vedic Ritual and also, Indian Medicine. One of his major contributions is his translation of Jolly's 'Medizin' into English. It shows his command over the subject matter as well as both the languages—German and English. 'A Survey of the Śrauta-sūtras', 'Bhāradvāja Śrauta-sūtra', 'Śrautadharmāchī Svarūpa-Cikitsā', 'Āyurvedīya Padārthavijñāna', editions of the Ṛgveda, Śrautakośa, Kauśikasūtra with Dārila's Bhāṣya are a few milestones among his publications.

In 1967, Prof. Kashikar was invited to join the Centre of Advanced Study in Sanskrit, in Pune. Personally I believe that this was the best part of his career— because, it was here that he could impart his vast knowledge to us students; it was here that we could learn so much from him. During this period, he delivered many lecture series—Ghorpade Series at BISM, Pune; Ashtekar series at the University of Pune; Kane series at Bombay University; Paranjpe series at Nagpur University; and so many others. Thus, he generously distributed his knowledge to common man too. He had a knack of making even a difficult subject simple and attractive.

After retiring from the CASS he joined Deccan College, Pune, as one of the Editors of the Sanskrit Dictionary. However, due to health problems, he resigned in 1982.

When I heard about his heart-trouble, I went to see him in a city hospital where he was admitted. The nurse warned me that he was advised complete bed-rest ......"so, no work and not much talking, please." I quietly tiptoed in the room only to find him sitting on the bed with some papers and a pencil in his hand. He quickly 'hid' everything under the pillow and said, "Please say nothing of this to the Doctor. Try to understand, I must send these proofs of Lāṭyāyana Śrauta-sūtra to the press by tomorrow. Anyway, how are you? And where are the kids"?

I just smiled. This is what he is! His work always comes before his health! To be honest, if I were treating him, I would prescribe three new books, for reading per week and at least one lecture per day. I bet this is the 'medicine' that would cure him faster. One more thing which is really unique to him—he would never say anything about himself, neither his ailments nor his honours. He is always concerned about the other person; he would always enquire about your studies and about your problems.

This, in fact, is the reason why he becomes a very respectable and at the same time, if I may say so, a very lovable person. There is no derth of scholastic giants in the field of Sanskrit studies—but this combination of great scholarship with a homely and warm relationship with everyone around is something that one very rarely comes across. We are really fortunate to be his students. The ritual tells me that one who imparts knowledge becomes thy Father; and I am proud to have Prof. C. G. Kashikar as my Father.

Along with his research and teaching, there are many other responsibilities that he has been carrying out actively for the last so many years. A life member of Vedaśāstrottejaka Sabhā, Pune and Vedapāṭhaśālā, Pune, he was also a member of the Organising Committee of Vājapeya sacrifice in 1955 in Pune and Sāgnicit Atirātra in 1975 in Kerala. There are many other fields where he pursues work with zeal and interest. Many of us would be surprised to know that he was an active freedom-fighter and was widely known in the political circles of Pune till recent times. His studies have not marred his interest in the fine arts. He is presently the Chairman of Bharat Gayan Samaj, Pune.

Prof. C. G. Kashikar—a learned scholar and a very good teacher, an active worker and a very kind and considerate man. May God give him a long and healthy life, so that he can continue doing his research and so that the coming generations of students would be fortunate to listen to Prof. Kashikar's lectures on Vedic Ritual—"एतद्वै यज्ञस्य समृद्धं, यद्रूपसमृद्धं, यत्कर्म क्रियमाणम्...."

PROF. C. G. KASHIKAR

BIODATA

1. Name

Chintaman Ganesh Kashikar

2. Address

Office Shri Balamukunda Sanskrit Mahavidyalaya,
Tilak Maharashtra Vidyapeeth,
1242 Sadashiv Peth, Pune 411 030.
Phone - 442774

Residence 1489 Sadashiv Peth, Pune 411 030.
Phone - 435330

3. Birth Date and Place

17th August, 1910, Satara, Maharashtra State.

4. Academic Qualifications

1) Vāṅmaya-Visharad (B. A.) - Sanskrit.
Tilak Maharashtra Vidyapeeth, Pune (1929).
2) Vaṅmaya-Parangat (M. A.) - Sanskrit.
Tilak Maharashtra Vidyapeeth, Pune (1934).
3) D. Litt. (Sanskrit) - University of Poona (1966).

5. Positions Held

1) Secretary and Editor, Vaidika Saṁśodhana Maṇḍala, Pune, 1933-1967.
2) Reader, Centre of Advanced Study in Sanskrit, University of Poona, 1967-1974.
3) Editor, Sanskrit Dictionary Project, Deccan College, Pune, 1974-1982.
4) Honorary Professor, Shri Balamukunda Sanskrit Mahavidyalaya, Tilak Maharashtra Vidyapeeth, Pune (since 1981); Editor in Chief, Vedic Concordance Project (since

1988).

6. **Publications**

Eighteen books and ov.,r a hundred research articles have been published so far. (A list is given seperately,)

7. **Students Guided**

Six students got Ph. D. (Sanskrit) of the University of Poona under his guidance.

8. **Participation in Conferences etc.**

1) Attended 18 sessions of All India Oriental Conference and read papers in the Vedic section.
2) Attended the Inernational Seminar held at Calcutta on the occasion of Vivekananda Centenary and read a paper (1964).
3) Attended two sessions of Viśva Saṁskṛta Sammelana held at Somnath and Varanasi.
4) Attended International Congress of Orientalists held at New Delhi in 1965 and read a research paper.
5) Deputed by the Ministry of Education, Govt. of India to attend the International Sanskrit Conference held at Berlin in 1975 and read a research paper.

9. **Special Lectures and other Academic Activites**

1) M. M. P. V. Kane Endowment Lectures at Bombay University on "A Survey of the Śrauta Sūtras" (1966).
2) R. B. Shridhar Ganesh Paranjape Memorial Lectures at Nagpur University on "The History of Plants in India" (1970).
3) Bhau Vishnu Ashtekar Vedic Lectures at the University of Poona on "A critical Analysis of the Vedic Sacrificial religion" (1972)
4) Murgudkar Shastri and A. K. Nulkar Lectures on "Ancient Indian Culture" at Tilak Maharashtra Vidypeeth.
5) Ichalkaranjikar Ghorpade Memorial Lectures at the Bharat Itihas Samshodhan Mandal, Pune.
6) Presided over the Vedic section of the All India Oriental

Conference, 24th session, Varanasi (1968).

7) Undertook a research tour in Orissa for the study of Paippalāda Atharvaveda tradition on behalf of the Centre of Advanced Study in Sanskrit, University of Poona (1968).

8) Organizer, Vājapeya Performance Committee and participated as a priest in Vājapeya sacrifice, Pune (1955).

9) Member of International Performance committee for the Atirātra Agnicayana, Kerala (1975).

10) Nominated as a scholar member on the Project Committee for the Sanskrit Dictionary Project at the Deccan College by the Department of Education, Ministry of Human Resource Development, Govt. of India.

11) Worked twice as the acting Vice-Chancellor of Tilak Maharashtra Vidyapeeth (1983 - 1984; August 1985 - April 1986)

10. **Honours, Awards, Memberships**

1) Honour for Vedic scholarship by Devadeveśvara Saṁsthāna, Pune (February 1987).

2) Honoured with the award (Vedavedāṅga Puraskāra) by Shri Guru Gaṅgeśvarānandajī Pratiṣṭhāna, Nasik for Vedic scholarship (January 1989).

3) Honoured with the award by the President of India for the scholarship in Sanskrit (March 1989).

4) Life Member and Member of Executive Board, Bhadarkar Oriental Research Institute; Life Member of Linguistic Society of India; Vedaśāstrottejaka Sabhā; Pune Vedapāṭhaśālā; Bhārata Itihāsa Saṁśodhaka Maṇḍala (all in Pune); Member of Sanskrit Standing Committee, Govt. of Maharashtra (1986-87).

11. **Present Position**

Hon. Professor and Chief Editor of Vedic Concordance Project, Balamukunda Sanskrit Mahavidyalaya, Tilak Maharashtra Vidyapeeth, Pune.

PROF. C. G. KASHIKAR

Bibliography of Books and Select Articles

Books

1 Cultural History of the Ṛgvedic Period (Marathi). Pune, 1935.
2 Ṛgveda Saṁhitā with Sāyaṇa's Commentary, Vols. II - V (in collaboration) Pune, 1936, 1941, 1946, 1951.
3 Indian Medicine. (English translation of J. Jolly's *Medizin*) Pune, 1952.
4 Āyurvedīya Padārthavijñāna. (in collaboration). Bombay, 1953.
5 The Śrauta Ritual and the Vājapeya sacrifice. Pune, 1955.
6 Śrautakośa. Vol. I (Sanskrit and English sections). Vol II, Part I (Sanskrit section) (in collaboration). Pune, 1958, 1962, 1970.
7 Sūtras of Bharadvāja. Parts I & II. Pune, 1964.
8 A Survey of the Śrautasūtras. Bombay, 1968.
9 Kauśikasūtra-Dārilabhāṣya. (in collaboration). Pune, 1972.
10 Some Aspects of the Vedic Culture (Marathi). Pune, 1972.
11 A critical analysis of the Vedic sacrificial religion (Marathi). Pune, 1972.
12 A History of Indian Plants (Marathi). Nagpur, 1975.
13 A Hundred Years of Vedaśāstrottejaka sabhā. Pune, 1975.
14 Ancient Indian Learning : A Review (Marathi) (in collaboration). Pune, 1980.
15 Keśavaviracitā Kauśikapaddhatiḥ (in collaboration). Pune, 1982.
16 Hautrika. Pune, 1984.
17 Vārāha Śrauta Sūtra. Pune, 1989.
18 Identification of Soma. Pune, 1990.

Articles

1 Sāyaṇa and the text of Ṛgveda Saṁhitā. *New Indian Antiquary* I (12), Bombay, 1939.

2 Untraced quotations in Sāyaṇa's Commentary on the Ṛgveda. *PAIOC* XII , Banaras, 1943-44.

3 The Problem of the Gaḷantas in the Ṛgveda padapāṭha *PAIOC* XIII, Nagpur, 1946.

4 The New Commentary on Vālakhilya hymns. *Poona Orientalist* IX (1 & 2). Pune, 1944.

5 Repetitions in the Ṛgveda padapāṭha. *ABORI* XXVIII (3 & 4), Pune, 1948.

6 An Examination of Max Müller's Saṁhitā and Pada-text. *Poona Orientalist* XIII (1 & 2). Pune, 1949.

7 The Text problem of the Baudhāyana Ādhāna Sūtra. *ABORI* XXIX (1 -4), Pune, 1949.

8 A comparative study of Udgītha's bhāṣya on the Ṛgveda. *Siddhabhāratī,* Hoshiarpur, 1950.

9 The revised Sautrāmaṇī text of the Vārāha Śrauta Sūtra. *JBBRAS* XXVI, Bombay, 1950.

10 Vaidika ṛṣīnce laukika nirīkṣaṇa (Marathi). *Kevalānanda Abhinandana Grantha,* Wai (Dist Satara), 1952.

11 Ritual Notes : A study of Bhāradvāja Śrauta Sūtra, Praśna VII. *D. V. Potdar Comm. Vol.,* Pune, 1950.

12 A critical study of the Ritualistic Sūtras : Bhāradvāja Śrauta sūtra Praśnas VI and VIII. *Sarūpabhāratī,* Hoshiarpur, 1954.

13 The Ritual of the Vājapeya Sacrifice. *Poona Orientalist* XIX, Pune, 1956.

14 A critical and exegetical study of the Ritualistic Sūtras. *S. K. Belvalkar Felicitation Volume,* Pune, 1959.

15 The Present day Vedic Rituals in India. *R. B. Trivedi Felicitation Volume,* Madras, 1958.

16 A critical and exegetical study of the Vārāha Śrauta Sūtra I, 1 - 3. *Adyar Library Bulletin* (1 - 4), Madras, 1961.

17 Baudhāyana Śrautasūtra II — A fresh study. *Journal of the Ganganath Jha Research Institute* XV (3-4), Allahabad, 1958.

18 The Pitṛmedhasūtra of Bharadvāja *vis-a-vis* Āpastamba and Satyāṣāḍha-Hiraṇyakeśin, *Journal of Oriental Research* XXVIII (Parts 1-4), Madras, 1959.

19 A critical study of the Ritualistic Sūtras : Bhāradvāja Śrautasūtra. *ABORI* XL, Pune, 1959(60).

20 A critical study of the Ritualistic Sūtras : Baudhāyana Śrautasūtra, Praśnas, I-V, XX, XXIII-XXIX, *P. K. Gode Commemoration Volume,* Pune, 1960.

21 The traditional Vedic Recitations : A wonder of Memory. *Bulletin of the Institute of Traditional Cultures* I, Madras, 1961.

22 Caraṇavyūha (Marathi). *Navabhārata,* Wai, 1963.

23 The ritual teachers : Āśmarathya and Ālekhana. *JBBRAS* XXXVI-XXXVII, Bombay, 1964.

24 The Vedic sacrificial rituals through the Ages. *Indian Antiquary* (III series) I (2), Bombay, 1964.

25 On the *khila* verse *arvāñcam indram. Vishveshwarananda Indological Journal* II (2), Hoshiarpur, 1965.

26 Mantrabrāhmaṇayor vedanāmadheyam (Sanskrit). *Vedavāṇī* 17 (10), Sonipat, 1965.

27 A rare manuscript of the Vārāha school. *Gopinath Kaviraj Abhinandana Grantha,* Lucknow, 1967.

28 Presidential Address to the Vedic Section of the 24th Session of the All India Oriental Conference, (Varanasi, 1968), Pune, 1973.

29 The Taittirīya Brāhmaṇa in relation to the Sūtrakāras. *Pratidānam,* The Hague, 1968.

30 *Pāpmano vinidhayaḥ* : Some unknown and less known words. *Indian Antiquary* (III series) III (1-4), Bombay, 1969.

31 Pottery in the Vedic Literature. *Indian Journal of History of Science* IV (1 &2), Calcutta, 1969.

32 Vedaśākhāmīmāṁsā (Sanskrit). *Ṛṣikalpanyāsa,* Allahabad, 1970.

33 The text of *Pāpmano vinidhayaḥ* with commentaries. *Journal of the University of Poona,* 33 (Humanities Section), Pune, 1970.

34 Veda men Pravṛttidharma (Hindi), *Prācya-Prajñā* 3, Aligarh, 1971.

35 A note on the Pada-text of Ṛ̣V 8.35.13-15. *ABORI* LI (1-4), Pune, 1971.

36 Śrauta Karmāce Svarūp (Marathi). *Saṁskṛtisugandha,* Pune, 1971.

37 A Fresh Study of the Āpastamba Śrautasūtra XXIV 11-14. *Indo-Iranian Journal* XIII (2), The Hague, 1971.

38 Introduction to the Bodhāyanīyabrahmakarmasamuccaya (Sanskrit). Gokarn, 1971.

39 Max Mueller : The doyen of Sanskrit Editors. *Bharatiya Vidya* XXXI (1-4), Bombay, 1971.

40 The Veda and the Vedic Tradition. *Sanskrit in Maharashtra,* Pune, 1972.

41 Āyurveda. *Sanskrit in Maharashtra,* Pune, 1972.

42 A critical and exegetical study of the Ritualistic sūtras : Vārāha Śrautasūtra I.4-5, *Vimarśa* I (3), Tirupati, 1972.

43 A propos of the Pravargya. *CASS Studies* 1, Poona, 1973.

44 Further Notes on the Vārāha Śrautasūtra I.1-3. *PAIOC* XXVI, Ujjain, 1972 : Also *V. Raghavan Felicitation Volume,* Delhi, 1975.

45 Jñānakośakāra Ketkar āṇi Vedavidyā (Marathi), *Ketkar Patrikā* II, Nanded, 1972.

46 An Examination of Max Müller's Ṛgveda Saṁhitā and Pada text. *CASS Studies* I, Pune, 1973.

47 The way to understand the Veda. *Saṁskṛta Vimarśa* I (1), Delhi, 1974.

48 Trikāṇḍamaṇḍana and the Bhāradvāja School. *CASS Studies* II, Pune, 1974.

49 Max Müller : the philosopher linguist. *BDCRI* XXXIV (1-4), Pune, 1974.

50 A Text critical Study of the Vārāha Śrautasūtra : The Animal Sacrifice. *Vishveshwarananda Indological Journal* XII (1&2), Hoshiarpur, 1974.

51 On the Bhāradvāja Gṛhyasūtra and its commentary. *BDCRI* XXXV (1-2), Pune, 1975.

52 The obscure in the Vedic sacrificial rituals (ii). *Saṁskṛta Vimarśa* III (1&2), New Delhi, 1975; also *Altorientalische Forschungen* VI, Berlin, 1979.

53 The Avāntaradīkṣā of the Pravargya, *BDCRI* XXXV (3-4),

Pune, 1976.

54 The Taittirīya text tradition : a study of verse-repetitions : *PAIOC* XXVIII, Dharwar, 1976.

55 On the adhimanthana (-śakala). *BDCRI* XXXVIII (1-4), Pune, 1978-79.

56 Baudhāyana Śyenaciti : A study in the Piling up of Bricks. *PAIOC* XXIX, Pune, 1978.

57 The idea of ultimate reality and meaning according to the Kalpa Sūtras (in) *Ultimate Reality and Meaning,* Toronto, 1979.

58 Vedic Ritualistic Studies : A Retrospect and prospect, Shri *Gopal Chandra Sinha Comm. Vol., Ṛtam* XVI - XVIII, Lucknow, 1980.

59 Agnicayana : The piling up of Svayamātṛṇṇā. *ABORI* LX, Pune, 1979.

60 The Concept of Mahāvīra in the Pravargya. *Vaidika Saṁśodhana Maṇḍala Golden Jubilee Volume,* Pune, 1981.

61 Agnicayana : Extension of Vedic Aryan rituals. *ABORI* LX, Pune, 1979.

62 Identification of the Vedic plant uśānā. *Journal of the History of Medicine,* Delhi.

63 Antecedents of the Vedic Soma. *Hamdard* XXIII (1-2), Karachi, 1980.

64 Yajñapārśve : an unpublished Pariśiṣṭa of the Śukla Yajurveda school. *Dr. Sternbach Felicitation Volume,* Lucknow, 1979.

65 On the verse *āśrāvitam atyāśrāvitam*. *BDCRI* XL, Pune, 1981.

66 Śrauta Tradition in Recent Times (in collaboration). *Agni* II Berkeley, 1983.

67 Vārāha Śrautasūtra I.9 : Cāturmāsyāni, A critical and exegetical study. *Dr. Baburam Saxena Felicitation Volume, Ṛtam* XI-XV, Lucknow, 1979 (1983).

68 Vārāha Śrautasūtra II : Agnicayana, A critical and exegetical Study. *ABORI* LXIV, Pune, 1983.

69 Vārāha Śrautasūtra III.1.1-2.2 : Vājapeya and Dvādaśāha, A critical and exgetical study. *Amṛtadhārā, R. N. Dandekar Felicitation Volume,* Delhi, 1984.

70 The Vedic Mataphor in the Churning of Ocean. *ABORI* LXV (I-IV), Pune, 1985.

71 Voice of Morality. (Article contributed to the) *Volume on 'Voice of Morality'*, Karachi, Pakistan, 1985.

72 Introduction in Sanskrit to Gṛhyāgnisāgara. Gokarn, 1986.

73 Man-World-Peace. (Article contributed to the) *Volume on 'Man-World-Peace'*, Karachi, Pakistan, 1988.

74 Meaning of Gataśrī. *ABORI* LXVII, Pune, 1986.

75 Soma drink *vis-a-vis* the ruling Class. *ABORI* LXVII, Pune, 1986.

76 On the Kaṭha Āraṇyaka. *ABORI* LXVIII (R. G. Bhandarkar 150th Anniversary Volume), Pune, 1987.

77 A Structural Analysis of Agniṣṭoma. *Sacrifice in India: Concept and Evolution,* Viveka Publications, Aligarh, 1987.

PART II

MAITRĀYAṆĪ SAṀHITĀ

Edited by
T. N. Dharmadhikari

INTRODUCTION

The text of the Maitrāyaṇī Saṁhitā has been critically edited on the basis of the then available manuscripts, by Dr. Schroeder in 1881-1886 and by Pt.. Satavalekar in 1943.

Early in 1969, in my thesis on the Maitrāyaṇī Saṁhitā (unpublished), I had pointed out that the text as presented in these two editions, needs to be bettered at many places. This was testified by a considerable long list of corrections and conjectures appended by Dr. Schroeder himself (partly by Dr.. Roth), at the end of volume IV of his edition. Dr. Delbrück, Prof. W. D. Whitney, Dr. W. Caland who could arrive at a more correct text after close study of the Maitrāyaṇī Saṁhitā, had also suggested some modifications in the text.

Apart from the corrections suggested by the above mentioned scholars, a few more modifications, not too bold, let us hope, had been suggested by me in my thesis.

Recently in 1986, Dr. Martin Mittwede has published a volume entitled 'Text-Kritiche Bemerkungen Zur Maitrāyaṇī Saṁhitā', giving a longer list of such corrections suggested by a host of scholars. This volume, in a way, supported my supposition of necessity for betterment of the text of the Maitrāyaṇī Saṁhitā.

Vaidika Saṁśodhana Maṇḍala of Pune, wherein I am working on research projects since 1957, have collected, during the last four decades, some manuscripts of the Maitrāyaṇī Saṁhitā and Padas, from Nandurbar, Bhadgaon, Nasik and Wai. These manuscripts were not collated and used for the earlier two editions of the Maitrāyaṇī Saṁhitā.

The availability of the fresh manuscript material cherished in me an ardent desire to edit the Saṁhitā and try, if possible, to make good the lacuna in the text of Maitrāyaṇī Saṁhitā, on the basis of these manuscripts.

For the following few specimen pages, I have used the below mentioned manuscripts of the Maitrāyaṇī Saṁhitā and of padas also.

Manuscripts of Saṁhitā :

V — Vaidika Saṁśodhana Maṇḍala, Pune. Xerox No. 13, Pṛṣṭhamātrā Character, Devanagari Kāṇḍa I, Prapāṭhakas 1-6, Paper, brought from Pt. Bhaskarrao Joshi, Nandurbar. Not dated.

V1 — Vaidika Saṁśodhana Maṇḍala, Pune. No. 10407, Devanagari, complete 4 kāṇḍas; Janorkar Collection, Nasik. Śake 1730.

V2 — Vaidika Saṁśodhana Maṇḍala, Pune. No. 4552, Devanagari, Paper, Kāṇḍa I. Abhyankar Collection, Wai, Śake 1709.

Manuscripts of Padas :

V3 — Vaidika Saṁśodhana Maṇḍala, Pune. No. 13617, Paper, Devanagari.

V4 — Vaidika Saṁśodhana Maṇḍala, Pune. No. 2744, Paper, Devanagari.

B1 — Bhandarkar Oriental Research Institute, Pune. No. 188, Paper, Devanagari.

I have also considered the earlier two printed editions of the Maitrāyaṇī Saṁhitā :

S — Satavalekar's edition.

Sc — Schroeder's edition.

Maitrāyaṇī Saṁhitā has a very peculiar system of accentuation-marks, which is characterised by showing Udātta with a vertical mark above the syllable and showing the various svaritas with additional distinctive marks. It is, however, strange to observe that all the above-mentioned three manuscripts of the Padapāṭha of the Maitrāyaṇī do not follow the accentuation system of the Maitrāyaṇī school. The accents are shown with the Ṛgvedic or Taittirīya system. This is obviously artificial. But in total absence of the oral tradition of the recitation of this Saṁhitā, these Pada-manuscripts help us determining the accents and splitting of the

Padas etc., to a certain extent.

In the following few pages I have the privilege to place before the scholars, the edited text of the Maitrāyaṇī Saṁhitā Kāṇḍa I, Prapāṭhaka1, by way of specimen. The comments of the scholars on these specimen pages will be useful in editing the further text..

मैत्रायणी संहिता

[प्रथमकाण्डे प्रथमः प्रपाठकः ।।]

[दर्शपूर्णमास-मन्त्राः]

श्री गणेशाय नमः ।। हरि ॐ ।।

इषे त्वा सुभूताय वायव स्थ देवो वः सविता प्रार्पयतु श्रेष्ठतमाय
कर्मणा आ प्यायध्वमघ्न्या देवेभ्या इन्द्राय भागं मा व स्तेन ईशत माऽघ-
शꣳसो ध्रुवा अस्मिन् गोपतौ स्यात बह्वीर्यजमानस्य पशून् पाहि ।।१।।
गोषदसि प्रत्युष्टꣳ रक्षः प्रत्युष्टोऽरातिः ।। प्रेयमगाद्धिषणा
बर्हिरच्छ मनुना कृता स्वधया वितष्टा । [1]-तया वहन्ते-[1] कवयः पुरस्तात् ।।
देवानां परिषूतमसि विष्णो स्तुपोऽतिसृष्टो गवां भागो देवस्य त्वा सवितुः
प्रस३वेऽश्विनोर्बाहुभ्यां पूष्णो हस्ताभ्यां बर्हिर्देवसदनं दामि ।। अतस्त्वं
बर्हिः [2]शतवल्शꣳ वि रोह [3]सहस्रवल्शा वि वयꣳ रुहेम ।। अयुपिता
योनिरदित्या रास्नासीन्द्राण्याः संनहनं पूषा ते ग्रन्थिं ग्रथ्नातु सं ते मा
स्थादिन्द्रस्य त्वा बाहुभ्यामुद्यच्छे [4]-बृहस्पतेर्मूर्ध्ना हराम्यु३र्वन्तरिक्षꣳ-[4]
३वीह्यदित्यास्त्वा पृष्ठे सादयामि ।।२।।
शुन्धध्वं दैव्याय कर्मणे वसूनां पवित्रमसि शतधारꣳ [5]सहस्रधार-
मच्छिद्रतनु ।। द्यौरसि पृथिव्यसि मातरिश्वनो घर्मः ।। विश्वहोतु-
र्धामन्त्सीद ।। पोषाय त्वाऽदित्या रास्नाऽसि कामधुक्षः सा विश्वायु-
रस्त्वसौ कामधुक्षः सा विश्वभूरस्त्वसौ कामधुक्षः सा विश्वकर्माऽस्त्वसौ

१-१. S -तयावहन्ते; Sc -तयावहन्ते । But cp S, Sc - MS 4.1.2 तया वहन्ते ।

२. S, V, V1, V2, V3, V4 - शतवलिशꣳ; MŚS I.1.1.38 - शतवल्शꣳ; B1 - शतवल्शं ।

३. S, V, V1, V2, V3, V4, - सहस्रवलिशा; MŚS I.1.1.39, VŚS I..2.1.20 - सहस्रवल्शा; B1 - सहस्रवल्शा ।

४-४. S, Sc -°मूर्ध्नाहिरा° ; V3, V4, B1 -°मूर्ध्ना । हरामि°।

५. S, V1, V2, V3, V4 - °तनुः ।

हुतं स्तोको हुतो द्रप्सोऽग्ने [६]पाहि विप्रुषः सुपचा देवेभ्यो हव्यं पचाग्नये त्वा बृहते नाकाय स्वाहा द्यावापृथिवीभ्यामिन्द्राय त्वा भागं सोमेना तनच्मि विष्णो हव्यं रक्षस्वाऽऽपो जागृत ॥३॥

वेषाय वां कर्मणे वां सुकृताय वां देवीरापोऽग्रेगुवोऽग्रेणीयो-ऽग्रेऽस्य यज्ञस्य [७]प्रैताग्रं यज्ञं नयताग्रं यज्ञपतिं युष्मानिन्द्रोऽवृणीत वृत्रतूर्ये यूयमिन्द्रमवृणीध्वं वृत्रतूर्ये प्रोक्षिता स्थ सं सीदन्तां दैवीर्विशो वानस्पत्याऽसि वर्षवृद्धमस्युर्वन्तरिक्षं व्रीहि प्रत्युष्टं रक्षः प्रत्युष्टा-ऽरातिर्धूरसि ध्वर ध्वरन्तं यो अस्मान् [८]ध्वराद्यं वयं ध्वराम तं ध्वर ॥४॥

देवानामसि वह्नितमं सस्नितमं पप्रितमं जुष्टतमं देवहूत-ममहुतमसि हविर्धानं दृंहस्व मा ह्वार्विष्णोः क्रमोऽस्युरु वाताय मित्रस्य वश्चक्षुषा प्रेक्षे देवस्य वः सवितुः प्रसवेऽश्विनोर्बाहुभ्यां पूष्णो हस्ताभ्यां यच्छन्तु पञ्च गोपीथाय वो नारातयेऽग्नये वो जुष्टान् निर्वपाम्यमुष्मै वो जुष्टानिदं देवानामिदमु नः सह दृंहन्तां [९]दुर्याः स्वाहा द्यावापृथिवीभ्यां निर्वरुणस्य पाशादमुक्षि स्वरभिव्यख्यं ज्योतिर्वैश्वानरमुर्वन्तरिक्षं [१०]वीह्यदित्या व उपस्थे सादयामि ॥५॥

देवो वः सवितोत्पुनात्वच्छिद्रेण पवित्रेण । वसोः सूर्यस्य रश्मिभिः ॥ अग्नये वो जुष्टान् प्रोक्षाम्यमुष्मै वो जुष्टान् यद्वोऽशुद्ध आलेभे तच्छुन्धध्व-मदित्यास्त्वगस्यवधूतं रक्षोऽवधूताऽरातिरदित्यास्त्वगसि प्रति त्वा-ऽऽदित्यास्त्वग्वेत्तु पृथुग्रावाऽसि वानस्पत्यः प्रति त्वाऽऽदित्यास्त्वग्वे-त्त्वग्नेर्जिह्वाऽसि वाचो विसर्जनमायुषे वो बृहद्ग्रावाऽसि वानस्पत्यो देवेभ्यो हव्यं शमीष्व सुशमि [११]शमीष्व कुटरुरसि मधुजिह्वस्त्वया वयं संघातं संघातं जेष्मेषमा वदोर्जमा वद रायस्पोषमा वद ॥६॥

वर्षवृद्धमसि प्रति त्वा वर्षवृद्धं वेत्तु परापूतं रक्षः परापूता-ऽरातिः प्रविद्धो रक्षसां भागोऽदित्यास्त्वगस्यवधूतं रक्षोऽवधूता-

---

६. [B1 -पाहि।] S, Sc, V, V1, V2, V3, V4 -पाहिं । Cp Sc's foot note.

७. S, V1, V2 - प्रेताग्रं ।

८. V, V1, V2 -ध्वरायं ; V3, V4, - ध्वर । अयं । B1 - ध्वरात् । यं ।

९. S, V1, V2 -दुर्या ।

१०. V, V1, V2 -वीह्यदित्या ।

११. B1 -शमीष्व । शमिष्वेति शमिष्व ।

ऽरातिरदित्यास्त्वगसि प्रति त्वाऽदित्यास्त्वग्वेत्तु धिषणाऽसि पार्वती प्रति त्वाऽदित्यास्त्वग्वेत्तु धिषणाऽसि पार्वती प्रति त्वा पार्वती वेत्त्वदित्या स्कम्भोऽसि धान्यमसि धिनुहि देवान् प्राणाय त्वाऽपानाय त्वा व्यानाय त्वा [१२]दीर्घामनु प्रसृतिं सं स्पृशेथामायुषे वो मित्रस्य वश्चक्षुषाऽवेक्षे देवो वः सविता [१३]हिरण्यपाणिरुप गृह्णातु ।।७।।

निर्दग्धं रक्षो निर्दग्धाऽरातिः समुद्रं मा [१४]धाग् ध्रुवमसि पृथिवीं दृं हापाग्नेऽग्निमामादं जहि निः क्रव्यादं नुदस्वाग्ने देवयजनं वह धरुणमस्यन्तरिक्षं दृं ह धर्त्रमसि दिवं दृंह धर्मासि विश्वा विश्वानि दृं-ह चिदसि परिचिदसि विश्वासु दिक्षु सीद सजातानस्मै यजमानाय परि वेशय सजाता इमं यजमानं परि विशन्तु वसूनां रुद्राणामादित्यानां भृगूणामङ्गिरसां घर्मस्य तपसा तप्यध्वम् ।।

यानि घर्मे कपालान्युपचिन्वन्ति वेधसः ।
पूष्णस्तान्यपि व्रत इन्द्रवायू वि मुञ्चताम् ।।८।।

देवस्य वः सवितुः प्रस३वेऽश्विनोर्बाहुभ्यां पूष्णो हस्ताभ्यां सं वपामि ।।

देवो वः सवितोत्पुनात्वच्छिद्रेण पवित्रेण ।
वसोः सूर्यस्य रश्मिभिः ।।
समापा ओषधीभिर्गच्छन्तां समोषधयो रसेन ।
सं रैवतीर्जगतीः शिवाः शिवाभिः समसृक्षतापः ।।

सीदन्तु विशो जनयत्यै त्वा घर्मोऽसि विश्वायुर्धर्म घर्मे श्रयस्वोरु प्रथस्वोरु ते यज्ञपतिः प्रथतां सं ते तन्वा तन्वः पृच्यन्ताम् ।।

परि वाजपतिः कविरग्निर्हव्यान्यक्रमीत् ।
दधद्रत्नानि दाशुषे ।।

देवस्त्वा सविता [१५]श्रपयतु वर्षिष्ठे अधि नाके पृथिव्या अग्ने ब्रह्म गृह्णीष्व ।।९।।

देवस्य त्वा सवितुः प्रस३वेऽश्विनोर्बाहुभ्यां पूष्णो हस्ताभ्यामा ददा

---

१२. S - दीर्घामनु ।
१३. S - हिरण्यपाणि॰ ।
१४. S, V1, V2, V3, V4 -धां ।
१५. S, V, V1, V2, -श्रपयतु ।

इन्द्रस्य बाहुरसि दक्षिणः सहस्रभृष्टिः शततेजा वायुस्तिग्मतेजाः पृथिवि देवयजनि मा हिंसिषं [१६]ता ओषधीनां मूलं व्रजं गच्छ गोस्थानं वर्षतु ते पर्जन्यो बधान देव सवितः शतेन पाशैः परमस्यां [१७]परावति यो अस्मान् द्वेष्टि यं च वयं द्विष्मस्तमत्र बधान सोऽतो मा मोचि मा वः शिवा ओषधयो मूलं हिंसिषं व्रजं गच्छ गोस्थानं वर्षतु ते पर्जन्यो बधान देव सवितः शतेन पाशैः परमस्यां [१७]परावति यो अस्मान् द्वेष्टि यं च वयं द्विष्मस्तमत्र बधान सोऽतो मा मोचि द्रप्सस्ते दिवं मा स्कान् व्रजं गच्छ गोस्थानं वर्षतु ते पर्जन्यो बधान देव सवितः शतेन पाशैः परमस्यां [१७]परावति यो अस्मान् द्वेष्टि यं च वयं द्विष्मस्तमत्र बधान सोऽतो मा मोचि वसवस्त्वा परि गृह्णन्तु गायत्रेण छन्दसा रुद्रास्त्वा परि गृह्णन्तु त्रैष्टुभेन छन्दसाऽदित्यास्त्वा परि गृह्णन्तु जागतेन छन्दसाऽपारं पृथिव्या अदेवयजनं सत्यसदस्यृतसदसि घर्मसदसि ।।

पुरा क्रूरस्य विसृपो [१८]विरप्शिन
उदादाय पृथिवीं जीरदानुम् ।
तामैरयं श्चन्द्रमसि स्वधाभि-
स्तां धीरासः [१९]कवयोऽनुदृश्यायजन्त ।।१०।।

प्रत्युष्टं रक्षः प्रत्युष्टोऽरातिरायुः प्राणं मा निर्मार्जीश्चक्षुः श्रोत्रं मा निर्मार्जीर्वाचं पशून् मा निर्मार्जीर्यज्ञं प्रजां मा निर्मार्जीस्तेजोऽसि शुक्रमसि ज्योतिरस्यमृतमसि वैश्वदेवमसि ।।

हविरसि [२०]वैश्वानरमुन्नीतशुष्मं सत्यौजाः ।
सहोऽसि सहस्वारातिं सहस्व पृतनायतः ।।

सहस्रवीर्यमसि [२१]तन्मा जिन्वाज्यस्याज्यमसि हविषो हविः सत्यस्य सत्यं [२२]सत्याभिघृतं सत्येन त्वाऽभि घारयाम्यदब्धेन त्वा चक्षुषाऽवेक्षे रायस्पोषाय सुप्रजास्त्वाय ।।

---

१६. S, V1, V2, V3, V4 -ताम्, [B1 - ते]; Cp S - MS IV.1.10 ता [औषधीनां]।
१७. V, V1, V2, V3, V4 - परावती ।
१८. V, V1, V2, V3, V4 - विरप्सिन ।
१९. Sc - ॰नुदिश्या॰ ।
२०. S, V, V1, V2 - ॰शुष्मं ।
२१. S, V - तन्वा; V1 - तन्वा; B1 - तत् । मा; V3, V4 - तन्वा ।
२२. S, V1 - सत्याभिहितं ।

धामासि प्रियं देवानामनाधृष्टं देवयजनम् ।

देववीत्यै त्वा गृह्णामि ।।

देवीरापः शुद्धा यूयं देवान् युयुध्वं शुद्धा वयं सुपरिविष्टाः परिवेष्टारो वो भूयास्म [२३]कृष्णोऽस्याखरेष्ठा अग्नये घृतं भव वेदिरसि बर्हिषे त्वा जुष्टं प्रोक्षामि बर्हिरसि वेद्यै त्वा जुष्टं प्रोक्षामि स्वाहा पितृभ्यो घर्मपावभ्यः ।।११।।

पूषा ते ग्रन्थिं विष्यतु विष्णो स्तुपोऽस्युरु [२४]प्रथस्वौर्णम्रदं स्वासस्थं देवेभ्यो गन्धर्वोऽसि विश्वावसुर्विश्वस्मादीषमाणो यजमानस्य परिधिरिडे ईडित इन्द्रस्य बाहुरसि दक्षिणो यजमानस्य परिधिरिडे ईडितो मित्रावरुणौ त्वोत्तरतः परि धत्तां यजमानस्य परिधिरसीडे ईडितः ।।

नित्यहोतारं त्वा कवे द्युमन्तः समिधीमहि ।।

वर्षिष्ठे अधि नाके पृथिव्याः सूर्यस्त्वा रश्मिभिः पुरस्तात् पातु कस्याश्चिदभिशस्त्या विश्वजनस्य विधृती स्थो वसूनां रुद्राणामादित्यानां सदोऽसि स्रुचां [२५]योनिर्द्यौरसि जन्मना जुहूर्नाम प्रिया देवानां प्रियेण नाम्ना ध्रुवे सदसि सीदान्तरिक्षमसि जन्मनोपभृन्नाम प्रिया देवानां प्रियेण नाम्ना ध्रुवे सदसि सीद पृथिव्युसि जन्मना ध्रुवा नाम प्रिया देवानां प्रियेण नाम्ना ध्रुवे सदसि सीद ऋषभोऽसि शाक्वरो वषट्कारस्य त्वा मात्रायां सादयामि ।। ध्रुवा [२६]असदन्नृतस्य योनौ सुकृतस्य लोके ता विष्णो पाहि ।। पाहि यज्ञं पाहि यज्ञपतिं पाहि मां यज्ञन्युम् ।। विष्णूनि स्थ वैष्णवानि धामानि स्थ प्राजापत्यानि ।।१२।।

[२७]सूयमे मेऽद्य स्तं स्वावृतौ सूपावृता अग्नाविष्णू वि जिहाथां मा मा हिं सिष्टं लोकं मे लोककृतौ कृणुतं मा मोदोषिष्टमात्मानं मे पातं शिवौ भवतमद्य नो विष्णो स्थामासीत इन्द्रस्तिष्ठन् वीर्युमकृणोद्देवताभिः [२८]समारभ्य ।।

---

२३. V - ०स्याषरेष्ठा ।

२४. S, V1 - स्वौर्णम्रदं ; [V3, V4, B1 -प्रथस्व। ऊर्णम्रदमित्यूर्ण-म्रदं।]।

२५. V - यौनिर्द्यौरसि; V1, V2 - योनिर्द्यौरसि ।

२६. S, V, V1, V2 - असदन्नृतस्य ।

२७. [Sc - foot note - सुयमे ईति सु-यमे; B1 - सुयम(?) ईति सु-यमे । But MŚS I.3.1.11 - सूयमे - All other mss - सूयमे]

२८. S, V, V1, V2 - समारभ्यः ।

ऊर्ध्वो अध्वरो दिविस्पृगह्रुतो यज्ञो यज्ञपते: ।
इन्द्रवान्त्स्वंवान् [२९]बृहद्भा: ।।
[३०]वीहि मधोर्घृतस्य स्वाहा सं ज्योतिषा ज्योति: ।।
वाजस्य मा प्रसवेनोद्ग्राभेणोदजिग्रभत् ।
अथा सपत्नानिन्द्रो मे निग्राभेणाधराँ अक: ।।
उद्ग्राभश्च निग्राभश्च ब्रह्म देवाँ अवीवृधत् ।
अथा सपत्नानिन्द्राग्नी मे विषूचीनान् व्युस्यताम् ।।

वसुरस्युपावसुरसि विश्वावसुरस्यप्तुभी रिहाणा व्यन्तु वयो वशा पृश्निर्भूत्वा मरुतो गछ ततो नो [३१]वृष्ट्याऽवत ।।

सꣳ स्रावभागा स्थेषा बृहन्त: प्रस्तरेष्ठा बर्हिषदश्च देवा: ।
इमाꣳ वाचमभि विश्वे गृणन्त: स्वाहा देवा अमृता मादयन्ताम् ।।

देवा गातुविदो गातुꣳ वित्त्वा गातुमित मनसस्पते सुधात्विमꣳ यज्ञं दिवि देवेषु वाते धा: स्वाहा ।।१३।।

।। इति प्रथमकाण्डे प्रथमस्थान: प्रथम: प्रपाठक: ।।

---

२९. S, V, V1, V2 - बृहद्भा:; [B1 - बृहद्भा इति बृहत्-भा:]; [Cp TS 1.1.12 - बृहत्-भा:]।

३०. V1, V2, - वीहि ।

३१. Sc - foot note - वृष्ट्यावत ।

GOPATHA BRĀHMAṆA

Edited by
Hukam Chand Patyal

INTRODUCTION

The Gopatha-Brāhmaṇa (GB.) is the only brāhmaṇa text of AV. belonging to both the recensions, viz. Śaunaka and Paippalāda. The GB. text, as it has come down to us, does not bear any accent marks. No commentary is available on this text. The text is divided into two parts, the pūrva-bhāga or brāhmaṇa in five prapāṭhakas, and the uttara-bhāga or brāhmaṇa in six prapāṭhakas. The prapāṭhaka is further divided into the kaṇḍikās. The pūrva shows more originality especially in the glorification of the Atharvan and its priests. Its subject-matter is different from that of the common Brāhmaṇa type. The uttara is comparatively less original. In the case of some legends the text gives Atharvanic colouring by introducing Atharvanic personages (see e.g. GB. 2. 1. 2 dealing with the prāśitra-legend, here the seers Idhma Āṅgirasa and Barhi Āṅgirasa are introduced; also see GB. 2.1.17; 2.2.6; 2.3.9 etc.)

The editions of the text

The GB. text was first edited by Rājendralāla Mitra and Haracandra Vidyābhūṣaṇa (abbr. to M.) in the Bibliotheca Indica, New Series Nos. 215 and 252 (work no. 69), Calcutta (1872). This edition is full of printing errors, and the editors have not taken any pains in emending the text even when it could have been possible for them.

The GB. was also edited by Jīvānanda Vidyāsāgara from Calcutta in 1891. I could not have access to this text. This edition and M.'s edition are utilised by Kṣemakaraṇadāsa Trivedī. This edition is practically the same as that of M.

Dutch scholar Dieuke Gaastra (abbr. to G.) brought out a critical edition of the text from Leiden in 1919. This edition provides a very exhaustive introduction in German. This edition is based on six Mss. (mentioned in her introduction, pp. 2-8). Despite the editor's utmost care some printing errors have crept in the text. She has also provided parallel text places, has noticed rare vocables not found in PW., pw. In the appendix the list of mantras, verses and sacrificial formulas is given in the Devanāgarī alphabetical order.

Paṇḍita Kṣemakaraṇadāsa Trivedī in 1924 brought out Hindi translation with Sanskrit Vyākhyā of this text from Allahabad. Second edition of this book appeared in 1977 from Allahabad. The editors of this second edition Prajñā Devī and Medhā Devī claim this edition to be a revised one, but in my opinion this does not contain revision of real value. The text is solely based on the editions of M. and Vidyāsāgara. This translation is based on sectarian and uncritical outlook. Hence this is not of much critical value.

Recently Vijayapāla Vidyāvāridhi (abbr. to V.) has brought out edition of this text. This is published by Ramlal Kapur Trust from Bahalgarh (Haryana) in 1980. V. has based his text on G.'s edition (to our great surprise he thinks Gaastra to be a male). He has made use of two Mss. from Pune(these are Diw. 1 and 2 in our list). He does provide parallel passages in his notes, but at times his comparisons are misleading. Even these two Mss. he has not collated meticulously. Let us point out such lacunae.

V. in fn. 3 on GB. 1.1.13 records the reading *prasākṣīd iti* from M., really speaking this reading is found in all Mss., the reading *pradhākṣīd iti* is suggested by Böhtlingk which is adopted by G. and also by V. (see note 55 on this reading in my text). In fn. 3 on 1.1.15 V. suggests *bhavati* (?) for *bhāti,* but here there is no need for emendation. V. at 2.3.20 accepts the reading *punarādāya* (whereas at 2.5.3 rightly *punarādāyam*), we have to accept *-am* form (cf. KB. 15.2; 15.4; AB. 3.17(12.6), he cites AB. 3.23 (?). Diw. 1 also reads *punarādāyam*. V. in GB. 2.6.14 adopts G's reading *śucam* and in his fn.11 records *sracam* from Mss., whereas Diw. 1 and 2 read *srucam*. I have left some printing errors. He has very tentatively utilised these two Mss.

The present writer has translated this text : Gopatha Brāhmaṇa--English Translation with Notes and Introduction, unpublished Ph. D. thesis, Poona University (1969). This translation is based on G's edition, but other editions as well as some Mss. are also used for this purpose.

Otto von Böhtlingk "Probe einer Kritik des Gopatha Brāhmaṇa" provides useful annotations on this text (G. records some of them under *Bemerkungen* in her *Einleitung*, pp. 27-36).

Maurice Bloomfield's *The Atharvaveda and the Gopatha Brāhmaṇa* in *Grundriss* series is a very important contribution on the subject. This provides a very good account of the Atharvaveda literature in general. Contents of GB. are provided in detail in this monograph. An attempt is also made to show mutual relationship with Vait. and Kauś. of GB.

Manuscripts used for this fascicule

The following Mss. are used in preparing this small *fascicule* of GB.

These Mss. were procured from Vaidika Saṁśodhana Maṇḍala, Pune (for their description, see *Descriptive Catalogue of Manuscripts* edited by T. N. Dharmadhikari, Vol. I (Veda and Vedic), (1974)).

Diw.1. S. No. 804, Acc. No. 8575, size 22.5 x 10 cms.; 168 folios, 8 lines, 35 letters in each line. Śaka 1642. This belongs to Diwekar Collection. This has Miri Markings. Paper, Devanāgarī script. The last folio is faded. A blank square with a hole is kept in the middle of each folio.

Diw.2. S. No. 803, Acc. No. 8576, size 20 x 10.5 cms., 201 folios, 7 lines, 35 letters in each lines. Śaka 1773-74. Paper, Devanāgarī script. Miri markings only in the Pūrva Brāhmaṇa. Scribe is Bāḷambhaṭṭa.

Go. Pūrva Bhāga alone. S. No. 805, Acc No. 4135, size 20.5 x 8.2 cms., 92 folios, 7 lines, 20 letters in each line. For each prapāṭhaka folio numbers are separately given. First two folios are missing, the third one srarts from °पत्समतपत् ताभ्यः (1.1.3). This Ms. is only up to a part of 1.5.24 (गीत्या स्तोमेन सह प्रस्तावेन च); this does not have the remaining part of 1.5.24 and 1.5.25. This Ms. belongs to Gore Collection.

There are two more Mss. of GB. in Gore Collection, see S. No. 806, Acc No. 4137 (14 foll.), and S. No. 807, Acc. No. 4136

(5 foll.), beginning of fifth prapāṭhaka of the uttarabhāga. I have not made use of both these fragmentary Mss.

Ad. *Descriptive Catalogue of Sanskrit Manuscripts in the Adyar Library* (Madras), Vol. I, p. 162. Acc No. 64310. 529 41B. 75, Paper, Devanāgarī script, 67 folia (marked 1-70, foll. 1, 2 and 29 are missing, size 8.1" x 4.5", 8 lines in a page. Good and large size writing. This Ms. is from a part of 1.1.4 to the end of 1.3. To our great surprise the Ms. is full of mistakes, and there are also many omissions and commissions of all sorts (see e.g. foll. 10 A, 28A). It appears to be comparatively new.

Ān. Ānandāśrama, Pune, Nos.4306 (folios 1-21) and 3661 (folios 22-119). Though the handwritten catalogue assigns two numbers, yet in reality this appears to be one manuscript, and it completes the text. At the beginning of the Ms. it is written : गोपथब्राह्मणं सादाशिवे: . This appears to be fairly old. It provides some good readings. Paper, Devanāgarī script. Folios 1-21 contain 15 lines on each page with small letters, whereas in later portion the number of lines varies from 11 to 14 on each page. Scribes for foll. 1-21 and 22-119 are two different persons, that is what appears obvious from handwriting.

Bh. This Ms. belongs to Bharat Itihas Mandal, Pune - 30 (see हस्तलिखितग्रन्थानुक्रमणिका, edited by G. H. Khare, (1970), p. 87 A). This Ms. belongs to S. N. Joshi Collection, Wai, Satara. Paper, Devanāgarī script. It contains only the uttarabhāga of the text. Excellent condition, 81 folios, 8 lines on each page. It has Miri markings. The scribe is one Nāgara Brāhmaṇa from Visala-nagara (modern Bisnagar in Gujrat).

W. *Descriptive Catalogue of Sanskrit Manuscripts* [Prājña Pāṭhaśālā Maṇḍala Collection], Pt. I, pp. 86-7, edited by Laxmanshastri Joshi, (1970), Prājña Pāṭhaśālā Maṇḍala, Wai. S. No. 670, L. No. 1-4 / 93. Paper, Devanāgarī script. Size 31.4 x 14.4 cms., folios 61, lines 12, letters per line 58. Good condition. Date is not mentioned.

In addition to these above mentioned Mss. I shall also be utilising some of the important Mss. of GB. mentioned in *Descriptive Catalogue of the Government Collection of Manuscripts* (deposited at Deccan College, Pune, but now in the possession of Bhandarkar Oriental Research Institute, Pune), Vol. I, Pt. 1, pp. 298-305, Bombay (1916), S. Nos. 409-420.

Shri Radhe Shyam Shastri also procured a xerox copy of GB. Ms. from Alwar (Rajasthan), but for this *fascicule* I could not make use of it.

For a detailed list of Gopatha Brāhmaṇa Mss., see *New Catalogus Catalogorum* VI. 128, Madras University, (1971).

Some better readings available in these Mss.

In the course of my study of these Mss. I have noticed some better readings in some of these Mss. For example, *svayaṁbhvekam eva* GB. 1.1.1 (Ān.); *udakrāmat* GB. 2.2.6 (Ān.,Bh) (G. erroneously *udakramat*, M. rightly has this reading); *nakṣatriyām* GB. 2.1.19 (Bh.) (G. adopts *nakṣatrīyām*, cf. KB. 5.1); majority of Mss. read *abhyaghārāt* GB. 2.5.5, but G. emends the reading to *abhyāgāram*, we have *abhyāgārāt* (in Bh).

It is true that some of the readings still will remain unintelligible despite our best efforts.

For the purpose of this *fascicule* I have taken GB. 1.1.1-15. This portion deals with an Atharvanic cosmogony in Upaniṣad manner (cf. BṛĀra U. 5.4). In the typical Brahmanical style the etymologies of the words like *sveda, aṅgirasa, bhṛgu, mṛtyu* etc. are provided through the *parokṣavṛtti*. Five *vyāhṛtis*, viz. *vṛdhat, karat, ruhat* (M. and also Bloomfield read *guhat*), *mahat*, and *tad* are associated with the *sarpaveda, piśācaveda, asuraveda, itihāsaveda*, and the *purāṇaveda* respectively. The scrifice is said to be 'threefold', seven-stringed consisting of 21 forms. The entire cosmogony establishes the Atharvan as the pivot around wich all creative acts revolve. Brahman-priest is the priest *par excellence* (for details of the contents of each kaṇḍikā, see Bloomfield, AV. and GB. sec, 67).

I hope that I have pointed out with sufficient clarity that there is need for a revised edition of the Gopatha Brāhmaṇa text.

Colophon

My thanks are due to Shri. Radhe Shyam Shastri. It was he who assigned the task of editing this text to me. He was kind enough in procuring xerox-copies of many Mss. of the text from different parts of the country. Dr. C. G. Kashikar, my guru, deserves heartfelt thanks with whom I has many fruitful discussions on technical aspects of editing. Dr. T. N. Dharmadhikari was kind enough in lending out to me three manuscripts mentioned above for my use.

अथ गोपथब्राह्मणम्

पूर्वभागः

प्रथमः प्रपाठकः

ओं नमोऽथर्ववेदाय नमः ॥

ओं ब्रह्म ह वा इदमग्र आसीत् स्वयंभ्वेकमेव[1] । तदैक्षत[2] महद्वै यक्षं यदेकमेवास्मि[3]। हन्ताहं मदेव मन्मात्रं द्वितीयं देवं निर्मिमा[4] इति। तदभ्यश्राम्यदभ्यतपत् समतपत् । तस्य श्रान्तस्य तप्तस्य संतप्तस्य ललाटे स्नेहो यदार्द्रमाजायत[5] । तेनानन्दत् तदब्रवीन्महद्वै यक्षं सुवेदमविदमहमिति[6] । तद्यदब्रवीन्महद्वै यक्षं सुवेदमविदमहमिति[6] तस्मात् सुवेदोऽभवत् । तं वा एतं सुवेदं सन्तं स्वेद इत्याचक्षते परोक्षेण । परोक्षप्रिया इव हि देवा भवन्ति प्रत्यक्षद्विषः[7] ॥१॥

स भूयोऽश्राम्यद् भूयोऽतप्यद् भूय आत्मानं समतपत् । तस्य श्रान्तस्य तप्तस्य संतप्तस्य सर्वेभ्यो रोमगर्तेभ्यः पृथक् स्वेदधाराः प्रास्यन्दन्त[8] । ताभिरनन्दत् । तदब्रवीदाभिर्वा अहमिदं सर्वं धारयिष्यामि यदिदं किं चाभिर्वा अहमिदं सर्वं जनयिष्यामि यदिदं किं चाभिर्वा अहमिदं सर्वमाप्स्यामि यदिदं किं चेति । तद्यदब्रीदाभिर्वा अहमिदं सर्वं धारयिष्यामि यदिदं किं चेति । तस्माद्धारा अभवन् । तद् धाराणां धारात्वं यच्चासु ध्रियते[9] । तद्यदब्रवीदाभिर्वा अहमिदं

---

1. G. rightly suggests this reading which is found in Ān, whereas other Mss. and M. have स्वयंत्वेकमेव.
2. Ān . तदीक्षत.
3. This reading is after G., all Mss. have तदे°.
4. This is after G., all Mss. read निर्मम.
5. This is suggested by Bohtlingk. Diw. 1 and 2 यदार्द्रियमा°, W.यदाद्रियमा°, Ān. यदर्द्रिमा°.
6. This is suggested by Böhtilingk. Diw. 1 and 2 °महा इति, Ān., W. °मह इति, and also repeated elsewhere.
7. Cf. this cosmogonic myth with that of Bṛ Āra U. 5.4.
8. W. प्राक्स्यंदंत.
9. W. ध्रियते.

सर्वं जनयिष्यामि यदिदं किं चेति तस्माज्जाया अभवन् । तज्जायानां जायात्वं यच्चासु[10] पुरुषो जायते यच्च पुत्रः । पुन्नाम नरकमनेकशततारं तस्मात् त्रातीति[11] पुत्रः । तत् पुत्रस्य पुत्रत्वम् । तद्यदब्रवीदाभिर्वा अहमिदं सर्वमाप्स्यामि यदिदं किं चेति तस्मादापोऽभवन्। तदपामप्त्वम्[12]। आप्नोति वै स सर्वान् कामान् यान् कामयते[13] ।।२।।

ता अपः[14] सृष्ट्वान्वैक्षत । तासु स्वां छायामपश्यत् । तामस्येक्षमाणस्य स्वयं रेतोऽस्कन्दत् । तदप्सु प्रत्यतिष्ठत् । तास्तत्रैवाभ्यश्राम्यदभ्यतपत् समतपत् । ताः श्रान्तास्तप्ताः संतप्ताः सार्धमेव रेतसा द्वैधमभवन् । तासामन्यतरा[15] अतिलवणा अपेया अस्वाद्व्यस्ता अशान्ता रेतः समुद्रं वृत्वातिष्ठन्[16] । अथेतराः पेयाः स्वाद्व्यः शान्तास्तास्तत्रैवाभ्यश्राम्यदभ्यतपत् समतपत् । ताभ्यः श्रान्ताभ्यस्तप्ताभ्यः[17] संतप्ताभ्यो यद्रेत आसीत् तदभृज्ज्यत[18] । यदभृज्ज्यत[18] तस्माद्भृगुः समभवत् । तद् भृगोर्भृगुत्वम् । भृगुरिव वै स सर्वेषु लोकेषु भाति य एवं वेद ।।३।।

स भृगुं सृष्ट्वान्तरधीयत । स भृगुः सृष्टः प्राङैजत[19] । तं वागन्ववदद्वायो वाय इति[20] । स न्यवर्तत स दक्षिणां दिशमैजत[21] । तं वागन्ववदन्मातरिश्वन् मातरिश्वन्निति । स न्यवर्तत । स प्रतीचीं दिशमैजत[21] । तं वागन्ववदत् पवमान पवमानेति । स न्यवर्तत । स उदीचीं दिशमैजत[21] । तं वागन्ववदद्वात वातेति । तमब्रवीन्न न्वविदमहमिति[22] । न हीति । अथार्वाङेनमेतास्वेवाप्स्वन्विच्छेति । तद् यदब्रवीदथार्वाङेनमेतास्वेवाप्स्वन्विच्छेति तदथर्वाभवत् । तदथर्वणो-

---

10. G. has printing error या °.
11. The form *trāti* class II. P. is irregular for regular class IV Ā.
12. Diw.1 °पामत्वम्, W. °पामपत्वम्.
13. G. expects य एवं वेद at the end after the style of subsequent kaṇḍikās, but there is no Ms. evidence. V. supplies this portion in square brackets in the text itself.
14. Diw.2, Ān. आपः.
15. All Mss. °मन्या अन्यतरा.
16. V. and Diw.1 वृत्त्वा°which is not desirable.
17. Diw.1 and 2, Go., W., Ān. श्रान्ताभ्यंःस्तप्ताभ्यः, this is an orthographic peculiarity, also repeated elsewhere.
18. All Mss. °भृज्यत.
19. All Mss. प्राङेजत°. This is G.' s suggestion.
20. All Mss. वायो वायो इति.
21. All Mss. दिशमेजत.
22. Diw.1 and 2, W. °विदामहा इति, Ān. °विदामह इति.

ऽथर्वत्वम् । तस्य ह वा एतस्य भगवतोऽथर्वण ऋषेर्यथैव ब्रह्मणो लोमानि यथाङ्गानि यथा प्राण एवमेवास्य सर्व[23] आत्मा समभवत् । तमथर्वाणं ब्रह्माब्रवीत् प्रजापतेः प्रजाः सृष्ट्वा पालयस्वेति तस्मात् प्रजापतिरभवत् । तत् प्रजापतेः प्रजापतित्वम् । अथर्वा वै प्रजापतिः । प्रजापतिरिव वै स सर्वेषु लोकेषु भाति य एवं वेद ।।४।।

तमथर्वाणमृषिमभ्यश्राम्य[24]दभ्यतपत् समतपत् । तस्माच्छ्रान्तात् तप्तात् संतप्ताद् दशतयानथर्वण ऋषीन् निरमिमीतैकर्चान्[25] द्व्यृचां-स्तृचांश्चतुर्ऋचान् पञ्चर्चान्त्षडर्चान्त्सप्तर्चानष्टर्चान् नवर्चान् दशर्चा-निति । तानथर्वण ऋषीनभ्यश्राम्यदभ्यतपत् समतपत् । तेभ्यः श्रान्तेभ्यस्तप्तेभ्यः संतप्तेभ्यो दशतयानाथर्वणानार्षेयान् निरमिमीतै-कादशान्[25] द्वादशांस्त्रयोदशांश्चतुर्दशान् पञ्चदशान् षोडशान्त्सप्तदशान् अष्टादशान् नवदशान् विंशानिति । तानथर्वण[26] ऋषीनाथर्वणां-श्चार्षेयानभ्यश्राम्यदभ्यतपत् समतपत् । तेभ्यः श्रान्तेभ्यस्तप्तेभ्यः संतप्तेभ्यो यान् मन्त्रानपश्यत् स आथर्वणो वेदोऽभवत् । तमाथर्वणं वेदमभ्यश्राम्यदभ्यतपत् समतपत् । तस्माच्छ्रान्तात् तप्तात् संतप्तादो-मिति मन एवोर्ध्वमक्षरमुदक्रामत् । स य इच्छेत् सर्वैरेतैरथर्व-भिश्चाथर्वणैश्च कुर्वीयेत्येतयैव तन्महाव्याहृत्या[27] कुर्वीत । सर्वैर्ह[28] वा अस्यैतैरथर्वभिश्चाथर्वणैश्च कृतं भवति य एवं वेद यश्चैवंविद्वाने-वमेतया महाव्याहृत्या कुरुते ।।५।।

स भूयोऽश्राम्यद् भूयोऽतप्यद् भूय आत्मानं समतपत् । स आत्मत एव त्रीँल्लोकान् निरमिमीत पृथिवीमन्तरिक्षं दिवमिति । स खलु पादाभ्यामेव पृथिवीं निरमिमीतोदरादन्तरिक्षं मूर्ध्नो दिवम् । स तांस्त्रीँल्लोकानभ्यश्राम्यदभ्यतपत् समतपत् । तेभ्यः श्रान्तेभ्यस्तप्तेभ्यः संतप्तेभ्यस्त्रीन् देवान् निरमिमीताग्निं वायुमादित्यमिति । स खलु पृथिव्या एवाग्निं निरमिमीतान्तरिक्षाद् वायुं दिव आदित्यम् । स

23. V. सर्वं, which is perhaps a p printing error.
24. Go. °मभ्यः श्राम्यद्, Diw. 1 and 2 °मभ्यश्रांम्यद् here and elsewhere.
25. All Mss. निरमिमत. This reading is after Böhtlingk's suggestion. G. accepts निरमिमीत in the subsequent kaṇḍikās but here twice she reads निरमिमत, which appears to be a printing error.
26. Ān. °थवण.
27. Mss. तं महा° here and elsewhere
28. Diw.2 सर्वैह.

तांस्त्रीन् देवानभ्यश्राम्यदभ्यतपत् समतपत् । तेभ्यः श्रान्तेभ्यस्तप्तेभ्यः संतप्तेभ्यस्त्रीन् वेदान् निरमिमीत ऋग्वेदं यजुर्वेदं सामवेदमिति । अग्नेर्ऋग्वेदं वायोर्यजुर्वेदमादित्यात् सामवेदम् । स तांस्त्रीन् वेदानभ्यश्राम्यदभ्यतपत् समतपत् । तेभ्यः श्रान्तेभ्यस्तप्तेभ्यः संतप्तेभ्यस्तिस्रो महाव्याहृतीर्निरमिमीत भूर्भुवः स्वरिति । भूरित्यृग्वेदाद् भुव इति यजुर्वेदात् स्वरिति सामवेदात् । स य इच्छेत् सर्वैरेतैस्त्रिभिः वेदैः कुर्वीयेत्येताभिरेव तन्महाव्याहृतिभिः कुर्वीत । सर्वैर्ह वा अस्यैतैस्त्रिभिर्वेदैः कृतं भवति य एवं वेद यश्चैवंविद्वानेवमेताभिर्महाव्याहृतिभिः कुरुते ॥६॥

ता या अमू रेतः वृत्वातिष्ठंस्ताः प्राच्यो दक्षिणाच्यः[29] प्रतीच्य[30] उदीच्यः समवद्रवन्त[31] । तद्यत् समवद्रवन्त[31] तस्मात् समुद्र उच्यते । ता भीता अब्रुवन् भगवन्तमेव वयं राजानं वृणीमह इति । यच्च वृत्वातिष्ठंस्तद्वरणोऽभवत् । तं वा एतं वरणं[32] सन्तं वरुण इत्याचक्षते परोक्षेण। परोक्षप्रिया इव हि देवा भवन्ति प्रत्यक्षद्विषः। स समुद्रादमुच्यत[33] । स मुच्युरभवत् । तं वा एतं मुच्युं सन्तं मृत्युरित्याचक्षते परोक्षेण । परोक्षप्रिया इव हि देवा भवन्ति प्रत्यक्षद्विषः । तं वरुणं मृत्युमभ्यश्राम्यदभ्यतपत् समतपत् । तस्य श्रान्तस्य तप्तस्य संतप्तस्य सर्वेभ्योऽङ्गेभ्यो रसोऽक्षरत्[34] । सोऽङ्गरसोऽभवत् । तं वा एतमङ्गरसं सन्तमङ्गिरा[35] इत्याचक्षते परोक्षेण । परोक्षप्रिया इव हि देवा भवन्ति प्रत्यक्षद्विषः ॥७॥

तमङ्गिरसमृषिमभ्यश्राम्यदभ्यतपत् समतपत् । तस्माच्छ्रान्तात् तप्तात् संतप्ताद्विंशिनोऽङ्गिरस ऋषीन् निरमिमीत । तान् विंशिनो[36]ऽङ्गिरस ऋषीनभ्यश्राम्यदभ्यतपत् समतपत् । तेभ्यः श्रान्तेभ्यस्तप्तेभ्यः[37] संतप्तेभ्यो[38] दशतयानाङ्गिरसानार्षेयान् निरमिमीत

29. Ān. दक्षिणाच्य.
30. Diw. 2 प्रतिच्य
31. Augmentless impf.
32. W. वरुणं.
33. Diw. 1 and 2, Ān., Ad. °मुच्युता; Go.°मुच्यता.
34. Diw. 2 °क्षर.
35. W. अङ्गिरा.
36. See Mahā Bh. on P. 5.2.37 which gives this as an example of secondary suffix—ḍin.
37. Diw. 1 तत्पेभ्यः, an orthographic error (similarly तत्पात्, संतत्पात्).
38. Diw. 1 संतत्पेभ्यः, an orthographic error.

षोडशिनोऽष्टादशिनो द्वादशिन एकर्चान् द्व्यृचांस्तृचांश्चतुरृचान्[39] पञ्चर्चान् षडर्चान् सप्तर्चानिति । तानङ्गिरस ऋषीनाङ्गिरसांश्चार्षेयानभ्यश्राम्यदभ्यतपत् समतपत् । तेभ्यः श्रान्तेभ्यस्तप्तेभ्यः संतप्तेभ्यो थान् मन्त्रानपश्यत् स आङ्गिरसो वेदोऽभवत् । तमाङ्गिरसं वेदमभ्यश्राम्यदभ्यतपत् समतपत् । तस्माच्छ्रान्तात् तप्तात् संतप्ताज्जनदिति द्वैतमक्षरं व्यभवत् । स य इच्छेत् सर्वैरेतैरङ्गिरोभिश्चाङ्गिरसैश्च कुर्वीयेत्येतयैवं तन्महाव्याहृत्या कुर्वीत । सर्वैर्ह वा अस्यैतैरङ्गिरोभिश्चाङ्गिरसैश्च कृतं भवति य एवं वेद यश्चैवंविद्वानेवमेतया महाव्याहृत्या कुरुते ॥८॥

स ऊर्ध्वोऽतिष्ठत् । स इमाँल्लोकान् व्यष्टभ्नात् तस्मादङ्गिरसो[40]ऽधीयान ऊर्ध्वस्तिष्ठति । तद् व्रतम् । स मनसा ध्यायेद् यद्वा अहं किं च मनसा ध्यास्यामि तथैव तद् भविष्यति । तद्ध स्म तथैव भवति । तदप्येतदृचोक्तम् –

श्रेष्ठो ह[41] वेदस्तपसोऽधि जातो
ब्रह्मज्यानां[42] क्षितये[42] संबभूव ।
ऋच्यृग्भूतं[43] यदसृज्यतेदं
निवेशनमनृणं दूरमस्येति ॥

ता वा एता अङ्गिरसां जामयो[44] यन्मेनयः । करोति मेनिभिर्वीर्यं य एवं वेद ॥९॥

स दिशोऽन्वैक्षत प्राचीं दक्षिणां प्रतीचीमुदीचीं ध्रुवामूर्ध्वामिति । तास्तत्रैवाभ्यश्राम्यदभ्यतपत् समतपत् । ताभ्यः श्रान्ताभ्यस्तप्ताभ्यः संतप्ताभ्यः पञ्च वेदान् निरमिमीत सर्पवेदं पिशाचवेदमसुरवेदमि-

39. Diw. 2 चतुरृ॰.
40. W. ॰ङ्गिरसो॰.
41. हि in Sāyaṇa's introduction (p.6) to Vishva Bandhu's ed. of AVŚ.
42. Sāyaṇa reads ब्रह्मज्ञानां हृदये, this reading is adopted by V. I prefer the reading of Mss. and render the text accordingly. 'This is the most excellent Veda born of fervour and(it) came into being in order to destroy the oppressors of (the knowers of) Brahman'. Cf. TB. 3.7.9.2 where the expression अपहतं ब्रह्मज्यस्य occurs. Bhaṭṭa Bhāskara: ब्राह्मणानां मंत्राणां वा जेतुः रक्षःपतेरपि अपहतं अपहतिरस्तु. See Mahā Bh. on Vār. 1 on P. 3.2.3, where the form ब्रह्मज्य is cited as an example of the suffix-ḍa.
43. M. and Ān. ऋज्यद्भूतं; W. ऋज्यग्भूतं; Ad. ऋग्यद्भूतम्.
44. M. यामयो.

तिहासवेदं पुराणवेदमिति । स खलु प्राच्या एव दिशः सर्पवेदं निरमिमीत दक्षिणस्याः पिशाचवेदं प्रतीच्या असुरवेदमुदीच्या इतिहासवेदं ध्रुवायाश्चोर्ध्वायाश्च पुराणवेदम् । स तान् पञ्च वेदानभ्यश्राम्यदभ्यतपत् समतपत् । तेभ्यः श्रान्तेभ्यस्तप्तेभ्यः[45] संतप्तेभ्यः पञ्च महाव्याहृतीर्निरमिमीत वृधत्करद्रुहन्म[46]हत्तदिति । वृधदिति सर्पवेदात् करदिति पिशाचवेदाद् रुहदित्यसुरवेदान्महदितीतिहासवेदात् तदिति पुराणवेदात् । स य इच्छेत् सर्वैरेतैः पञ्चभिर्वेदैः कुर्वीयेत्येताभिरेव तन्महाव्याहृतिभिः कुर्वीत । सर्वैर्ह[47] वा अस्यैतैः पञ्चभिर्वेदैः कृतं भवति य एवं वेद यश्चैवंविद्वानेवमेताभिर्महाव्याहृतिभिः कुरुते ॥१०॥

स आवतश्च परावतश्चान्वैक्षत । तास्तत्रैवाभ्यश्राम्यदभ्यतपत् समतपत् । ताभ्यः श्रान्ताभ्यस्तप्ताभ्यः संतप्ताभ्यः शमित्यूर्ध्वमक्षरमुदक्रामत् । स य इच्छेत् सर्वाभिरेताभिरावद्भिश्च परावद्भिश्च कुर्वीयेत्येतयैव तन्महाव्याहृत्या कुर्वीत । सर्वाभिर्ह अस्यैता[48]भिरावद्भिश्च परावद्भिश्च कृतं[49] भवति य एवं वेद यश्चैवंविद्वानेवमेतया महाव्याहृत्या कुरुते ॥११॥

स भूयोऽश्राम्यद् भूयोऽतप्यद् भूय आत्मानं समतपत् । स मनस एव चन्द्रमसं निरमिमीत नखेभ्यो नक्षत्राणि लोमभ्य ओषधिवनस्पतीन् क्षुद्रेभ्यः प्राणेभ्यो[50]ऽन्यान् बहून् देवान् । स भूयोऽश्राम्यद् भूयोऽतप्यद् भूय आत्मानं समतपत् । स एतं त्रिवृतं सप्ततन्तुमेकविंशतिसंस्थं यज्ञमपश्यत् । तदप्येतदृचोक्तम् – अग्निर्यज्ञं त्रिवृतं सप्ततन्तुमिति[51] । अथाप्येष प्राक्रीडितः[52] श्लोकः[52] प्रत्यभिवदति – सप्त सुत्याः सप्त च पाकयज्ञा इति[53] ॥१२॥

---

45. Ān. श्रोतेभ्यस्तप्तेभ्यः.
46. M. गुहन् for रुहन्. Bloomfield, Ved. Con. 899b, records गुहन्, but in Kauś. 91.12 rightly has रुहत् Ad. has ब्रह्मन् for रुहन्, but later on rightly रुहदित्य°.
47. Ān सर्वेर्ह. 48. Ān. अस्ये°.
49. Ad. क्रतं. 50. Ān. प्रोणेभ्यो.
51. AV. (P.) 5. 28. 1.
52. Ān. प्राक्रीडीत श्लोकः; Ad. प्राक्रीडितश्लोकः; Diw. 1 प्राक्रीडितं श्लोकः. Böhtlingk suggests प्राक्रोडितः.
53. Cf. GB. 1.5.25 which further reads हविर्यज्ञाः सप्त तथैकविंशतिः. Diw. 2 पावक इति for पाकयज्ञा इति.

तमाहरत् । तेनायजत । तस्याग्निर्होतासीद् वायुरध्वर्युः सूर्य उद्गाता चन्द्रमा ब्रह्मा पर्जन्यः सदस्य ओषधिवनस्पतयश्चमसाध्वर्यवो विश्वे देवा होत्रका अथर्वाङ्गिरसो गोप्तारः । तं ह स्मैतमेवंविद्वांसः[54] पूर्वे श्रोत्रिया यज्ञं ततं सावसाय ह स्माहेत्यभिव्रजन्ति मा नोऽयं घर्म उद्यतः प्रमृत्तानाममृताः प्रजाः प्रधाक्षीदिति[55] । तान् वा एतान् परिरक्षकान्त्सदःप्रसर्पकानित्याचक्षते दक्षिणासमृद्धान् । तदु ह स्माह प्रजापतिः । यद्वै यज्ञेऽकुशला ऋत्विजो भवन्त्यचरितिनो[56] ब्रह्मचर्यमपराग्या[57] वा तद्वै यज्ञस्य विरिष्टमित्याचक्षते । यज्ञस्य विरिष्टमनु यजमानो विरिष्यते । यजमानस्य विरिष्टमन्वृत्विजो विरिष्यन्ते । ऋत्विजां विरिष्टमनु दक्षिणा विरिष्यन्ते । दक्षिणानां विरिष्टमनु यजमानः पुत्रपशुभिर्विरिष्यते । पुत्रपशूनां विरिष्टमनु यजमानः स्वर्गेण लोकेन विरिष्यते । स्वर्गस्य लोकस्य विरिष्टमनु तस्यार्धस्य योगक्षेमो विरिष्यते यस्मिन्नर्धे यजन्त इति ब्राह्मणम् ॥१३॥

तं ह स्मैतमेवंविद्वांसं ब्रह्माणं यज्ञविरिष्टी वा यज्ञविरिष्टिनो वेत्युपधावेरन् । नमस्ते अस्तु भगवन्[58] । यज्ञस्य नो विरिष्टं संधेहीति[59] । तद् यत्रैव विरिष्टं स्यात् तत्राग्नीनुपसमाधाय शान्त्युदकं कृत्वा पृथिव्यै श्रोत्रायेति[60] त्रिरेवाग्नीन्त्संप्रोक्षति त्रिः पर्युक्षति त्रिः कारयमाणमा[61]चामयति च संप्रोक्षति च यज्ञवास्तु च संप्रोक्षति । अथापि वेदानां रसेन यज्ञस्य विरिष्टं संधीयते । तद्यथा लवणेन सुवर्णं

54. G. and V. read separetely एवं विद्वांसः, which is not desirable.

55. All Mss. and M. read प्रसाक्षीदिति. G. follows Böhtlingk's suggestion प्रघाक्षीविति. *prādhākṣit* is s-aor. 3 / 1 of *pra- dah* —; see J. Narten, Die sigmatischen Aoriste im Veda, p. 134; K. Hoffmann, Der Injunktiv im Veda, p. 61. Ch U. 4.1. 2 has *pradhākṣīḥ* 'one expects here too *prādhākṣīt*, also see JB. 1.39.

56. Diw. 2 °चरतिनो.

57. Ad.ब्रह्मचर्यमृपराग्या°. Böhtlingk conjectures ब्रह्मचर्येऽपराध्या°.

58. VS. 16.52b; MS. 2.9.9; KS. 17.16b; TS. 4.5.10.5 (all these texts read *bhagavaḥ*). See Ved. Con. 533a.

59. Its source is not known.

60. Extraction of AVŚ. 6.10.1.

61. G. has a printing error कारयमानम्.

संदध्यात् सुवर्णेन रजतं रजतेन लोहं लोहेन सीसं सीसेन त्रप्वे[62]वमेवास्य यज्ञस्य विरिष्टं संधीयते । यज्ञस्य संधितिमनु यजमानः संधीयते । यजमानस्य संधितिमन्वृत्विजः संधीयन्ते[63] । ऋत्विजां संधितिमनु दक्षिणाः संधीयन्ते । दक्षिणानां संधितिमनु यजमानः पुत्रपशुभिः संधीयते । पुत्रपशूनां संधितिमनु यजमानः स्वर्गेण लोकेन संधीयते । स्वर्गस्य लोकस्य संधितिमनु तस्यार्धस्य योगक्षेमः संधीयते यस्मिन्नर्धे यजन्त इति ब्राह्मणम् ॥१४॥

तदु ह स्माहाथर्वा देवो विजानन्[64] यज्ञविरिष्टानन्दानी-त्युपशमयेरन् । यज्ञे प्रायश्चित्तिः क्रियतेऽपि च यदु बह्विव[65] यज्ञे विलोमं[66] क्रियते न चैवास्य काचनार्तिर्भवति न च यज्ञविष्कन्ध-मुपयात्यपहन्ति पुनर्मृत्युमपात्येति पुनराजातिं कामचारोऽस्य सर्वेषु लोकेषु भाति[67] य एवं वेद यश्चैवंविद्वान् ब्रह्मा भवति यस्य चैवं-विद्वान् ब्रह्मा दक्षिणतः सदोऽध्यास्ते यस्य चैवंविद्वान् ब्रह्मा दक्षिणत उदङ्मुख आसीनो यज्ञ आज्याहुतीर्जुहोतीति ब्राह्मणम् ॥१५॥

---

62. Cf. Ch U. 4.17.7; JUB. 3.17. 3.
63. W. संधीयते.
64. Source of this formula is not known.
65. W. बह्वीव.
66. M., Diw. 1 and 2, Go., Ān., Ad. read` बिलोमः; W. विलोम.
67. V. suggests भवति(?). This is unncessary.

ऐतरेयारण्यकम्

[सायणभाष्यसंवलितम्]

संपादकः
मुनीश्वरदेवः

भूमिका

तदानीमुपलभ्यमानानां हस्तलेखानां स्वल्पानेव कांश्चिदुपयुज्य संस्कृत्य राजेन्द्रलालमित्रेण १८७६ खिस्ताब्दे कलिकातात ऐतरेयारण्यकं सायणभाष्येण सहितं प्रकाशितम् । ततः कांश्चिदन्यान् हस्तलेखानवलम्ब्य राजेन्द्रलालमित्र-संस्करणम् अदृष्ट्वैव पुण्यपत्तनस्थेनानन्दाश्रमेण स्वपण्डितैः संपाद्य १८९८ खिस्ताब्दे प्रकाशितम् । ते उभे संस्करणे समवलोक्य तयोः पाठैरसंतुष्टेन कीथेन पूर्वप्रयुक्तहस्तलेखेभ्योऽन्यान् हस्तलेखान् संगृह्य संमेल्य समालोच्य च मूलमैतरेयारण्यकम् आङ्ग्लभाषया अनुवादेनाऽङ्ग्लभाषानिबद्धया भूमिकया, बहुभिः परिशिष्टैश्चालंकृत्य १९०९ खिस्ताब्दे लन्दनतः प्रकाशितम् । नूनं तत्संस्करणं पूर्वसंस्करणाभ्यां शोभनतरं विद्यते ।

कीथसंस्करणात् पूर्वयोर्द्वयोरपि संस्करणयोर्विषये कीथवद् अन्येषामपि पाठकानाम् इयं धारणा संभाव्यते यत् तयोः कतरदपि शुद्धं संस्करणं नास्तीति।

राजेन्द्रलालमित्रेण संगृहीतहस्तलेखैः सह स्वीयां स्वतंत्रेच्छामपि संमिश्र्य तत्र रोचकान् शोभनान् पाठान् मनसा प्रकल्प्य स्वसंस्करणं प्रकाशितम् (द्र. कीथभूमिका पृ. ९) । तत्र पाठेषु कतरो हस्तलेखपाठः कतरश्च मनःप्रकल्पित इति ज्ञातुं न शक्यते यावत् ते हस्तलेखा न दृश्येरन् । आनन्दाश्रमसंस्करणं त्रुटितान् पाठान् तत्र तत्र भाव्यान् अन्यांश्च पाठान् प्रकल्प्य तान् कोष्ठबद्धान् करोति । प्रकल्पनाभावे तान् प्रश्नचिह्नाङ्कितान् करोति । राजेन्द्रलाल-संस्करणेन न तथा क्रियते ।

आनन्दाश्रमसंस्करणम् अपेक्षितान् सर्वान् पाठभेदान् न परिगृह्णाति । भूतेऽपि बहुत्र महत्योऽशुद्धयः सन्ति। तासु काश्चिन्निदर्शिता अपि कीथेन (द्र. तस्य भूमिका पृ. ९), तथापि स सर्वं विविच्याऽऽनन्दाश्रमसंस्करणं राजेन्द्र-

लालसंस्करणाच्छोभनतरं मन्यते ।

अस्यां स्थितौ पूर्वोक्तसंस्करणगुणयुक्तस्य तद्दोषरहितस्य च संस्करणस्य नितान्तमपरिहार्याऽपेक्षा विद्यते । सायणभाष्य उद्धृतानां पूर्वमनिर्दिष्टग्रन्थस्थलानां २०० वाक्यानां ग्रन्थस्थलानि निर्देष्टव्यानि सन्ति भाविसंस्करणे । अड्यार-पुस्तकालयादुपलब्धस्यैकस्यातिरिक्तहस्तलेखस्यापि साहाय्यं ग्रहीष्यते । षड्गुरु-शिष्यस्य, द्वितीयतृतीयारण्यकयोः शंकरमध्वाचार्ययोश्च पाठभेदाः, आधुनिक-रीत्या विरामादिचिह्नानि च विवक्षितार्थस्पष्टप्रतिपत्त्यर्थं प्रदर्शयिष्यन्ते।

पूर्वोक्तसंस्करणानां पाठेषु परस्परं भेदानां निदर्शनानि तालिकया प्रदर्श्यन्ते —

(मूले) पृष्ठम्	पङ्क्तिः	(१८९८ खिस्ताब्दे प्रकाशिते) आनन्दाश्रमसंस्करणे पाठः	कीथपाठः
१०	१७	°कयानत्रिंश°	°कया न त्रिंश°
१६	२३	°न्द्रो गच्छति	°न्द्रो यज्ञं गच्छति
१४	६	°काहः शान्त्या	°काहःशान्त्या
१९	११	°काहः शान्त्या	°काहःशान्त्या
२७	११	°काहः शान्त्या	°काहःशान्त्या
७९	८	°काहः शान्त्या	°काहःशान्त्या
५९	१३	स्तोमौ	स्तोमो
७८	५-६	रथस्त्रिचक्र इति पदे तत्त्रिवत्तदन्तो वै त्रिवदन्त एतदहरेतस्याह्नो रूपम्	रथस्त्रिचक्र इति यदेतत्त्रिवत्तदन्तो वै त्रिवदन्त एतदहरेतस्याह्नो रूपम्
८७	८	°न्र्यवन्या	°न्र्यन्या
१०८	२२	विष्टब्धानीत्येवं	°त्येव (शङ्करश्च)
११४	१०	ते परा°	ते ह परा° (अन्यत्रापि सर्वत्र)
१२२	१०	उपनिषससाद	उपनिषसाद
१२९	१२	°नुविधा	°नुविधां
१४०	८	प्राणे न	प्राणेन
१४२	२०	नवम्रक्ति	नवम्रक्तिः
१४३	२१	वृथा वाक्	वृथावाक्
१४३	२२	ओमिति	ओ३मिति
१५१	२०	शृधेऽधि (शङ्करषड्गुरुशिष्यौ)	श्रुतेऽधि (सायणश्च)
१५२	३	शृधेऽधि (शङ्करषड्गुरुशिष्यौ)	श्रुतेऽधि (सायणश्च)

१६९	२५	°व्यैख्यत्	°व्यैक्षत्
१६९	२६	ब्रह्मततमम्	ब्रह्म ततमम्
१७३	१५,२०	°धिमाव°	°धि भाव°
१८०	१२	°चोद्भिजानि	°चोद्भिज्जानि
१८९	१३	अनूद्गृहणन्	अनुद्गृहणन्
१९०	३	तस्मिन् हस्मिन्नाकाशे	तस्मिन् हास्मिन्नाकाशे
१९३	२२	ब्रुवन् वाऽब्रुवन्तं वा	ब्रुवन् वा ब्रुवन्तं वा
१९५	२१	ब्रुवन् वाऽब्रुवन्तं वा	ब्रुवन् वा ब्रुवन्तं वा
१९५	३	प्राणवंशम्	प्राणं वंशम्
१९५	४	समधा३म्	समधाँ३
१९९	४,२१,२६	तार्क्ष्यः	तारुक्ष्यः
२०७	१०	षष्टि शतानि	षष्टिशतानि
२०८	१३	षष्टि शतानि	षष्टिशतानि
२२४	११	विरुरुचुषेत	विरुरुचिषेत
२२४	१९	न कुलीदन्तैः	नकुलीदन्तैः
२२७	२, १३	°षकारावुपाप्ता°	°षकारा उपाप्ता°
२३४	९	ही३न्द्रम्	ही३न्द्रा
२३९	२४	माध्यन्दिनः	माध्यन्दिने
२४१	२७	उदाभिषिक्ताः	उताभिषिक्ताः
२४१	२८	माऽनु	मा नु
२४४	२४	प्रभूर्भूयासम्	प्रभुर्भूयासम्
२४६	२२	°र्वेदि	°र्वेदीति
२५२	२४	°मन्वीङ्ख°	°मनुवीङ्ख°
२५३	२१	नानापाणिभ्याम्	नाना पाणिभ्याम्
२५४	२०	°कर्मिणे	°कर्मणे
२६१	१०	°सोमिति	°सो३मिति
२६५	१६	पुरुवारं	पुरु वारं
२६५	१७	विजुरो	विजरो
२७०	१२	देवतास्वर्का	देवताः स्वर्का
२८३	२२	वरुणवय्वितमं	वरुणवाय्वितमं
२८३	२३	ह्यायतनमासीनो	ह्यायतन आसीनो
२९३	१५	पुराणे नाऽऽपीते	पुराणेनापीते
२९३	१९	रात्रौ च न च कीर्तयिषेत्	रात्रौ चन चिकीर्तयिषेत्

१८९८ खिस्ताब्दे प्रकाशित आनन्दाश्रमसंस्करणे स्थितानाम् अशुद्धपाठानां स्थाने भाविसंस्करणाय शोधिताः पाठः –

पृष्ठम्	पङ्क्तिः	मुद्रितः पाठः	शोधितः पाठः
२	१४	आत्मसंग्रहात्	अतिसंग्रहात् (तु. रा.)
६	४	[सिद्धमर्थं कथयति]	सिद्धान्तं निगमयति(तु. रा.)
७	१७	भागद्वयार्थता	भानाद् द्वयार्थता
८	२४	वाच्येन	(व्यर्थपाठः)
११	२८	उत	°दुत
११	२९	अन्यः	अन्यत्
११	३१	पूर्ववन्न्यायेन न	पूर्ववन्न्यायेन तद् दधि न
१४	१३	दासीवृत्तबटुमैथुन°	दासीनृत्यबहुभूतमैथुन° (तु. रा.)
१५	२३	वेति	चेति
१६	२३	°न्द्रो गच्छति	°न्द्रो यज्ञं गच्छति
२०	१८	उक्थपदं	उक्थ्यपदं
२०	२१	नूनं वेदस्वरूपं	नूनं मंत्रं वेदस्वरूपं
२१	११	सुविद्यते	विद्यते
२१	१८	मिह	मिहे
२१	२५	युक्तमेत°	युक्तमेव त°
२२	९	ब्रह्माऽऽर्चतेति	ब्रह्माऽर्चतेति
२३	११	प्रगाथनेन	प्रग्रथनेन
३१	११	तत्तेनोद्धरणेना°	तत्तेनोद्भरणेना°
३३	१४	°षा स्वर्गप्रापिका	°षा स्वर्गयाणी स्वर्गप्रापिका
३४	२६	प्रेङ्खं	प्लेङ्खं (तु. तैसं.)
३६	८	देवरेत [:] सं प्रजायते	देवरेतसं प्रजायते (तु. षड्गुरुशिष्यकीयौ)
३६	२३	°शस्त्रप्रशंसनार्थं	°शस्त्रशंसनार्थं
३६	२४	पक्षिणामित्येतस्य	हिमित्येतस्य (तु. रा.)
३७	९	तदुक्तमुखे	तदुक्थमुखे
४१	२५	°छरीरे	°छरीरेषु
४१	४४	[मूले त्यक्तम्]	सर्वं ह्येतस्माद् बीभाय
५३	१८	पकारादिः	यकारादिः
५९	१३	स्तोमौ	स्तोमो (तु. षड्गुरुशिष्यकीयौ)
६६	४	पुरुषशरीरः(?)	पुरुषशरीरे

६८	२६	वशाख्या	वशोऽश्व्य
७२	२६	संपन्नानां	बृहतीसंपन्नां
८२	५	आत्मनैवा°	आत्मन्येवा°
८२	२०	चेन्मानसं तु तत्	चेन्न स तत्त्ववित्
८९	२५	°नर्त्विक्	नर्त्विजः
८९	२८	°शेषकर्तव्यानु°	°शेषकर्मानु°
११०	२९	°यती ँ३	°यन्ती ँ३
११४	१०	ते पराबभूवुः	ते ह पराबभूवुः
११५	१७	कारणाद्वयं	कारणाद्ध्ययं
१२२	१०	उपनिषससाद	उपनिषसाद
१२९	१२,१६	°नुविधा	°नुविधां
१४०	८	प्राणे न	प्राणेन
१५२	२१	चोद्यते	रक्ष्यते
१५७	१५	°त्यस्य सर्वा	°त्यस्य लोकस्य सर्वा°
१५७	१७	६	९
१६१	२८	ईक्षतेमे लोका	ईक्षतेमे नु लोका
१६९	७	जागरितं...समादिशेत्	जाग्रतं...विनिर्दिशेत्
१६९	९	स्त्यन्न°	स्त्रियन्न°
	१०	स्वप्नेषु...विश्वलोके	स्वप्ने स...जीवलोके
१८०	१२	चोद्भिजानि	चोद्भिज्जानि
२१७	२१	अथापि पिधाया°	अथाप्यपिधाया°
२३७	१२	°भ्यासाय	°भ्यासङ्ग्यः
२३८	१९	°पश्वाधानमिति	पशुबन्धानामिति (द्र. आपश्रौ)
२४२	१७	पृश्निर्ये वैष यशो मरुतो हुताः (?)	पृश्नियै वै पयसो मरुतो जाताः (तैसं २.२.११.४)
२४२	२०	पृश्नये	पृश्नियै (तैसं २.२.११.४)
२४९	२१	प्राणमात्रः	बाणमात्रः
२५४	२०	°कर्मिणो	(सायणः) कर्मिणे, (कीथः) कर्मणे
२५८	५	वदन्त्युत्कोचं.... प्रश्नयो	वदन्त्युत्क्रोद.... पत्नयो (तु. आपश्रौ)
२५८	६	वीणाशङ्खानाधीं तूणवाः	वीणावादाः शङ्खान् नाळीस्तूण-वानिति (आपश्रौ १९.२१.४)
२५८	१४-१६	संघातेना°..शयनार्थं	संघाते वा .. व्यधनार्थं...

		...च्छ्वसन्ति...तच्च	च्छ्वयन्ति...(आपश्रौ२१.१८.५)
		कर्म..प्रवात्सीर्मा निर्वा-	तच्चर्म...ऽपरात्सीर्मा..तिवात्सी°
		त्सी°.. विधानाति	....विद्धानाति पातयन्ति
		पादयन्ति	(आपश्रौ २१.१९.१३-१५)
२५८	१७-१८	°ग्नीध्रीयं ... परि-	°ग्नीध्रं ... परिणिहत्या°
		निहत्या°	(आपश्रौ २१.१८.२-३)
२६४	७	°दधर्षन्नैव	°दधर्ष नैव
२६४	८	सत्तु (?) म°	शत्रुम°
२८३	२१	°भर्तृमन्न°	°भर्तृकमन्न°
२९४	३	पौर्णमास्यां च चोपा°	प्रौष्ठपद्यां वाऽप्युपा° (मनु ४.९५)

आनन्दाश्रमसंस्करणे पाठः			**राजेन्द्रलालमित्रसंस्करणे पाठः**
पृष्ठम्	पङ्क्तिः		
२	१४	°ऽऽत्मसंग्रहात्	°तिसंग्रहात्
	१७	अरण्य एव पठ्यं (पाठ्यं)	अरण्य एव पाठ्यत्वा-
		स्यादारण्यकमितीर्यताम्	दारण्यकमितीर्यते
३	२४	त्विच्छया	स्वेच्छया
५	१८	अत्र सिद्धान्तत्वेन	अत्र सिद्धान्तत्वेनैत-
		तस्य सूक्तस्य प्रसङ्गं	त्सूक्तविधानार्थं
		च विधत्ते –	प्रतिप्रसवं विधत्ते
''	२४	अत्रास्तिवाची	सत्तावाची
७	५	तन्त्रेण	तत् तेन
''	२६	डिण्डिमः	विदितम्
११	२७	चिन्तितः	प्रपञ्चितः
१२	१३	सर्वे पक्षाः	सप्त पक्षाः
१३	२६	माक्षिकवाची	मादकवाची
१४	२३	°दिकं प्रापयन्तम् ।	दिकं, प्रापयन्तीं मन्त्र-
		मन्त्ररूपां वा वाचं	रूपां वाचं संपाद-
		संपादयन्तम्	यन्तीम्
२२	२३	गतः	शत्रुः
२३	६-८	अहनि..गतानि...	अहानि.. गतानि ।....
		उक्थानि । ...स्तोत्राणि	उक्थानि स्तोत्राणि ।

		..पृष्ठानि । स्तोत्राणि	पृष्ठानि ...स्तोत्राणि ।
२८	२२	एकैकस्यामङ्गुलौ चत्वारि पर्वाणि	एकस्यामङ्गुलौ चत्वारि पर्वाणि
२९	२८	पवते संचरति	चलन्त्या दोलायाः
३०	२३-२४	द्वावेव पृथिवी द्यौश्चेतीमौ लोकौ	द्वे एव पृथिवी द्यौश्चे-ति, इमौ लोकौ
३१	६	फलकयोर्लम्बमानतां	फलकयोरन्नसाधनतां
३१	९	वीतयनाम°	वीवधनाम°
३१	१३	प्रेङ्खबन्धनाय	प्रेङ्खधारणाय
३३	२९	तद्दर्शनार्थं	तद्भर्त्सनार्थं
३४	२५	अतः श्रीरासन्दी	अतः अन्नमेव प्रेङ्खः श्रीरासन्दी

ऐतरेयारण्यकम्

[सायणभाष्यसंवलितम्]

अथ शान्तिः

भूमिमुपस्पृशेद् अग्न इळा नम इळा नम ऋषिभ्यो मन्त्रकृद्भ्यो मन्त्रपतिभ्यो नमो वो अस्तु देवेभ्यः ।

शिवा नः शंतमा भव सुमृळीका सरस्वति । मा ते व्योम संदृशि ।।
भद्रं कर्णेभिः शृणुयाम देवा भद्रं पश्येमाक्षभिर्यजत्राः ।
स्थिरैरङ्गैस्तुष्टुवांसस्तनूभिर्व्यशेम देवहितं यदायुः ।।
शं न इन्द्राग्नी भवतामवोभिः शं न इन्द्रावरुणा रातहव्या ।
शमिन्द्रासोमा सुविताय शं योः शं न इन्द्रापूषणा वाजसातौ ।।
स्तुषे जनं सुव्रतं नव्यसीभिर्गीर्भिर्मित्रावरुणा सुम्नयन्ता ।
त आ गमन्तु त इह श्रुवन्तु सुक्षत्रासो वरुणो मित्रो अग्निः ।।
कया नश्चित्र आ भुवदूती सदावृधः सखा । कया शचिष्ठया वृता ।।
कस्त्वा सत्यो मदानां मंहिष्ठो मत्सदन्धसः । दृव्हा चिदारुजे वसु ।।
अभी षु णः सखीनामविता जरितृणाम् । शतं भवास्यूतिभिः ।।
स्योना पृथिवि भवानृक्षरा निवेशनी । यच्छा नः शर्म सप्रथः[1] ।।
ओष्ठापिधाना नकुली दन्तैः परिवृता पविः ।
सर्वस्यै वाच ईशाना चारु मामिह वादयेत् ।। इति वाग्रसः ।।
ओं शान्तिः शान्तिः शान्तिः ।। इति शान्तिः ।।

---

१. इत ऊर्ध्वं क्वचिदधिकः पाठः, स यथा—'उदितः शुक्रियं दधे । तमहमात्मनि दधे । अनु मामैत्विन्द्रियम् । मयि श्रीर्मयि यशः । सर्वः सप्राणः सबलः । उत्तिष्ठाम्यनु मा श्रीः । उत्तिष्ठत्वनु माऽऽयन्तु देवताः । अदब्धं चक्षुरिषितं मनः । सूर्यो ज्योतिषां श्रेष्ठो दीक्षे मा मा हिंसीः। तच्चक्षुर्देवहितं शुक्रमुच्चरत् । पश्येम शरदः शतं जीवेम शरदः शतम् । त्वमग्ने व्रतपा असि देव आ मर्त्येष्वा । त्वं यज्ञेष्वीड्यः । शं नो मित्रः शं वरुणः शं नो भवत्वर्यमा । शं न इन्द्रो बृहस्पतिः शं नो विष्णुरुरुक्रमः । वाङ्मे मनसि प्रतिष्ठिता मनो मे वाचि प्रतिष्ठितमावीरावीर्म एधि वेदस्य म आणी स्थः श्रुतं मे मा प्र हासीरनेनाऽऽधीतेन । अहोरात्रान्त्संदधाम्यृतं वदिष्यामि सत्यं वदिष्यामि तन्मामवतु तद्वक्तारमवत्ववतु मामवतु वक्तारमवतु वक्तारम्' इति ।

[ऐतरेयारण्यकम्]

अथ महाव्रतम् । इन्द्रो वै वृत्रं हत्वा महानभवद् यन्महानभवत्

[सायणभाष्यम्]

वागीशाद्याः सुमनसः सर्वार्थानामुपक्रमे ।
यं नत्वा कृतकृत्याः स्युस्तं नमामि गजाननम् ॥१॥
यस्य निश्वसितं[२] वेदा यो वेदेभ्योऽखिलं जगत् ।
निर्ममे तमहं वन्दे विद्यातीर्थमहेश्वरम् ॥२॥
तत्कटाक्षेण तद्रूपं दधद् बुक्कमहीपतिः ।
आदिशत् सायणाचार्यं वेदार्थस्य प्रकाशने ॥३॥
ये पूर्वोत्तरमीमांसे ते [३]व्याख्यायात्मसंग्रहात्[३] ।
कृपालुः सायणाचार्यो वेदार्थं वक्तुमुद्यतः ॥४॥
ऐतरेयब्राह्मणेऽस्ति काण्डमारण्यकाभिधम् ।
अरण्य एव[४]पाठ्यं स्यादारण्यकमितीर्यताम्[४] ॥५॥
आरण्यकानि पञ्चेति प्रोक्तान्यर्थविभेदतः ।
महाव्रतमहः प्रोक्तं प्रथमारण्यके स्फुटम् ॥६॥
गवामयनमित्युक्ते सत्रे संवत्सरात्मके ।
उपान्त्यमस्ति यदहस्तन्महाव्रतनामकम् ॥७॥
[५]सत्रप्रकरणेऽनुक्तिररण्याध्ययनादिति[५] ।
महाव्रतस्य तस्यात्र हौत्रं कर्म विविच्यते ॥८॥

तत्रादौ विवक्षितमर्थं प्रतिजानीते—**अथ महाव्रतम्** इति । अथशब्द आरम्भवाची । महाव्रताख्यं कर्म प्रारब्धमित्यर्थः । अथवाऽयमानन्तर्यार्थोऽथशब्दः । प्रकृतिज्ञानानन्तरं विकृतिरूपं महाव्रताख्यं कर्माभिधीयत इति शेषः । प्रकृतिज्ञाने हि सति तत्सकाशाद्[६] विकृतावतिदिष्टा धर्माः साकल्येनावबोद्धुं शक्यन्ते। विश्वजिच्चतुर्विंशादीनि कर्माणि महाव्रतस्य प्रकृतयः । आज्यप्रउगनामके द्वे शस्त्रे विश्वजिदाख्यात्[७] कर्मणो महाव्रतेऽतिदिश्येते । होत्रकाणां शस्त्राणि तु[८] चतुर्विंशाख्यात् कर्मणोऽतिदिश्यन्ते । तथा च पञ्चमारण्यके पठिष्यते— 'आज्य-

---

२. **निःश्व°** क.
३-३. **व्याख्यायातिसंग्रहात्** रा.
४-४. **पाठ्यत्वादारण्यकमितीर्यते** रा. (राजेन्द्रलाल मित्र संस्करणम्)
५-५. **°नुक्तकरणाध्य°** घ. अ.
६. **ततो** रा.
७. **ख्याञ्च** ख.ग.घ.अ (=अडियार पुस्तकालय-हस्तलेखः)
८. नास्ति रा.

तन्महाव्रतस्य महाव्रतत्वम् ।

प्रउगे विश्वजितः । होत्राश्चतुर्विंशत्' । (ऐआ ५. १.१) इति।

महाव्रतं प्रशंसितुमाख्यायिकामुखेन तच्छब्दनिर्वचनं दर्शयति–**इन्द्रो वै वृत्रं हत्वा महानभवद् यन्महानभवत् तन्महाव्रतमभवत् तन्महाव्रतस्य महाव्रतत्वम्** इति। वृत्रवधस्य श्रुत्यन्तरप्रसिद्धिद्योतनार्थो वैशब्दः । तैत्तिरीयके दर्शपूर्णमासब्राह्मणशेषे 'त्वष्टा हतपुत्रः' (तैसं २.४.१२) इत्यस्मिन्ननुवाके वृत्रनाम्नोऽसुरस्योत्पत्तिवृद्ध्यादिकं बहुना प्रपञ्चेनाभिधायान्ते द्यावापृथिवीभ्यामनुज्ञातेनेन्द्रेण कृतो वृत्रवध एवमाम्नायते–'स आभ्यामेव प्रसूत इन्द्रो वृत्रमहन्' (तैसं २.५.२.६) इति । एवमन्यत्रापि –'इन्द्रो वृत्राय वज्रं प्राहरत्' (तैसं २.५.६.२), 'इन्द्रो वृत्राय वज्रमुदयच्छत्' (तैसं ६.५.१.१), 'इन्द्रो वृत्रं हत्वा' (तैसं २.५.३.१) इत्यादिषु प्रसिद्धिर्द्रष्टव्या । ईदृशात् प्रसिद्धाद् वृत्रवधाद् ऊर्ध्वम् इन्द्रो महानभवत् । भीतिराहित्यमस्य महत्त्वम् । वृत्रवधात्पुरा तु स्वकीयां भीतिं स्वयमेव प्रजापतेरग्रे प्रोवाच । तथा च तैत्तिरीया आमनन्ति–'तस्मादिन्द्रोऽबिभेत् स प्रजापतिमुपाधावच्छत्रुर्मेऽजनि' (तैसं २.५.२.५) इति । इत्थं भीतस्य त्विच्छया[९] बहुषु देशेषु संचारासंभवात् स्वगृहे च निद्राभोजनादौ बिभ्यतः स्वास्थ्याभावादल्पत्वम् । अतो निर्भयत्वमेव महत्त्वम् । यद् यदाऽसाविन्द्रो महानभवत् [१०]तत् तदानीम्[१०] इन्द्रार्थं क्रियमाणं सोमपानविशेषात्मकं कर्म महाव्रतमभवत्, तत् तस्मात्कारणाद् याज्ञिकैर्महाव्रतमिति व्यवह्रियमाणस्य कर्मणो महाव्रतनामकत्वं संपन्नम् । तस्य च नाम्नस्त्रेधा निर्वचनं द्रष्टव्यम् – महान्भवत्यनेन व्रतेनेति महाव्रतं, महतो देवस्य व्रतमिति महाव्रतं, महच्च तद्व्रतमिति महाव्रतमिति । एतानि त्रीणि निर्वचनानि तैत्तिरीया आमनन्ति–' प्रजापतिः प्रजाः सृष्ट्वा वृत्तोऽशयत्। तं देवा भूतानां रसं तेजः संभृत्य । तेनैनमभिषज्यन् । महानववर्तीति। तन्महाव्रतस्य महाव्रतत्वम् । महतो व्रतमिति । तन्महाव्रतस्य महाव्रतत्वम्' (तैब्रा १.२.६.१) इति । वृत्तोऽशयत् श्रान्तो भूमावपतत् । तदानीं ते देवास्तेजोभूतं तं द्युलोकाद् गायत्र्या समानीतं रसायनरूपं सोमं महाव्रताङ्गभूतैर्मन्त्रैः संपाद्याथ प्रजापतिं तेन सोमेन चिकित्सित्वा महानववर्तीति श्रमरहितो वृत्तोऽनेन कर्मणेत्युक्तवन्तः । छन्दोगैरपि महद्व्रतं महतो व्रतमिति निरुक्तिद्वयमाम्नातम् –'प्रजापतिः प्रजा असृजत । सोऽरिच्यत । सोऽपद्यत । तं देवा अभिसंगच्छन्त । तेऽब्रुवन् । महदस्मै व्रतं संभराम । यदिमं धिनवदिति । तस्मै तत्संवत्सरमन्नं पच्यते । तत्संभरदस्मै प्रायच्छंस्तदव्रजयन्त तदेनमधिनोन्महन्मर्या व्रतं यदिममधिन्वीदिति । तन्महाव्रतस्य महाव्रतत्वम् । प्रजापतिर्वाव महांस्तस्यै-

---

९. **स्वेच्छया** रा.

१०-१०. **तदिदा**° क.

द्वे एतस्याह्न आज्ये कुर्यादिति हैक आहुरेकमिति त्वेव स्थितम् । प्र वो देवायाग्नय इति राद्धिकामः । विशोविशो वो अतिथिमिति पुष्टिकामः ।

तद्व्रतम्' (तांब्रा ४.१०.१) इति । अरिच्यत शक्त्या रिक्तोऽभूत् । अपद्यत भूमौ पतितः । धिनवत् प्रीणयति[११] अव्रजयत् प्राप्नोत् । अधिनोद् अप्रीणयत् । हे मर्या मरणयोग्या मनुष्या यद् व्रतमिमं प्रजापतिमधिन्वीदप्रीणयत् तद् व्रतं महदिति देवा उक्तवन्त इत्यर्थः ।

इत्थं महाव्रतं प्रशस्य तत्र प्रातःसवने होत्रा शंसनीय आज्यनामके शस्त्रे पूर्वपक्षसिद्धान्तौ दर्शयति – **द्वे एतस्याह्न आज्ये कुर्यादिति हैक आहुरेकमिति त्वेव स्थितम्** इति । एतस्य महाव्रताख्यस्याह्नः प्राकृतं वैकृतं चेत्येवं द्वे आज्यशस्त्रे कुर्यात् । 'प्र वो देवायाग्नये' (ऋ ३.१३.१) इति सप्तर्चं सूक्तमाज्यशस्त्रत्वेनाग्निष्टोमेऽभिहितत्वात्[१२] प्राकृतम् । 'अग्निं नरो दीधितिभिः' (ऋ ७.१.१) इति पञ्चविंशत्यृचं सूक्तम् आज्यशस्त्रत्वेन विश्वजिति विधानाद्[१३] वैकृतम् । ते द्वे अपि प्राकृतवैकृते आज्ये अस्मिन् महाव्रते कुर्यादित्येवमेके शाखान्तरीया[१४] आहुः । सोऽयं पूर्वः पक्षः । तस्य पूर्वपक्षस्य व्यावृत्त्यर्थस्तुशब्दः। द्वे आज्ये न कुर्यात्, किन्तु विशेषविधानाद् वैकृतमेकमाज्यं कुर्यादित्येव सिद्धान्तरहस्यं स्थितम् । यदाऽऽज्ये शस्त्रद्वयमङ्गीक्रियेत तदानीमग्निष्टोमसंस्थेऽस्मिन् महाव्रते प्रकृतितः प्राप्तेभ्यो द्वादशभ्यः शस्त्रेभ्योऽधिकं शस्त्रं प्राप्नुयात् । तच्चायुक्तम्, 'द्वादशाग्निष्टोमस्य स्तोत्राणि, द्वादश शस्त्राणि[१५] इति श्रुत्यन्तरविरोधात् । तदेवमत्र नित्यमाज्यशस्त्रं व्यवस्थापितम् ।

अथ काम्यान्याज्यशस्त्राण्युच्यन्ते । तत्र समृद्धिफलाय शस्त्रविशेषं विधत्ते–**'प्र वो देवायाग्नये' (ऋ ३.१३.१) इति राद्धिकामः** इति । तच्च सप्तर्चं सूक्तमिति पूर्वमेवाभिहितम् ।

पुष्टिफलाय सूक्तान्तरं विधत्ते – **विशोविशो वो अतिथिम् (ऋ ८.७४.१) इति पुष्टिकामः** इति । एतच्च सूक्तं पञ्चदशर्चम् ।

तस्य पुष्टिहेतुत्वमुपपादयति–**पुष्टिर्वै विशः पुष्टिमान् भवतीति** इति । विशो वैश्यास्ते हि वाणिज्येन बहुधनमर्जयन्तः करमपि बहुलं प्रयच्छन्ति । अतो विशां पुष्टित्वम् । अस्मिन्नर्थे लोकप्रसिद्धिर्वैशब्देनोच्यते । सूक्ते तु विशोविश इति वीप्सया बहुविधानां वैश्यानामभिहितत्वात् तेन सूक्तेनायं यजमानः पुष्टिमान्

---

११. **प्रीणयत्** रा.

१२. द्र. आश्रौ ५.९. १५

१३. द्र. आश्रौ ८.७.१

१४. द्र. शांआ १.२

१५. द्र. तांब्रा ६.३.३

पुष्टिर्वै विशः पुष्टिमान् भवतीति । अतिथिमिति पदं भवति नैतत् कुर्यादित्याहुरीश्वरोऽतिथिरेव चरितोः । तदु ह स्माऽऽह कुर्यादेव । यो वै भवति यः श्रेष्ठतामश्नुते स वा अतिथिर्भवति । न वा असन्त-

---

भवतीत्येतदुपपन्नम् । इतिशब्दो हेत्वर्थः । यस्मात् पुष्टिमान् भवति तस्मात् पुष्टिकामस्तत्सूक्तं कुर्यात् ।

अत्र पूर्वपक्षत्वेन तत्सूक्तं दूषयति – **अतिथिमिति पदं भवति नैतत् कुर्यादित्याहुरीश्वरोऽतिथिरेव चरितोः** इति । अस्मिन् सूक्ते दरिद्रस्य वाचकम् अतिथिमिति पदं वर्तते । तस्मान्नैतत्सूक्तं कुर्यादित्येवं केचित् पण्डितंमन्या आहुः । तत्रोपपत्तिं च वर्णयन्ति–य एतदाज्यं कुर्यात् सोऽयमतिथिरेव दरिद्र एव भूत्वा याच्ञार्थं परगृहेषु सर्वदा चरितुं प्रभुर्भवतीति ।

[१६]अत्र सिद्धान्तत्वेन तस्य सूक्तस्य प्रसङ्गं च विधत्ते[१६] –**तदु ह स्माऽऽह कुर्यादेव** इति । अतिथिपदतात्पर्याभिज्ञः सिद्धान्ती [१७]तदु ह[१७] सूक्तमवश्यं कुर्यादित्याह स्म ।

पूर्वपक्षोक्तदूषणशमनार्थम् अतिथिशब्दतात्पर्यं दर्शयति–**यो वै भवति यः श्रेष्ठतामश्नुते स वा अतिथिर्भवति** इति । [१८]अत्रास्तिवाची[१८] भूधातुः सन्मार्गवर्तिनं ब्रूते । यस्तु पुमान् सन्मार्गवर्ती भवति तस्मिन्नपि सन्मार्गवर्तिसंघे यः पुमान् अतिशयेन प्राशस्त्यं प्राप्नोति स एवातिथिर्भवति । अतः प्राशस्त्यमत्र शब्दप्रवृत्तिनिमित्तं न तु दारिद्र्यम् ।

एतदेव व्यतिरेकमुखेन स्पष्टयति[१९] –**न वा असन्तमातिथ्यायाऽऽद्रियन्ते** इति। सन्मार्गरहितं व्रात्याभिशस्तादिकं पुरुषम् अत्यन्त–दरिद्रमप्यातिथ्यसत्काराय[२०] नाऽऽद्रियन्ते ।

सिद्धान्तं निगमयति–**तस्मादु काममेवैतत् कुर्याद्** इति । यस्माद् अतिथिशब्दो न दुष्टः, किन्तु प्रशस्तस्तस्मादेव कारणाद् विस्रम्भेणैवैतत्सूक्तं कुर्यात् ।

तत्सूक्तप्रयोगे कंचिद् विशेषं विधत्ते–**स यद्येतत् कुर्याद् 'आगन्म वृत्रहन्तमम्' (ऋ ८.७४.४) इत्येतं तृचं प्रथमं कुर्याद्** इति । तस्मिन् सूक्ते 'विशो विशः' (ऋ ८.७४.१) इत्यादिकः प्रथमस्तृचः । 'आगन्म' इत्यादिको द्वितीयस्तृचः । प्रयोगकाले त्वागन्मेत्यादिकं प्रथमत्वेन पठेत् ।

तत्रोपपत्तिमाह– **एतद्वा अहरीप्सन्तः संवत्सरमासते त आगच्छन्ति** इति । ये

१६-१६. **अत्र सिद्धान्तत्वेनैतत्सूक्तविधानार्थं प्रतिप्रसवं विधत्ते** रा.

१७-१७. **तदु ह तदेव** रा.

१८. **सत्तावाची** रा.

१९. **व्यवस्यति** अ.

२०. °**तिथ्याय सत्काराय** अ.

मातिथ्यायाऽऽद्रियन्ते । तस्मादु काममेवैतत् कुर्यात् । स यद्येतत् कुर्याद् 'आगन्म वृत्रहन्तमम्' इत्येतं तृचं प्रथमं कुर्यात् । एतद् वा अहरीप्सन्तः संवत्सरमासते त आगच्छन्ति । त एतेऽनुष्टुप्शीर्षाणस्त्रयस्तृचा भवन्ति ब्रह्म वै गायत्री वागनुष्टुब् ब्रह्मणैव तद् वाचं संदधाति । 'अबोध्यग्निः

गवामयननामकं संवत्सरसत्रमनुतिष्ठन्ति ते महाव्रताख्यम् एतदेवोपान्त्यम् अहः प्राप्तुमिच्छन्तोऽनुतिष्ठन्ति । तथा सत्यागन्मेति प्राप्तिवाचकं शब्दं प्रयुञ्जानास्ते पुरुषा एतदहरागच्छन्ति तस्माद् एतस्य प्राथम्यं युक्तम् ।

अतिथिमागन्मेति पदद्वयतात्पर्यदर्शनेन तृचद्वयं व्याख्यातम् । अथावशिष्टानां तृचानां तात्पर्यं दर्शयति– **त एतेऽनुष्टुप्शीर्षाणस्त्रयस्तृचा भवन्ति ब्रह्म वै गायत्री वागनुष्टुब् ब्रह्मणैव तद् वाचं संदधाति** इति । पञ्चदशर्चे 'विशोविशः'(ऋ ८.७४.१) इत्यादिके सूक्ते प्रथमतस्तृचद्वये गते सति तत ऊर्ध्वं त्रयस्तृचाः शिष्यन्ते[२१], तेष्वन्तिमस्तृचः 'अहं हुवानः' इत्यादिकोऽनुष्टुप्छन्दस्कः । [२२]तत्रानुष्टुप्छन्दसि तदुत्तमाङ्गस्थानं[२२] येषां तृचानां[२३] तेऽनुष्टुप्शीर्षाणः । एते तृचास्त्रिसंख्याकाः । तत्रोपान्त्यतृचे ततः पूर्वतने तृचे च गायत्री छन्दो विद्यते। सा च गायत्री ब्रह्मैव, 'तत् सवितुर्वरेण्यम्' (ऋ ३.६२.१०) इत्यनया गायत्र्या परब्रह्मणः प्रतिपाद्यत्वात्। येयं तृचगताऽनुष्टुप् सा वाग्रूपा चतुष्पात्त्वसामान्यात्। 'चत्वारि वाक् परिमिता पदानि' (ऋ १.१६४.४५) इति वाचः पादचतुष्टयमाम्नातम्। परा पश्यन्ती मध्यमा [२४]वैखरीत्युक्तं यत्पादचतुष्टयम्[२४] अन्यैर्व्याख्यातम्(द्र.वा.प. १.१४३)। अनुष्टुभस्तु चतुष्पात्त्वं प्रसिद्धम्। एवं सत्यस्मिन् सूक्ते गायत्र्यनुष्टुभोर्मेलने सति तन्त्रेण[२५] सूक्तपाठेन ब्रह्मणैव वाचं संयोजयति।

अथ कीर्तिफलार्थं सूक्तान्तरं विधत्ते– **अबोध्यग्निः समिधा जनानाम्** (ऋ ५.१.१) **इति कीर्तिकामः** इति। अबोधीत्यादिकं द्वादशर्चं सूक्तम्।

प्रजापशुफलार्थम् अन्यत्सूक्तं विधत्ते– **होताऽजनिष्ट चेतनः** (ऋ २.५.१) **इति प्रजापशुकामः** इति। होतेत्यादिकम् अष्टर्चं सूक्तम्। यथोक्तानां[२६] काम्यसूक्तानां गोदोहनन्यायेन फलार्थत्वमेव न तु[२७] क्रत्वर्थत्वम्।

स च न्यायश्चतुर्थाध्यायस्य प्रथमपादे चिन्तितः।

" गोदोहनं द्वयार्थं स्यान्न वा[२८] भानाद् द्वयार्थता।

---

२१. **अवशिष्यन्ते** रा.
२२-२२. **°छन्दः शिर उत्तमा°** रा.
२३. **स्थानं** ख.
२४-२४. **वैखरीत्येवं पाद°** रा.
२५. **तत्तेन** रा.
२६. **अत्र यथो°** रा.
२७. नास्ति क.
२८. **च** क.

समिधा जनानाम्' इति कीर्तिकामः। 'होताऽजनिष्ट चेतनः' इति प्रजापशुकामः।

।।इत्यैतरेयब्राह्मणारण्यकाण्डे प्रथमारण्यके प्रथमेऽध्याये प्रथमः खण्डः।।

अन्यथाऽपि क्रतोः सिद्धेः केवलं पुरुषाय तत् ।। ''

दर्शपूर्णमासयोः श्रूयते – 'चमसेनापः प्रणयेत्' (आपश्रौ १.१५.३), 'गोदोहनेन पशुकामस्य' (आपश्रौ १.१६.३) इति। तत्र गोदोहनस्य क्रत्वर्थत्वं पुरुषार्थत्वं चेत्याकारद्वयमस्ति। पशुफलजननेन पुरुषप्रीतिर्भाति, अपां प्रणयनेन क्रतुपौष्कल्यमपि भातीति चेत्, मैवम्। गोदोहनमन्तरेण फलासिद्धेर्भवतु पुरुषार्थत्वं क्रतुस्तु तदभावेऽपि[२९] चमसेन सिध्यतीति न क्रत्वर्थता'' (जै. न्या. ४.१.२) । एवमत्रापि[३०] यथोक्तानि काम्यसूक्तानि फलार्थान्येव न तु क्रत्वर्थानि। एवं तर्हि क्रतोरङ्गवैकल्यं प्रसज्येतेति चेत्, मैवम्। काम्यानामेतेषां क्रत्वङ्गभूतं शंसनमाश्रित्य विधानमिति[३१] काम्यैरपि[३२] सूक्तैः क्रत्वङ्गस्य शंसनस्य निष्पत्तेः, काम्येन नित्यसिद्धिरिति तान्त्रिकाणां डिण्डिमः[३३]। तस्मात् फलसाधनत्वेन विधानात् एतैः फलं साक्षात् सिध्यति। अर्थात् क्रतोः साङ्गत्वमित्युपपन्नम्[३४]।

।।इति श्रीमत्सायणाचार्यविरचिते माधवीये वेदार्थप्रकाश ऐतरेयब्राह्मणारण्यककाण्डभाष्ये प्रथमारण्यके प्रथमाध्याये प्रथमः खण्डः।।१।।

अन्नाद्यफलाय सूक्तान्तरं विधत्ते– **'अग्निं नरो दीधितिभिररण्योः' (ऋ ७.१.१) इत्यन्नाद्यकामः** इति। अत्तुं योग्यं आद्यं शाल्यादिनिष्पन्नमन्नम्। अन्नं च तदाद्यं चेत्यन्नाद्यं तस्मिन् कामोऽस्य। अग्निं नर इत्यादिकं पञ्चविंशत्यृचम् आज्यशस्त्रम् अवगन्तव्यम्।

अस्य सूक्तस्यान्नहेतुत्वं संभावयति– **अग्निर्वा अन्नादः** इति । अग्नेरन्नभोजकत्वे[१] लोकप्रसिद्धिद्योतनार्थो वैशब्दः। अग्नेः स्वयमन्नभोजकत्वेनान्नप्रियत्वात् तद्विषयसूक्तेनान्नलाभो युक्त इत्यर्थः।

ननु 'प्र वो देवायाग्नये' (ऋ ३.१३.१) इत्यादिसूक्तेष्वप्यग्निर्विद्यत इत्या-

---

२९. **°ऽपि नास्ति** क.
३०. **एबमन्यान्यपि** अ.
३१. **बिघाने सति** रा.
३२. **काम्यैः** अ.
३३. **बिदितम्** रा.
३४. **°मित्युभयमुप°** रा.
१. **°न्नभक्षकत्वे** रा.

अग्निं नरो दीधितिभिररण्योरित्यन्नाद्यकामः। अग्निर्वै अन्नादः। चिरतरमिव वा इतरेष्वाज्येष्वग्निमागच्छन्त्यथेह मुखत एवाग्निमागच्छन्ति मुखतोऽन्नाद्यमश्नुते मुखतः पाप्मानमपघ्नते। हस्तच्युती जनयन्तेति जातवदेतस्माद्वा अह्नो यजमानो जायते तस्माज्जातवत्। तानि चत्वारि

शङ्क्य तेभ्योऽस्ये[२] सूक्तस्य विशेषं दर्शयति— **चिरतरमिव वा इतरेष्वाज्येष्वग्निमागच्छन्त्यथेह मुखत एवाग्निमागच्छन्ति मुखतोऽन्नाद्यमश्नुते मुखतः पाप्मानमपघ्नते** इति। इतरेषु [३]'प्र वो देवायाग्नये' (ऋ ३.१३.१) इत्यादिष्वाज्यशस्त्रेषु यजमाना अत्यन्तविलम्बो यथा*भवति तथैवाग्निं प्राप्नुवन्ति[३] सूक्तादावग्निपदाभावात्। इह तु तत्सद्भावाद् आदावेव सहसाग्निं प्राप्नुवन्ति। [४]अतो भवदा (?°तोऽन्ना) द्यमादौ[४] विलम्बमन्तरेणैव यजमानसंघः प्राप्नोति। तथा ते यजमाना आदावेव पाप्मानं नाशयन्ति।

सूक्तस्य प्रथमपादेऽग्निं शब्दं प्रशस्य द्वितीयपादे जनयन्तेति शब्दं प्रशंसति —**हस्तच्युती जनयन्तेति जातवदेतस्माद्वा अह्नो यजमानो जायते तस्माज्जातवद्** इति। हस्तेत्यादिर्द्वितीयपादस्तस्यायमर्थः[५]—हस्तव्यापारेणैवे[६] जनयन्त यजमाना अग्निमुत्पादयन्त इति। तत्र जनयन्तेत्यनेन शब्देनेदं सूक्तं जातवज्जन्मवाचकशब्दोपेतं[७] भवति। एतस्माज्जन्मवाचिशब्दोपेतसूक्तयुक्ताद् अह्नो महाव्रताख्यात् कर्मणो यजमानोऽयं तत्फलयोग्यजन्मवान् भवति। तस्मात् कारणात् तथाविधजन्मसाधनभूतं सूक्तम्[८]।

अस्मिन् पञ्चविंशत्यृचे सूक्ते (ऋ ७.१) आदावष्टादशर्चो विराट्छन्दस्काः। अवशिष्टास्तु 'मा नो अग्नेऽवीर ते' इत्यादिकाः सप्तर्चस्त्रिष्टुप्छन्दस्काः। तास्वेकैकस्यामृचि पादचतुष्टययुतानि[९] च्छन्दांसि प्रशंसति— **तानि चत्वारि च्छन्दांसि भवन्ति चतुष्पादा वै पशवः पशूनामवरुद्ध्यै** इति। 'एकादशाक्षरा त्रिष्टुप्' (तैसं ३.४.९.७) इति श्रुत्यन्तराद् एकैकस्मिन् पाद एकैकं त्रिष्टुबाख्यं छन्दोऽस्ति। ततश्चतुर्षु पादेषु चत्वारि त्रिष्टुप्छंदांसि संपद्यन्ते। ततः पशूनां [१०]चतुष्पात्त्वात् तेन[१०] तत्साम्यात् पशुप्राप्तिर्भवति।

यास्तु सूक्तादिगता विराट्छन्दस्का ऋचस्तासां पादगतानि च्छन्दांसि

---

२. **ततोऽस्य** रा.

३-३. **नास्ति** अ. ***यथा न** क. ख

४-४. **अतोऽनवद्यम् । आदौ** रा.

५. **°तीयः पाद°** क.

६. **°णैव बाध्येन आन, °णेव बाध्येनं अ.,** **हस्तच्युती हस्तंव्यापारेण मथनाख्येन** रा.

७. **°शब्दवद्** रा.

८. **सूक्तं जन्मवाचिशब्दोपेतमित्येतद् युक्तम्** रा.

९. **°युक्तानि** क. ख. ग. **°ष्टयगतानि** रा.

१०-१०. **चतुष्पात्त्वेन** रा.

च्छन्दांसि भवन्ति चतुष्पादा वै पशवः पशूनामवरुद्ध्यै । तानि त्रीणि च्छन्दांसि भवन्ति त्रयो वा इमे त्रिवृतो लोका एषामेव लोकानामभिजित्यै। ते द्वे छन्दसी भवतः प्रतिष्ठाया एव द्विप्रतिष्ठो वै पुरुषश्चतुष्पादाः पशवो यजमानमेव तद् द्विप्रतिप्रतिष्ठं चतुष्पात्सु पशुषु प्रतिष्ठापयति। ताः पराग्वचनेन पञ्चविंशतिर्भवन्ति पञ्चविंशोऽयं पुरुषो दश हस्त्या अङ्गुलयो दश पाद्या द्वा ऊरू द्वौ बाहू आत्मैव पञ्चविंशस्तमिममात्मानं पञ्चविंशं संस्कुरुते । अथो पञ्चविंशं वा एतदहः पञ्चविंश एतस्याह्नः

प्रशंसति – **तानि त्रीणि च्छन्दांसि भवन्ति त्रयो वा इमे त्रिवृतो लोका एषामेव लोकानामभिजित्यै** इति। यथा 'चतुष्पदा त्रिष्टुप्' (तैसं ३.२.९.१.), 'एकाक्षरा त्रिष्टुप्' (तैसं ३.४.९.७.) इति श्रुत्योः पादसंख्याऽक्षरसंख्या च श्रुता तथा 'त्रिपदा विराट्' (मैसं ३.४.६.), 'दशाक्षरा विराट्' (तैसं २.६.१.२.) इति श्रुत्योः[११] संख्याद्वयं श्रुतम्। ततस्त्रिष्वपि पादेषु दशाक्षरसंख्याकानि त्रीणि विराट्च्छन्दांसि संपद्यन्ते। लोकाश्च पृथिव्यन्तरिक्षं द्यौरित्येवं त्रिसंख्याकाः, उत्तममध्यमाधमैः सात्त्विकराजसतामसैः प्राणिभिरुपेतत्त्वात् त्रिवृतश्च। ततः[१२] संख्यासाम्याल्लोकजयो भवति।

सूक्ते पूर्वोत्तरभागयोर्वर्तमाने विराट्त्रिष्टुबित्येते द्वे छन्दसी प्रशंसति – **ते द्वे छन्दसी भवतः प्रतिष्ठाया एव द्विप्रतिष्ठो वै पुरुषश्चतुष्पादाः पशवो यजमानमेव तद् द्विप्रतिष्ठं चतुष्पात्सु पशुषु प्रतिष्ठापयति इति।** छन्दोद्वयं[१३] प्रतिष्ठार्थमेव संपद्यते। लौकिकः पुरुषः सर्वोऽपि भूमौ द्वाभ्यां पादाभ्यां प्रतिष्ठितत्वाद् द्विप्रतिष्ठो भवति। पशवस्तु चतुष्पादाः। एवं सति च्छन्दोद्वित्वेन पादचतुष्ट्वेन च द्विपादं यजमानं चतुष्पात्सु पशुषु होता प्रतिष्ठापयति।

इदानीं सर्वास्वृक्ष्ववस्थितां पञ्चविंशतिसंख्यां प्रशंसति – **ताः पराग्वचनेन पञ्चविंशतिर्भवन्ति पञ्चविंशोऽयं पुरुषो दश हस्त्या अङ्गुलयो दश पाद्या द्वा ऊरू द्वौ बाहू आत्मैव पञ्चविंशस्तमिममात्मानं पञ्चविंशं संस्कुरुते** इति। आवृत्ति-मन्तरेणोर्ध्वपाठः पराग्वचनम्। आत्मा मध्यदेहः[१४], 'मध्यं ह्येषामङ्गानामात्मा' (ऐआ २.३.५.) इति वक्ष्यमाणत्वात्। तेनात्मना सहितैरवयवैः सर्वैरयं पुरुषः पञ्चविंशतिसंख्योपेतः। अतस्तादृशं पुरुषम् ऋग्गतया पञ्चविंशतिसंख्यया संस्करोति[१५]।

प्रकारान्तरेण तां संख्यां प्रशंसति– **अथो पञ्चविंशं वा एतदहः पञ्चविंश**

---

११. श्रुत्योस्तु रा. १२. अतः रा.
१३. छन्दोद्वित्वं रा.
१४. देहम् ख. ग.
१५. संस्कृतं करोति अ.

स्तोमस्तत्समेन समं प्रतिपद्यते तस्माद् द्वे एव पञ्चविंशतिर्भवन्ति। तास्त्रिः प्रथमया त्रिरुत्तमयैकयानत्रिंशन्न्यूनाक्षरा विराण् न्यूने वै रेतः सिच्यते न्यूने प्राणा न्यूनेऽन्नाद्यं प्रतिष्ठितमेतेषां कामानामवरुद्ध्यै। एतान् कामानवरुन्द्धे य एवं वेद। ता अभिसंपद्यन्ते बृहती च विराजं च

एतस्याह्नः[१६] **स्तोमस्तत्समेन समं प्रतिपद्यते तस्मात् द्वे एव पञ्चविंशतिर्भवन्ति** इति। अथो अपि चेत्यर्थः। यन्महाव्रताख्यमहस्तदेतत् पञ्चविंशतिसंख्योपेतमेव। तत्कथमिति तदुच्यते – एतस्याह्नो यः स्तोमः सामगैः स्तोत्रकाले[१७] तृचस्याऽऽवृत्त्या संपद्यते सोऽयं त्रिवृत्पञ्चदशादिरूपो न भवति किन्तु पञ्चविंशस्तस्मात् कारणात् पञ्चविंशतिसंख्यया समेन सूक्तेन पञ्चविंशतिस्तोमयुक्तं समं तदहः [१८]प्राप्नोतीति तस्माद्[१८] एतदहः सूक्तं चेत्युभयं समं तस्माद् एते द्वे अहःसूक्ते पञ्चविंशतिसंख्याप्रयुक्ते[१९] एव भवतः। अन्यथा साम्यासंभवात्। भवन्तीति बहुवचनं तु सूक्तगतानामृचां स्तोत्रगतानां चापेक्षया द्रष्टव्यम्।

तस्मिन् सूक्ते प्रथमोत्तमयोर्ऋचोरावृत्तिविधिमभिप्रेत्य तदावृत्तिसहितां संख्यां प्रशंसति– **तास्त्रिः प्रथमया त्रिरुत्तमयैकयानत्रिंशन्**[२०] **न्यूनाक्षरा विराण् न्यूने वै रेतः सिच्यते न्यूने प्राणा न्यूनेऽन्नाद्यं प्रतिष्ठितमेतेषां कामानामवरुद्ध्यै** इति। ताः सूक्तगताः पञ्चविंशतिसंख्याका ऋचस्त्रिरावृत्तया प्रथमया त्रिरावृत्तया चोत्तमया सहिताः सत्यो मिलिता एकोनत्रिंशत्संख्याकाः संपद्यन्ते। एकयर्चा न संपूर्णा त्रिंशदित्येकयोनत्रिंशत्[२१], त्रिंशदक्षरा विराट् (तैब्रा १. ६. ३. ४) इति श्रुतेर्विराट्छन्दसस्त्रिंशत्संख्योपेतत्वाद् अत्र त्रिंशत्संख्यायाम् एकया न्यूनत्वाद् इयमृक्संख्या न्यूनाक्षरा विराट् संपद्यते। लोकेऽपि न्यूने वै स्वल्प एव गर्भाशये प्रजोत्पादनार्थं रेतः सिच्यते। तथा स्वल्पे हृदयपुण्डरीके प्राणाः प्रतितिष्ठन्ति, स्वल्पे चोदरेऽन्नाद्यं प्रतिष्ठितं[२२], तस्मादियं न्यूना[२३] विराड् एतेषां प्रजोत्पत्तिप्राणान्नप्रतिष्ठारूपाणां कामानां प्राप्त्यै संपद्यते।

यथोक्तार्थवेदनं प्रशंसति– **एतान् कामानवरुन्द्धे य एवं वेद** इति। यः पुमान् एवम् ऋग्गताम् एकोनत्रिंशत्संख्यां वेद स पुमान् उक्तान् कामानाप्नोति। वेदनमात्रेण फलप्राप्तिर्यजुर्वेदार्थप्रकाशे (उपोद्घाते) उपपादिता।

प्रकारान्तरेण सूक्तगता ऋचः प्रशंसति– **ता अभिसंपद्यन्ते बृहतीं च विराजं च च्छन्दो यैतस्याह्नःसंपत् तामथो अनुष्टुभमनुष्टुबायतनानि ह्ययाज्यानि** इति। या

---

१६. °ह्न कीयः
१७. **स्तोमकाले** रा.
१८. **प्राप्नोति । यस्माद्** रा.
१९. **संख्यायुक्ते** रा.
२०. **°कया न त्रिंश°** कीयः
२१. **°त्रिंशदिति योजना** रा.
२२. **°तं भवति** रा.
२३. **न्यूनाक्षरा** रा.

च्छन्दो यैतस्याह्नः संपत् ताम् अथो अनुष्टुभम् अनुष्टुबायतनानि ह्याज्यानि।

।।इत्यैतरेयब्राह्मणारण्यकाण्डे प्रथमारण्यके प्रथमाध्याये द्वितीयः खण्डः ।।२।।

ऋचः सूक्ते प्रोक्ताः 'अग्निं नरः' (ऋ ७.१) इत्यादिकास्ताः सर्वा ऋचो मिलित्वा बृहत्याख्यच्छन्दोऽ[२४]भिसंपद्यन्ते। तथा विराडाख्यं छन्दोऽभिसंपद्यन्ते। एवं सत्येतस्य महाव्रतस्याह्नोऽपेक्षिता[२५] या संपत् तां प्राप्ता भवन्ति। तत्राऽऽदावष्टादशानामृचां स्वत एव विराडभिसंपत्तिः सिद्धा। यास्तूत्तराः सप्त त्रिष्टुभस्तासु बृहतीछन्दः संपादनीयम्। अन्तिमाया ऋचस्त्रिरावृत्तौ सत्यां नव त्रिष्टुभः संपद्यन्ते। तासु प्रत्येकम् अष्टाक्षरेष्वतीतेष्ववशिष्टा[२६] नव बृहत्यो भवन्ति। अपनीताश्च नवसंख्याका अष्टाक्षरपादा मिलित्वा द्वासप्ततिरक्षराणि संपद्यन्ते[२७]। तत् षट्त्रिंशदक्षरोपेते द्वे बृहत्यौ निष्पद्येते। तदेवं बृहतीछन्दःसंपत्तिः। अपि[२८]चैवम् आद्यायामृच्यनुष्टुप्त्वस्य[२८] संपादयितुं शक्यत्वात् ताः सूक्तगता ऋचोऽनुष्टुभमभिसंपद्यन्ते । यद्यप्याद्यायास्त्रयस्त्रिंशदक्षरत्वात् एकमक्षरम् अनुष्टुभोऽधिकं तथापि नैतावताऽनुष्टुप्त्वं हीयते, न वा एकेनाक्षरेण च्छन्दांसि वियन्ति न द्वाभ्याम्' (ऐब्रा १.६.) इति श्रुतेः। यथैवास्यामृच्यक्षरत्रयाधिकत्वेऽपि विराट्त्वम् अनुक्रमणिकाकारैरुक्तम् एकाक्षराधिक्येऽनुष्टुप्त्वं किं न स्यात् । न चैतावता प्रयासेनानुष्टुप्संपादने[२९] प्रयोजनाभावः । यस्माद् आज्यशस्त्राण्यनुष्टुबाश्रितानि 'प्र वो देवायाग्नये' (ऋ ३.१३.१) इत्यादौ तथा दृष्टत्वात् तस्माद् अनुष्टुप्संपत्त्या प्रशस्तमिदं सूक्तमित्यभिप्रायः। नन्वेतत्सूक्तम् अन्नाद्यकामस्य विधीयत इति पुरुषार्थमिदं तथा क्रत्वर्थत्वमप्यस्य चोदकेन[३०] प्रापितम् । तथा हि 'आज्यप्रउगे विश्वजितः' (ऐआ ५.१.१) इति पञ्चमारण्यके वक्ष्यते। विश्वजिन्नाम्न एकाहाच्छस्त्रद्वयमतिदेष्टव्यमिति तस्य वाक्यस्यार्थः 'विश्वजितोऽग्निं नरः' (आश्रौ ८.७.१) इति सूत्रकारेणाभिधानाद् विश्वजिद्विकृतिरूपे महाव्रतेऽपि तदेवातिदिश्यते । तस्माद् एकस्यैव 'अग्निं नरः' (ऋ ७.१.१) इति सूक्तस्य क्रत्वर्थत्वं पुरुषार्थत्वं चेत्युभयविधत्वम् अनुपपन्नम्। नायं दोषः, दधिन्यायेनोपपत्तेः[३१]।

---

२४. °ख्यं छ° रा.
२५. °व्रताख्यस्या° रा.
२६. °ष्वपनीतेष्व° रा. २७. भवन्ति ख. ग.
२८-२८. च प्रथमायामृ° रा.
२९. °नुष्टुप्त्वसं° रा.
३०. चोदकः = अतिदेशः प्रकृतिवद् विकृतिः कर्तव्येत्यादिरूपः।
३१. दध्यादिन्या° रा.

गायत्रं प्रउगं कुर्यादित्याहुस्तेजो वै ब्रह्मवर्चसं गायत्री तेजस्वी ब्रह्मवर्चसी भवतीति। औष्णिहं प्रउगं कुर्यादित्याहुरायुर्वा उष्णिग् आयुष्मान् भवतीति। आनुष्टुभं प्रउगं कुर्यादित्याहुः क्षत्त्रं वा अनुष्टुप् क्षत्त्रस्याऽऽप्त्या इति। बार्हतं प्रउगं कुर्यादित्याहुः श्रीर्वै बृहती श्रीमान् भवतीति। पाङ्क्तं प्रउगं कुर्यादित्याहुरन्नं वै पङ्क्तिरन्नवान् भवतीति।

स च न्यायश्चतुर्थाध्यायस्य तृतीयपादे चिन्तितः[३२]।

'दध्ना त्विन्द्रियकामस्य नित्योऽन्यदुत तद्दधि ।

अन्यत् स्यात् पूर्ववन्नैवं संयोगस्य पृथक्त्वतः ।।

अग्निहोत्रे श्रूयते–''दध्नेन्द्रियकामस्य जुहुयात्'' (तैब्रा २.१.५.६) इति। तत्र दध्नः काम्यत्वान्नित्येऽग्निहोत्रे पूर्वन्यायेन तद् दधि न प्रयोक्तव्यं किन्त्वन्यदेव किंचिद् द्रव्यमिति चेत्, मैवम्। 'दध्ना जुहोति' इत्यस्मिन् वाक्यान्तरे कामसंयोगमुपन्यस्य नित्यहोमसंयोगेन दधिविधानात्। तस्माद् एकस्यापि दध्नो वाक्यद्वयेन नित्यत्वं काम्यत्वं चाविरुद्धम् । एवमग्नीषोमीयपशौ 'खादिरे बध्नाति'; खादिरं वीर्यकामस्य यूपं कुर्वीत' (तु. आपश्रौ ७.१.१६) इत्युदाहरणीयम्'' (जैन्या ४.३.३)। अनेन दधिन्यायेनात्रापि काम्येन 'अग्निं नरो दीधितिभिररण्योः' (ऋ ७.१.१) इति सूक्तप्रयोगेण पुरुषार्थेन क्रतुरपि निष्पद्यत इत्येकस्यैव सूक्तस्य चोदकप्रत्यक्षवचनाभ्याम् उभयार्थत्वम् अविरुद्धम्।

।।इति श्रीमत्सायणाचार्यविरचिते माधवीये वेदार्थप्रकाश ऐतरेयब्राह्मणारण्यकभागे प्रथमारण्यके प्रथमाध्याये द्वितीयः खण्डः।।२।।

ऋतुग्रहभक्षणादूर्ध्वं निवित्पदान्युच्चार्य होत्रा शंसनीयं यदाज्यशस्त्रं तन्निरूपितम्। वैश्वदेवग्रहणादूर्ध्वं होत्रा शंसनीयं प्रउगनामकं यच्छस्त्रं तद्विषयं छन्दोविशेषमाश्रित्य नानाशाखानुसारेण सर्वे[१] पक्षाः संभाविताः, गायत्र्युष्णिगनुष्टुब्बृहती पङ्क्तिस्त्रिष्टुब्जगती चेति च्छन्दोविशेषास्तत्र प्रथमं पक्षमाह – **गायत्रं प्रउगं कुर्यादित्याहुस्तेजो वै ब्रह्मवर्चसं गायत्री तेजस्वी ब्रह्मवर्चसी भवतीति** इति । तेजः शरीरकान्ती राज्ञां सामर्थ्यं वा, ब्रह्मवर्चसं श्रुताध्ययनसंपत्तिः, तदुभयहेतुत्वाद् गायत्र्यास्तद्रूपत्वम् । अतो यजमानस्तदुभयवान् भवत्वित्यनेनाभिप्रायेण प्रउगशस्त्रं गायत्रीछन्दोविशिष्टं कुर्यात् । तस्य गायत्रस्य प्रउगस्य स्वरूपमाश्वलायनेन पूर्वषट्के पञ्चमाध्यायेऽभिहितम्–''वायुरग्रेगा यज्ञप्रीः (ऋखि ५.६.१-७; शांश्रौ ७.१०.९-१६) इति सप्तानां पुरोरुचां तस्यास्तस्या उपरिष्टात्

---

३२. **प्रपञ्चितः** रा.

१. **सप्त** रा.

त्रैष्टुभं प्रउगं कुर्यादित्याहुर्वीर्यं वै त्रिष्टुब् वीर्यवान् भवतीति। जागतं प्रउगं कुर्यादित्याहुर्जागता वै पशवः पशुमान् भवतीति। तदु गायत्रमेव कुर्याद् ब्रह्म वै गायत्री ब्रह्मैतदहर्ब्रह्मणैव तद् ब्रह्म प्रतिपद्यते। तदु माधुच्छन्दसम् । मधु ह स्म वा ऋषिभ्यो मधुच्छन्दाश्छन्दति तन्मधुच्छन्दसो मधुच्छन्दस्त्वम् ।

तृचं तृचं शंसेद् 'वायवा याहि दर्शत' (ऋ १.२.१) इति सप्त तृचाः'' (आश्रौ ५.१०.४-५) इति ।

द्वितीयादिपक्षानाह– **औष्णिहं प्रउगं कुर्यादित्याहुरायुर्वा उष्णिग् आयुष्मान् भवतीति । आनुष्टुभं प्रउगं कुर्यादित्याहुः क्षत्त्रं वा अनुष्टुप् क्षत्त्रस्याऽऽप्त्या इति । बार्हतं प्रउगं कुर्यादित्याहुः श्रीर्वै बृहती श्रीमान् भवतीति । पाङ्क्तं प्रउगं कुर्यादित्याहुरन्नं वै पङ्क्तिरन्नवान् भवतीति । त्रैष्टुभं प्रउगं कुर्यादित्याहुर्वीर्यं वै त्रिष्टुब् वीर्यवान् भवतीति । जागतं प्रउगं कुर्यादित्याहुर्जागता वै पशवः**[२] **पशुमान् भवतीति** इति। क्षत्त्रं बलम् । अन्यत् पूर्ववद् व्याख्येयम् ।

एवं नानाविधब्राह्मणसिद्धानि मतान्युपन्यस्य तेषु प्रथमं स्वकीयत्वेन स्वीकरोति–**तदु गायत्रमेव कुर्याद् ब्रह्म वै गायत्री ब्रह्मैतदहर्ब्रह्मणैव तद्ब्रह्म प्रतिपद्यते** इति।

तदु तेषां तु सप्तानां मध्ये यत्[३] प्रथमम् उपन्यस्तं गायत्रं तदेवास्मिन् महाव्रते कुर्यात्। गायत्र्या ब्रह्मत्वं पूर्वमेवोक्तम् (१.१) । अस्य चाह्नो ब्रह्मत्वं तत्प्राप्तिहेतुत्वाद् अवगन्तव्यम्। तद्गायत्रप्रउगरूपेण ब्रह्मणा तन्महाव्रतरूपं ब्रह्म प्राप्नोति।

दाशतय्यां[४] गायत्रीछन्दस्कानां बहूनां विद्यमानत्वात् तद्विशेषं दर्शयति- **तदु माधुच्छन्दसम्** इति। तदपि गायत्रीछन्दस्कं प्रउगं मधुच्छन्दोनाम्न ऋषेः सम्बन्धि द्रष्टव्यम् । तेनर्षिणा दृष्टं[५] 'वायवा याहि' (ऋ १.२.१.) इत्यादिकं यन्मन्त्रजातं तदित्यर्थः।

ऋषेर्नाम निर्वक्ति– **मधु ह स्म वा ऋषिभ्यो मधुच्छन्दाश्छन्दति तन्मधुच्छन्दसो मधुच्छन्दस्त्वम्** इति । योऽयं मधुच्छन्दोनामक[६] ऋषिः सोयऽमितरेभ्य ऋषिभ्यो मधु च्छन्दति मधुरं भोग्यं संपादयितुमिच्छति । ह स्म वा इति निपातत्रयसमूह ऐतिह्यार्थः । यस्माद् अयं मध्विच्छति[७]तस्माद् अस्य[७] तन्नाम

---

२. पशूनां जगत्याऽऽहृतत्वात् 'जगती हि तानाहरत्' (ऐब्रा ३.२५) इति हि ब्राह्मणम्।
३. **यत्तु** अ.
४. **दशतयीनां** रा.
५. **दृष्टं हि** रा.
६. °**न्दो नाम** रा.
७-७. तस्मात् तस्य रा.

अथो अन्नं वै मधु सर्वं वै मधु सर्वे वै कामा मधु तद् यन्माधुच्छन्दसं शंसति सर्वेषां कामानामवरुद्धयै । सर्वान् कामान् अवरुन्द्धे य एवं वेद ।

तद्वैकाहिकं रूपसमृद्धं बहु वा एतस्मिन्नहनि किंच किंच वारणं क्रियते शान्त्या एव शान्तिर्वै प्रतिष्ठैकाहः शान्त्यामेव तत् प्रतिष्ठायामन्ततः

सम्पन्नम्।

ऋषिसंबन्धेन शस्त्रं प्रशस्य फलसंबन्धेनापि प्रशंसति–**अथो अन्नं वै मधु सर्वं वै मधु सर्वे वै कामा मधु तद् यन्माधुच्छन्दसं शंसति सर्वेषां कामानामवरुद्धयै** इति। माक्षिकवाची[८] मधुशब्दस्तन्निष्ठं प्रियत्वं लक्षयति। अन्नस्य प्रियत्वं प्रसिद्धम्। तद्वद् वस्त्रादेः सर्वस्यापि भोग्यस्य प्रियत्वं प्रसिद्धम्। यस्मात् प्रियत्वेन सर्वेऽपि कामा मधुरूपास्तस्मात् कारणान्मधुत्वसामान्यान्माधुच्छन्दसं शंसतीति यदस्ति तत् सर्वकामप्राप्त्यै संपद्यते।

माधुच्छन्दसवेदनं प्रशंसति-**सर्वान् कामानवरुन्द्धे य एवं वेद** इति।

पुनः प्रकारान्तरेण शस्त्रं प्रशंसति – **तद्वैकाहिकं रूपसमृद्धं बहु वा एतस्मिन्नहनि किंच किंच वारणं क्रियते शान्त्या एव शान्तिर्वै प्रतिष्ठैकाहः शान्त्यामेव तत् प्रतिष्ठायामन्ततः प्रतितिष्ठन्ति** इति । तदु तदपि यथोक्तं गायत्रं प्रउगम् ऐकाहिकम् एकाहे प्रकृतिभूतेऽग्निष्टोमे निष्पन्नं तदेव विश्वजिद्-द्वारेणास्मिन् महाव्रते प्राप्तमन्तत[९] ऐकाहिकत्वाद् एतद् रूपसमृद्धम् । प्रकृतिरूपे ह्येकाहे कृत्स्नस्यानुष्ठेयस्य प्रत्यक्षवचनप्रापितत्वाद् अविस्मरणेन सर्वमनुष्ठातुं शक्यम् । सेयं रूपसमृद्धिः । न च किमनेनैकाहिकत्वेनेति[१०] शङ्कनीयम् । तस्यानिष्टशमनार्थत्वात् एतस्मिन् महाव्रताख्येऽहनि वारणं शिष्टैर्निवारणीयं वर्जनीयं किमपि बहुविधं दासीनृत्यबहुभूतमैथुनब्रह्मचारिपुंश्चलीसंप्रवादादिकं[११] (द्र. ऐआ. ५.१.५) क्रियतेऽतस्तस्य[१२] शान्त्यर्थमेव सरूपसमृद्धस्यैकाहिकस्य[१३] प्रउगशंसनम् । एकाहस्य तु सर्वविकृतिप्रतिष्ठापकत्वाच्छान्तिहेतुत्वम् उपपन्नम् । अतो यजमाना अप्यन्ततः संवत्सरसत्रस्यावसान[१४] उपान्त्येऽस्मिन्नहनि तत् तेन शस्त्रपाठेन प्रतिष्ठारूपायाम् अनिष्टशान्त्यामेव प्रतितिष्ठन्ति प्रतिष्ठिता भवन्ति ।

अस्य शस्त्रस्य प्रतिष्ठाहेतुत्ववेदनं तत्पूर्वकानुष्ठानं च प्रशंसति – **प्रतितिष्ठति य एवं वेद येषां चैवं विद्वान् एतद्धोता शंसति** इति । येषां

---

८. **मादक°** रा.

९. **प्राप्तम्। अत** रा.

१०. **°हिकवचनेनेति** रा.

११. **दासीवृत्तवटुमैथुन°** आन.

१२. **°स्य सर्वस्य** रा.

१३. **रूप°** रा.

१४. **°सानभागे** रा.

प्रतितिष्ठन्ति। प्रतितिष्ठति य एवं वेद येषां चैवं विद्वान् एतद्धोता शंसति।

।।इत्यैतरेयब्राह्मणारण्यकाण्डे प्रथमारण्यके प्रथमाध्याये तृतीयः खण्डः।।३।।

शस्त्रिणामर्थ एवम् उक्तप्रकारेण शस्त्रमहिमानं विद्वान् होतैतच्छस्त्रं[१५] शंसति तेऽपि सत्रिणः प्रतितिष्ठन्तीति द्रष्टव्यम् ।

।। इति श्रीमत्सायणाचार्यविरचिते माधवीये वेदार्थप्रकाश ऐतरेयब्राह्मणारण्यकभाष्ये प्रथमारण्यके प्रथमाध्याये तृतीयः खण्डः ।।३।।

१५. °**द्धोता तदेत**° रा.

बौधायनश्रौतसूत्रम्

[भवस्वामिकृतविवरणसहितम्]

संपादकः
विजयपालः

आमुखम्

परःसहस्रैर्विपरीतझञ्झावातं सासह्यमानं वैदिककर्मकाण्डवाङ्मयमद्यापि स्वविशालग्रन्थराशिना सुसमृद्धं वर्त्तते । अद्यत्वेऽपि दक्षिणापथे स्पृहणीयश्रद्धया दर्शपूर्णमासादारभ्य आहीनयागं यज्ञा अनुष्ठीयन्ते। सहस्रशो ब्राह्मणा अद्यापि श्रौतवाङ्मयमहर्निशमभ्यस्यन्ति । तत्र श्रौतवाङ्मये बौधायनस्य महत्त्वविशेषो वर्त्तते प्राचीनतमत्त्वात् सुखावबोधत्वाच्च । प्राचीनानूचानैरप्यस्यैव प्राथम्यं प्रत्यपादि । तथा च भट्टभास्करः स्वकीयतैत्तिरीयसंहिताभाष्योपक्रमे बोधायनमेव प्रथमतः प्रणनाम—

प्रणम्य शिरसाचार्यान् बोधायनपुरस्सरान् ।
व्याख्यैषाध्वर्युवेदस्य यथाबुद्धि विधीयते ।। इति

सत्याषाढवैजयन्तीव्याख्याकृतो महादेवस्यापि कठिनी इदम्प्रथमतया बोधायननाम्न्येव पतति । तथाहि —

यत्राकरोत्सूत्रमतीवगौरवात् बोधायनाचार्यवरोऽर्थगुप्तये ।
तथा भरद्वाजमुनीश्वरस्तथाऽपस्तम्ब आचार्य इदं परं स्फुटम् ।। इति ।

सुप्रतिष्ठस्यास्य त्रिंशत्प्रश्नात्मकस्य बौधायनसूत्रस्य विवरणभाष्यवृत्ति-व्याख्याप्रयोगकृत्सु भवस्वामि-सायण-महादेव-दामोदर-रामस्वामि-गोपाल-वेङ्कटे-श्वर-वासुदेव-द्वारकानाथ-सुदर्शनाचार्यप्रभृतीनां विंशत्यधिकसंख्याकानि नामानि प्रख्यायन्ते, तेषां च कृतयोंऽशतो हस्तलिखितमातृकासु समुपलभ्यन्ते । सम्पूर्णस्य ग्रन्थस्य विवृतिस्त्वेकापि न श्रूयते क्वचित् । एता हस्तलिखितमातृकाः खल्वपि कर्मकाण्डविदां विप्राणां पुस्तकवेष्टनेषु निबद्धाः प्रायशः प्रकाशं प्रतीक्षन्ते। एतासु व्याख्यासु भवस्वामिकृता विवरणाभिधा कृतिः प्राचीनतमा प्रतीयते । भव-स्वामिनः प्राचीनतमः उल्लेखो भट्टभास्करमिश्रेण स्वकीये तैत्तिरीयसंहितायाः भाष्ये नामग्राहमकारि— 'वाक्यार्थैकपराण्यधीत्य च भवस्वाम्यादिभाष्याण्यतो

भाष्यं सर्वपथीनमेतदधुना सर्वीयमारभ्यते' इति । भट्टभास्करो दशम्यां शताब्द्यां स्व-भाष्यं रचयामासेत्यभियुक्ताः; अतो भवस्वामी नवमशताब्द्यां दक्षिणापथं सनाथ-याञ्चकारेति सम्भाव्यते । एकादशशताब्द्यां लब्धयशाः केशवस्वामी भव- स्वामिनमनुसरति, तथा हि स स्वकीये बौधायनश्रौतसूत्रप्रयोगसार उल्लिखति —'भवस्वामिमतानुसारिणा मया तूभयमप्यङ्गीकृत्य प्रयोगसारः क्रियते' इति । सुप्रख्यातः कारिकाकारो गोपालोऽपि स्वकीयं गोपालकारिकाख्यं ग्रन्थं भवस्वामि-विवरणमेवानुसृत्य रचयामासेति —'इति द्वैधोदिताः पक्षा भवस्वामिमतानुगाः' — इत्युल्लिख्य प्रकटयाञ्चकार । सायणाचार्योऽपि एनं विवरणकृतम् अभियुक्तपदेन स्मृत्वा समाद्रियते बौधायनश्रौतसूत्रभाष्ये । अतो वैदिकविद्वत्सम्मानभाक् विवरणकारो भवस्वामी बौधायनश्रौतसूत्रव्याख्यातृषु प्राचीनतमः, शोभनतमा चास्य कृतिः ।

विवरणस्य शैली संक्षिप्तवाक्यबहुला, सुप्राञ्जलभाषानिबद्धा, निगूढार्थप्राया, कर्मकाण्डरहस्योद्भेदिका, वैकल्पिकविधीनां तत्त्व निर्णायिका, सुव्यक्ताभिप्राया च वर्त्तते । सम्प्रत्युपलभ्यमानास्तु विवरणस्य हस्तलिखितमातृका दुश्शोधत्रुटिबहुला अशुद्धभ्रष्टपाठाकीर्णाश्च वर्त्तन्ते । इदं विवरणमादितश्चतुर्दशसु प्रश्नेषु अतिरात्र-एकादशिनी-सौत्रामणी-अप्तोर्यामयागेषु द्वैधकर्मान्तसूत्रयोश्च सुरक्षितमस्तीति कालन्दमहोदयः सूचयामास बौधायनश्रौतसूत्रामुखे १९०३ ख्रीष्टाब्दे । तस्य महाविदुषो महती मनःकामना आसीत् भवस्वामिविवरणस्य प्रकाशनस्य, परं न सा फलवती बभूवे तस्य जीवनकाले । डा. सीताराम-सहगलशास्त्रिमहाभागेन कतिपयवर्षेभ्यः पूर्व बौधायनश्रौतसूत्रस्य प्रथमप्रश्ने भव-स्वामिविवरणं समपादि, तस्य प्रकाशनं सायणभाष्येण सार्धं रामलाल-कपूरट्रस्टाख्यया बहालगढस्थया (जिला-सोनीपत, हरियाणा) संस्थया व्यधीयत । तदनन्तरमनयैव संस्थया बौधायनश्रौतसूत्रस्य द्वितीयप्रश्नो महादेवकृत सुबोधिनी-वृत्त्या सहितः प्रकाशितः । ततोऽग्रेऽपि यावदुपलब्धसुबोधिनीवृत्तिसहितस्य बौधा-यनसूत्रस्य प्रकाशनस्य योजना आसीत् । गतवर्षे श्रीराधेश्यामशास्त्रिमहाभागस्य परमस्नेहसिक्तसन्तताग्रहभूरीकृत्य मया यथोपलब्धं भवस्वामिविवरणस्य सम्पादन-कर्म इन्दिरागांधिराष्ट्रीयकलाकेन्द्रसाहाय्येन समारम्भि । श्रीराधेश्यामशास्त्रि-महोदयानां प्रयासेनैव पाण्डुलिपयः सङ्कलिताः । तत्रोपयुज्यमानानां पाण्डुलिपीनां विवरणमधस्तात् प्रस्तूयते —

(१)

गोकर्णः (गो०) I दर्शपूर्णमासादिसोमान्तम् (१-९ प्रश्नाः) । नागरी लिपिः । आकारः - २५ × ११ से. मी., पत्रसंख्या १३९, प्रतिपृष्ठं ८-१० पङ्क्तयः । प्रतिपङ्क्ति १२-१४ शब्दाः । लेखः सुपठः प्रायः शुद्धः । **प्रारम्भे** -

श्रीगणेशाय नमः । ब्राह्मणानां बहुत्त्वादेकैकस्यां शाखायां अपरिसमाप्तित्त्वादर्थस्य .....। प्रत्यध्यायं समाप्तिनिर्देशः । अन्ते – अत ऊर्ध्वं प्रकृतिवदेव प्रसिद्धम् । इति श्रीस्वामीविरचितः समाप्तोऽग्निष्टोमः ! संवत् १९७९ साल पौषसुरी १ रोज गुरुवार ।।

गोकर्णः (गो०) II अग्निचयन-राजसूय-वाजपेय-इष्टिकल्पाः (१०–१३ प्रश्नाः)। नागरी लिपिः । आकारः ३५ × १३ से.मी. । पत्रसंख्या ५७ । प्रतिपृष्ठं ९ पङ्क्तयः । प्रतिपङ्क्ति १५ शब्दाः । लेखः सुपठः । पाठः शुद्धः । प्रारम्भे - श्रीगणेशाय नमः । अग्निचयनं । अग्नेरनारभ्याधीतत्वा-दनारभ्याधीतानां प्रकृत्यर्थत्वाद् दीक्षादिसम्बन्धात् । अन्ते - परस्परतः अन्यस्य वाग्निभिः । इति भवस्वामिकृते इष्टिकल्पे द्वादशोऽध्यायः ।।१२।। इति कल्पः समाप्तः। औपानुभाष्यं समाप्तः । ....संवत् १९३७ शके १८०२ नंदन-नामसंवत्सरे दक्षिणायने हेमन्त ऋतौ मार्गशीर्षे कृष्णपक्षे चतुर्थ्यां तिथौ इन्दु-वासरे प्रातःकाले श्रीगङ्गाकाशीविश्वेश्वरसन्निधौ समाप्तः ।

गोकर्ण (गो०) III भवस्वामिद्वैधविवरणम् (२०-२३ प्रश्नाः) । नागरी लिपिः । आकारः २२ × ११ से. मी. । पत्रसंख्या ११७ । प्रतिपृष्ठं १० पङ्क्तयः । प्रतिपङ्क्ति शब्दाः १२ । सुपठः शुद्धः लेखः । प्रारम्भे – उपवसथ इत्यादि द्वैधानां पूर्वनिरपेक्षत्वं विशेषणविशेषित्वं....। अन्ते – सर्वस्य वाचनिक-त्त्वादिति । १४ । इति भवस्वामिकृते चतुर्थस्य दशकस्य दशमोऽध्यायः ।।

(२)

पाचवड (वैदिकसंशोधनमण्डलम्) (पा०) I दर्शपूर्णमासादिसोमान्तः (१-९ प्रश्नाः) । नागरी लिपिः । आकारः – २२ × १० से. मी. । पत्रसंख्या १७१ । प्रतिपृष्ठं पङ्क्तयः १० । प्रतिपङ्क्ति शब्दाः १२ । लेखः सुपठः, प्रायः शुद्धः । प्रारम्भे – श्रीदुंढिराजाय नमः । श्री विश्वेश्वराय नमः । श्री गोपालं गुरुं भजे । ब्राह्मणा बहुत्वदेकैकस्यां.....। अन्ते-अत ऊर्ध्व प्रकृतिवदेव सिद्धं ।। इति श्रीभवस्वामिविरचितः समाप्तोऽग्निष्टोमः । शुभं भवतु । शके १७०५ वर्षे शोभकृतनामसम्वत्सरे फाल्गुणशध पञ्चम्यां समाप्तः ।।

पाचवड (वै.सं.म.) (पा०) II द्वैधसूत्रविवरणम् (२०-२३ प्रश्नाः) । नागरी लिपिः । आकारः -२२ × १० से. मी. । पत्रसंख्या १७६ । प्रतिपृष्ठं पङ्क्तयः ८ । प्रतिपङ्क्ति शब्दाः १२ । लेखः सुपठः, शुद्धः । प्रारम्भे – श्रीगणेशाय नमः । श्रीसरस्वत्यै नमः । उपवसथ इत्यादि द्वैधानां पूर्वनिरपेक्षत्त्वं विशेषेण...। अन्ते – सर्वस्य वाचनिकत्त्वादिति । इति भवस्वामिकृते द्वैधविवरणे चतुर्थस्य दशकस्य दशमोध्यायः । समाप्तिमगमत् । शुभमस्तु ।

पाचवड (वै.सं.म.) (पा०) III कर्मान्तविवरणम् (२४-२६ प्रश्नाः) । नागरी लिपिः । आकारः २२ × १० से. मी. । पत्रसंख्या ७५ । प्रतिपृष्ठं

पङ्क्तयः ९ । प्रतिपङ्क्ति शब्दाः १२ । लेखः सुपठः, शुद्धः । प्रारम्भे – श्रीगणेशाय नमः । श्रीसरस्वत्यै नमः । पञ्चतयेन कल्पमवेक्षेतेत्यादिकर्मान्त इत्यन्वर्थकसंज्ञा कर्मणामन्त इति...। अन्ते– प्रतिपादितं यज्ञेन यज्ञमुपलक्षयतेत्यभ्यासः समाप्तितुष्टिमंगलार्थः । इति भवस्वामिकृते कर्मांतविवरणे तृतीयस्य कर्मान्तस्य विंशोध्यायः । समाप्तश्च मूलकल्पाद्वैधकर्मांताः ॥

पाचवड (वै. सं. म.) (पा०) IV अग्निकल्पः । नागरी लिपिः । आकारः ३४ × ११ से. मी. । पत्रसंख्या १२ + १८ । अनिश्चितम् ?

(३)

वाई (प्राज्ञपाठशाला) (वा०) दर्शपूर्णमासादि अग्निष्टोमान्तम् (१-९) । नागरी लिपिः । आकारः २२ × १८ से. मी. । पत्रसंख्या १२९ । प्रतिपृष्ठं पङ्क्तयः १४ । प्रतिपङ्क्ति शब्दाः १० । पाचवडस्यैव प्रतिलिपिमात्रम् ।

(४)

मुद्रितः कोशः (मु०) सीतारामसहगलसंपादितः, पाण्डुलिपिचतुष्टयाधारभूतः, रामलालकपूरट्रस्ट, बहालगढ, जि. सोनीपत(हरियाणा) द्वारा प्रकाशितः ।

(५)

बडौदा (ओरियण्टल इन्स्टिट्यूट ४५११) (ब०) I दर्शादिसोमान्तः (१-९ प्रश्नाः) । नागरी लिपिः । आकारः - ३० × ११ से. मी. । पत्रसंख्या ११३ । प्रतिपृष्ठं पङ्क्तयः ९ । प्रतिपङ्क्ति शब्दाः २० । सुपठः शुद्धः । प्रारम्भे – श्रीगणेशाय नमः । ब्राह्मणाणां बहुत्वादेकैकस्यां शाखायां ....। अन्ते –अत ऊर्ध्वं प्रकृतिवदेव प्रसिद्धम् । इति श्री भवस्वामिविरचितः समाप्तोग्निष्टोमः । श्री सांबसदाशिवार्पणमस्तु ।....शके १७६२ शार्वरीनामसंवत्सरे दक्षिणायने शरदृतौ आश्विने शुक्लपक्षे द्वादशां तिथौ गुरुवासरे इदं पुस्तकं समाप्तम् ।

बडौदा (ओ. इ. ४५२) (ब०) II अतिरात्र – एकाहान्तः (१२, १५-१८ प्रश्नाः) नागरी लिपिः । आकारः ३५ × ११ से. मी. । पत्रसंख्या ५३ । प्रतिपृष्ठं पङ्क्तयः ९ । प्रतिपङ्क्ति शब्दाः १५ । सुपठः शुद्धः । प्रारम्भे – श्रीगणेशाय नमः । ॐ । अतिरात्रिंकरिष्यनित्यादि ......। अन्ते – इत्यादिनैतत् क्रियते त्रयोपि कर्त्तव्या इति । एकाहे एकादशोध्यायः । शके १७६२ शार्वरीनाम सम्वत्सरे दक्षिणायने हेमंत ऋतौ पौषे मासे शुक्ल पक्षे द्वितीयां तिथौ भृगुवासरे तद्दिने इदं पुस्तकं समाप्तम् ।

बडौदा (ओ. इ. ११३९५) (ब०) III द्वैधसूत्रविवरणम् (२/१०–४ प्रश्नाः) । देवनागरी लिपिः । आकारः - ३० × ११ से. मी. । पत्रसंख्या १५६ । प्रतिपृष्ठं पङ्क्तयः १४ । प्रतिपङ्क्ति शब्दाः ८ । सुपठः, शुद्धः । प्रारम्भे– प्रत्यभिमर्शनं प्रत्यभिमर्शद्रव्यभेदानामात्मनोऽपि संस्थानभेदः । कालभेदा-

च्चेति । अन्ते – एवं सति यत्राप्युपपत्त्याभावा सा उक्तः तत्रापि न दोषः । सर्वस्य वाचनिकत्वादिति । इति भवस्वामिविरचितायां द्वैधवृत्तौ दशमोध्यायः समाप्तः । द्वैधवृत्तिः समाप्ता ।

बडौदा (ओ. इ. २९-९-२१) (ब०) IV द्वैधविवरणम् (२०-२२ प्रश्नाः) । देवनागरी लिपिः । आकारः ३३ × २१ से. मी. । पत्रसंख्या ४० । प्रतिपृष्ठं पङ्क्तयः ९ । प्रतिपङ्क्ति शब्दाः २२ । सुपठः, शुद्धः । प्रारम्भे -- उपवसथ इत्यादि द्वैधानां पूर्वनिरपेक्षत्वं विशेष विशेषित्वं.... । अन्ते -- दीक्षासमाप्तिः न काललक्षणात्ततश्च सोपि प्रतिषेधकाल एवेति न प्रतिहोम इति ।।२०।। इति भवस्वामिविरचितायां द्वैधवृत्तौ द्वितीयस्य दशकस्य दशमोऽध्यायः।। द्वितीयः प्रश्नः समाप्तः ।।

बडौदा (ओ. इ. ४४२) (ब०) V कर्मान्तविवरणम् (२४-२६ प्रश्नाः) । नागरी लिपिः । आकारः ३३ × २१ से. मी. । पत्रसंख्या ३७ । प्रतिपृष्ठं पङ्क्तयः ९ । प्रतिपङ्क्ति शब्दाः २२ । सुपठः, शुद्धः । प्रारम्भे -- श्रीगणेशाय नमः । पंचतयेन कल्पमवेक्षेतेत्यादिकर्मान्त इत्यन्वर्थसंज्ञा.... । अन्ते – प्रतिपादितं यज्ञे यज्ञमुपलक्षयतेत्यभ्यासः समाप्तितुष्टिमंगलार्थः। इति भवस्वामिकृते कर्मांतविवरणे तृतीयस्य कर्मांतस्य विंशोऽध्यायः । समाप्ताश्च मूलकल्पा द्वैधकर्मान्ताः ।।

(६)

मद्रास (GOML R. 3781) **(म०)** I दर्शपूर्णमासादिसोमान्तम् (१-९ प्रश्नाः) । नागरी लिपिः । आकारः - १६ × १८ से. मी. । पत्रसंख्या २०७ । प्रतिपृष्ठं पङ्क्तयः १८ । प्रतिपङ्क्ति शब्दाः १० । बहुधा दुष्पठः, अपूर्णः । प्रारम्भे– ब्राह्मणानां बहुत्वादेकैकस्यां ..... । अन्ते – हृदयशूलोद्वासने गच्छत्यत ऊर्ध्वं प्रकृतिवत् सिद्धम् । समाप्तोऽग्निष्टोमः ।। .....

मद्रास (GOML R. 5497) **(म०)** II प्रवर्ग्य-चयन-कर्मान्ताः । नागरी लिपिः । आकारः - १६ × १८ से. मी. । पत्रसंख्या ८१ । प्रतिपृष्ठं पङ्क्तयः २० । प्रतिपङ्क्ति शब्दाः १० । बहुशः त्रुटितः । सुपठः । अपूर्णः । प्रारम्भे -- प्रवर्ग्यं संभरिष्यन्नित्यादि अनारभ्याधीतत्वात्.... । अन्ते – ओषधस्य निवायोकर .... । १९२९-३० ।

इत्थं प्रथमे प्रश्ने षण्णां पाण्डुलिपीनां (कोशानां) उपयोगो भविष्यति । ततोऽग्रे केवलानां चतुर्णामेव । एवं विनिवेद्य प्रस्तौमि स्थालीपुलाकन्यायेन भवस्वामिकृतं बौधायनसूत्रविवरणस्य प्रारम्भिकं स्वल्पांशं विद्वद्विमर्शार्थम् ।

बौधायनश्रौतसूत्रम्

[भवस्वामिकृतविवरणसहितम्]

प्रथमोऽध्यायः

आमावास्येन वा पौर्णमासेन वा हविषा यक्ष्यमाणो भवति ।। स पुरस्तादेव हविरातञ्चनमुपकल्पयते ।। एकाहेन वा द्व्यहेन वा यथर्तु ।। अथ वै ब्राह्मणं भवति – दध्नातनक्ति सेन्द्रत्वायाग्निहोत्रोच्छेषणमभ्यातनक्ति यज्ञस्य संतत्यै **(तै. सं. २।५।३।५,६) इति ।। चन्द्रमसं वाऽनिर्ज्ञाय सम्पूर्णं वा विज्ञाय ।। अग्नीनन्वादधाति त्रीणि काष्ठानि गार्हपत्येऽभ्यादधाति त्रीण्यन्वाहार्यपचने त्रीण्याहवनीये ।। परिसमूहन्ति ।। उपवसथस्य रूपं कुर्वन्ति ।। अथास्य व्रतोपेतस्य पर्णशाखामाच्छैति प्राङ्वोदङ् वा वाचंयमो यत्र वा वेत्स्यन्मन्यते ।। सा या प्राची वोदीची वा बहुपर्णा बहुशाखाप्रतिशुष्काग्रा भवति तामाच्छिनत्ति –** इषे त्वोर्जे त्वा **(तै. सं. १।१।१।१) इति ।। तया वत्सानपाकरोति –** वायव स्थोपायव स्थ **(तै. सं. १।१।१।१) इति ।। अथैषां मातॄः प्रेरयति –** देवो वः सविता प्रार्पयतु श्रेष्ठतमाय कर्मण आप्यायध्वमघ्निया देवभागमूर्जस्वतीः पयस्वतीः प्रजावतीरनमीवा अयक्ष्मा मा व स्तेन ईशत माऽघशंसो रुद्रस्य हेतिः परि वो वृणक्तु **(तै. सं. १।१।१।१) इति ।।** ध्रुवा अस्मिन् गोपतौ स्यात बह्वीः **(तै. सं. १।१।१।१) इति यजमानमीक्षते ।। अथैतां शाखामग्रेणाहवनीयं पर्याहृत्य पूर्वया द्वारा प्रपाद्य जघनेन गार्हपत्यमग्निष्ठेऽनस्युत्तरार्धे वाग्न्यगारस्योद्गूहति –** यजमानस्य पशून् पाहि **(तै. सं. १।१।१।१) इति ।। इति नु यदि संनयति । यद्यु वै न संनयति बहिंःप्रतिपदेव भवति ।।**

भवस्वामिविवरणम्

ब्राह्मणानां बहुत्वादेकैकस्यां शाखायामपरिसमाप्तत्वादर्थस्य[१] च दुर्बोधत्वादसार्वत्रिकत्वाच्च[२] संहृत्य विवरणार्थं सुखं बुद्ध्वा कर्मसाङ्गमनुष्ठाय[३] फलं सर्वे प्राप्नुयुरिति फलकल्प आरब्ध आचार्येण । वाक्यसम्बन्धश्च गर्भाधानादिसंस्कारैः संस्कृतोऽधीत्य वेदान् न्यायतः कृतदार आहिताग्निरामावास्येन वेति चोदितस्य[४] कर्मणोऽधिकारी । तानि च कर्माणि नानाविधानि । तत्र दर्शपूर्णमासाग्निहोत्रज्योतिष्टोमप्रवर्ग्याण्यपूर्वाणि । तत्र दर्शपूर्णमासविकारा इष्टयोऽग्नीषोमीयश्च पशुः । ज्योतिष्टोमविकारा एकाहा द्वादशाहश्च[५] । अग्निहोत्रं न[६] प्रकृतिः । प्रकृतिर्नाम सर्वधर्माणामातिदेशिकं प्रवर्ग्याधानकुण्डपायिनामयनेषु[७] प्रवर्ग्यश्च न प्रकृतिः । दधिघर्मे धर्मातिदेशं[८] केचिदिच्छन्ति ''परिश्रित्योभयतः शान्तिं कृत्वा'' (बौ. श्रौ. २१/२२) इति । दर्शपूर्णमासज्योतिष्टोमौ प्रकृती एव । अग्नीषोमीयद्वादशाहसवत्सरादयः प्रकृतिविकृतयः । इष्टयः एकाहश्चोद्भिदादयो विकृतय एव । दर्विहोमादयो न प्रकृतयो न विकृतयः ।

आमावास्येन वा पौर्णमासेन वा हविषा यक्ष्यमाणो भवति । दर्शपूर्णमासारम्भो मन्त्रक्रमात् निरपेक्षत्वात् । आधानादीनां सांगानां समस्तविधानाभावादेतदपेक्षत्वाच्च । अनयोर्ज्ञानेन तेषां गतकल्पत्वात्[९] । पौर्णमासस्यादित्वेऽप्यमावास्यायाः[१०] प्रथमग्रहणं मन्त्रक्रमात् । दाक्षायणयज्ञादौ शाखाहरणाद्यारम्भस्य पौर्णमास्यामप्युपकारात् पौर्णमासीधर्मारम्भे क्वचिदप्यामावास्यस्यानुपकारात् असाधारण्यादादिपदार्थस्य[११] ।

अथातो दर्शपूर्णमासौ व्याख्यास्याम इत्यप्रतिज्ञातमारम्भादेव गम्यत इति अथेत्यधिकाराकरणं तयोरेवारम्भात् । तद्धितश्च कालप्रकृतेः 'तस्येदम्' (अष्टा. ४।३।१२०) इति वा 'भवार्थे' (अष्टा. ४।३।५३) वा विध्यपेक्षः । एवं सति य इष्ट्या पशुना सोमेनाग्रयणेन यक्ष्यमाणः सोऽमावास्यायां पौर्णमास्यां वा[१२] यजेतेत्यप्रसङ्गः । प्रयोजननिमित्ता संज्ञा इत्येतस्य व्याख्यापनम् । एवं च सत्याग्नेयादीनां प्राधान्यात् दर्शपूर्णमासाभ्यां स्वर्गकामफलसम्बन्धत्वान्निमित्तत्वे[१३] च ज्ञापिते सति निमित्ते नैमित्तिकेन भवितव्यम् इति यावज्जीविताप्युक्ता भवति। तेषां च परस्परानपेक्षाणामुत्पत्तौ भेदप्रसङ्गेऽपि दर्शपूर्णमासाभ्यामिति

---

१. '°समाप्ति°' कोशेषु ।
२. '°सार्वजन्यत्वा°' मु०, म० ।
३. 'कर्माण्यनुष्ठाय' म० ।
४. 'चोदितस्वकर्मणि' गो० ।
५. '°हाश्च' मु०, म० ।
६. 'च' म० ।
७. इतोऽग्रे 'च' अधिकः मु०।
८. 'धर्मा°' पा०, म० ।
९. 'ज्ञात°' पा०, वा० ।
१०. 'इह पौ°' मु०।
११. '°रणादा°' गो० । '°रणपदा°' मु०।
१२. 'पौर्णमास्यां वा' नास्ति पा०, मु० ।
१३. इतोऽग्रे 'अपि' अधिकः म० ।

द्विवचननिर्देशात् तत्कालसम्बद्धौ द्वौ समुदायौ न प्रत्येकमाग्नेयादयः । तयोश्च समुदितयोः फलसम्बन्धात् समुदितौ फलसाधनमिति[१४]गम्यते । उभयोरत्रैकवचन-निर्देशाद्दर्शपूर्णमासाभ्यामिति सिद्धे न[१५] समासकरणं भिन्नकालत्वात् । समुच्चयार्थो वा शब्दः वायुर्वात्वेति (तै. सं. १।७।७।२) यथा । सत्यपि समुच्चये प्रत्येकं यक्ष्यमाणसंबन्धो भिन्नकालविधानात् । अमावास्यायां वा पौर्णमासीं वातिपादयेदिति (तै. सं. २।२।२।१) लिङ्गान्नसंगतप्रसङ्गः[१६] । देवदत्तस्य यज्ञदत्तस्य च भुञ्जानस्य दधि कर्त्तव्यमिति तयोरुद्दिश्यमानत्वात् स्वकाल एव भुञ्जानयोरिति गम्यते । कर्तृविषयो वा विकल्पः । आमावास्येन यक्ष्यमाणो वा पौर्णमासेन यक्ष्यमाणो वेति कर्त्तृव्यापारस्य कादाचित्कत्वादुपपन्नो विकल्पः । एकेन सिध्यतीति चेत् दध्ना पयसा वा पात्नीवतमिति (बौ. श्रौ. २१।२३) यथा न क्वचिन्मुख्यानुकल्पदर्शनाद् दशाहमाशौचम् (मनु. ५।९) इत्यादौ पयसा भोजयेत् तक्रेण वेति च । ननु दध्ना पयसा वा पात्नीवतमिति समत्वेऽपि दृष्टः । तत एवासन्देहार्थमुभावुक्तौ बैल्वो वा खादिरो वेति यथा । हविषेति साधनेन साध्यसमुदायो लक्ष्यते आयुर्घृतमिति यथा । समुदाय-नामधेयत्वाद्दर्शपूर्णमासयोरुक्तयोश्च प्रयोगाभावात् निर्वर्त्यवक्तव्यम् अन्यथा-नर्थक्यं अविशेषणस्यां[१७] हविर्ग्रहणं विनापि सिद्धे हविर्मात्रेणाप्यशक्तौ कर्त्तव्या-वित्येतत् ख्यापयति[१८] । अतिपत्तौ च प्रधानमात्रस्य प्रायश्चित्तविधानादपि वाप्येकदेशे स्यादित्येष न्यायः संगृहीतो भवति । कर्तृनिर्देशादेकवचनं यक्ष्यमाण इत्यवश्यं कर्त्तव्यं हविष उपकल्पनस्यकरणत्वमाविज्ञापयति[१९] ।

यो यक्ष्यमाणः स पुरस्तादेवेति सिद्धे[२०] भवतिग्रहणस्यैतत्प्रयोजनम् — भवतेः सत्तार्थत्वात् असतश्च प्रसङ्गाभावात् सत एवाधिकारविशिष्ट-सत्तापरिग्रहार्थं वचनं न सन्मात्रस्याधिकारः अर्थिनः समर्थस्य शास्त्रेण वा पर्युदस्तस्येति । द्वयोराख्यातयोः परस्परेण सम्बन्धार्थं स इति ब्रुवन्नात्मीयेनैव सिध्यति कर्म न परकीयेनेति ज्ञापयति । ततश्च द्वादशाहे एकस्य द्रव्येणापि साधारणयागनिर्वृत्तौ[२१] सर्वेषामात्मीयत्वेन कर्त्तव्यम् इति ज्ञापितं भवति । साधनस्य साध्यात्पूर्वकालत्वे सिद्धे पुरस्ताद्ग्रहणं कर्मारम्भात्पूर्वस्मिन् काले यथा स्यात् । इतरथाऽरब्धे कर्मणि द्रव्यालाभे दोषः स्यात् । एतेनैव ज्ञापितत्वात् अन्यत्राधानादिषु पुरस्ताद्ग्रहणं न करोति । एव शब्दश्च न्यायादेव पूर्वकालत्वे सिद्धे यस्याप्रतिबन्धेन द्रव्यं सम्भवति तस्य तस्मिन्नपि काले ग्रहणे न दोष इति

१४. 'साधन' नास्ति म० म० ।
१५. 'असमा' पा० ब० ।
१६. '°संत°' पा०, वा०। '°संहत°' म०।
१७. 'विशेष°' मु० म०।
१८. 'व्यापारयति' म० ।
१९. '°त्वं मा विज्ञायीति' म० ।
२०. 'सिद्धे भवति' नास्ति मु० ।
२१. '°योग°' गो० ।

ज्ञापनार्थम् । यत्र क्वचित्[२२] पुरस्ताद्ग्रहणेन ज्ञापने सिद्धे इह वचनं प्रयत्नार्थं, न यतः कुतश्चित्तस्मिन् काले उपादेयं शुद्धिकामत्वाद्देवानामिति । हविरातञ्चनग्रहणं प्रदर्शनार्थं सर्वद्रव्याणां पुरोडाशादीनामनेनोपलक्षणादेकाहादीनां विशेषविवक्षया सहसोत्पादयितुमशक्यत्वात् प्रदर्शनार्थम् । उभाभ्यां यक्ष्यमाण उपकल्पयत इति वचनाद्दधिग्रहणाल्लाघवेन सामान्यवचनं तदभावेऽन्यस्यापि उपकल्पनार्थं पुनस्तस्यापि नाशशङ्कायां च । उपकल्पयत इति चौरादिकात् व्यन्ताद्धेतुमणिच्[२३] कर्त्रभिप्राये क्रियाफले इत्यात्मनेपदमुपकल्पयन्ति कर्मकरास्तानुपकल्पयते यजमान इति भौवादिकाद्वा क्लृपेस्तथैवात्मनेपदम् । भृत्यैरपि[२४] कारयन्[२५] करोत्येव यथाभक्तं ददातीति[२५] ।

यथर्त्वित्येव सिद्धे यावताह्ना विना न भवति तावतः प्रदर्शनार्थं विप्रकर्षस्य । एवं च सति प्राजापत्यानामङ्गानि यावता विप्रकर्षेण विना न सम्भवति तावदेव विप्रकृष्टकालानीति । यथर्त्विति सर्वत्रायमेव विकल्पो मा भूद् व्यवस्थितो यथा स्यात् ग्रीष्मे एकाहेन हेमन्ते द्व्यहेनेति[२६] । एको वाशब्दो विकल्पार्थः द्वितीयः अनियमार्थः[२७] । यथर्त्वेकाहेन द्व्यहेन वेत्युक्ते अत्रैव द्व्याश्रयविकल्पः स्यात् । द्वितीये पुनर्वाशब्दे सति[२८] अयमपि नियमो नास्ति यथासम्भवमासन्नकाले उपकल्पनं कर्त्तव्यं दृष्टार्थत्वादातञ्चनस्येति । उभयोः प्रकृतत्वेपि सन्नयत इति न वक्तव्यं प्रदर्शनार्थं यथासम्भवं सर्वद्रव्याणामित्युक्तत्वात्[२९] ।

अथ वै भवतीत्यवचनेऽपि ब्राह्मणत्वेऽवगते, अन्यत्राथ[३०] वै भवतीत्युक्ते ब्राह्मणं द्रष्टव्यमिति यथाथ वै भवत्यष्टावत्तः स्विष्टकृद्द्वादशावत्तेडा (बौ. श्रौ. ६।११।१४) इत्यादौ । ब्राह्मणोक्तानां यत्पूतीकैः (तै. सं. २।५।३।५) इत्यादीनां दध्नोऽभावे सदृशद्रव्योत्पादनार्थम् । एवं च सति तस्मिन्नविद्यमाने एतेषामेकेनातञ्च्यादिति, तेषामप्यभावे सामान्यवचनेनान्यस्योपसङ्ग्रहः । दध्नातनक्तीति[३१] दधिनियमार्थम् । अग्निहोत्रोच्छेषणोपादानं ब्राह्मणवाक्ये सम्बन्धत्वात् । यज्ञस्य सन्तत्या इत्यर्थवादत्वात् सायन्तनमिति गम्यते । तस्मिन् काले अविस्मरणार्थं च यथा दध्ना तथैवेत्यपरः । स यदि अग्निहोत्रोच्छेषणात् (बौ. श्रौ. २४।२३।९) इत्याद्यप्रमादार्थमेव नह्युभयार्थम् । अग्निहोत्रं प्रधानकर्मत्वा-

---

२२. 'क्वचित् नास्ति गो० । 'तत्र क्वचित्' मु० । 'यः क्वचित्' म० ।

२३. '°णिच्च' गो० । '°तिच' अन्यत्र ।

२४. 'वाच्येन हि' गो०। 'वाक्येन हि' मु०, म० । इतोऽनन्तरं 'मृत्यैदपि कारयन्' मु० ।

२५. 'तातैव' मु० ।

२६. 'यथा...नेति' नास्ति मु० ।

२७. 'द्वि...र्थः' नास्ति म०।

२८. 'सति' नास्ति गो०, पा०, ब० ।

२९. 'सर्वत्रद्र°' गो० । 'द्रव्य°' म० ।

३०. 'अन्यत्र' नास्ति गो० ।

३१. 'इति' नास्ति गो०, पा०, ब०।

न्नैव गुणार्थमावर्त्तितुमर्हति । आवर्त्यमानमप्यग्निहोत्रमेव न स्यादतत्कालत्वात् ।

चन्द्रमसं वानिर्ज्ञायेति अनिर्गतं ज्ञात्वा नास्त्यद्येति बुद्ध्वा सम्पूर्णं वा विज्ञाय सम्पूर्णो भविष्यतीति ज्ञात्वा शास्त्रादन्यतो वेति क्त्वाप्रत्ययोपपत्तिः । वाशब्दाभ्यां दृश्यमानेऽप्यपूर्णेऽपीति ज्ञापयति । दर्शनापूर्णत्वयोः सर्वतिथिषु भावात् सर्वत्र प्रसङ्ग इति चेन्न अमावास्यापौर्णमास्योरेव विधानात् तत्रैव द्वैविध्यं न सर्वत्र प्रसङ्गः । कथं तयोर्विधानम्? आमावास्येन वेत्यत्रोक्तं कालनिमित्ता संज्ञेति कुतोऽन्यत्र प्रसङ्गः? ब्राह्मणे चोच्यते – यदाग्नेयोऽष्टाकपालः (तै. सं. २।६।३।३) इत्येवमादि, तस्मात्सदृशीनां रात्रीणाममावास्यायां पौर्णमास्यां च देवा इज्यन्ते (तै. सं. २।५।६।६)। पौर्णमास्यां पौर्णमास्या यजेत अमावास्याया-ममावास्यया यजेत (द्र. आप. यज्ञपरि. २।२०, १९) इति मन्त्रलिङ्गं पञ्चदशीं ये प्रविष्टाः (बौ. श्रौ. २०।१) इति छन्दसा ब्राह्मणेन (बौ. श्रौ. २४।१।१) इत्यभ्युपगमात् । प्रातरग्निहोत्रं हुत्वा इडा देवहूः (तै. सं. ३।३।२।१) इति जपित्वा देवा गातुविदः (तै. ब्रा. ३।७।४।१) इति च अग्नीन्पुनर्विहृत्य तूष्णी-मग्नीनन्वादधाति यो वै दधाति[३२] यो वै देवताः पूर्वः परिगृह्णाति (तै. सं. १।६।७।१) इति वचनात् अग्निहोत्रानन्तरमेवेति गम्यते । आचार्याभिप्रायश्च पुरा प्रातरग्निहोत्रात् पिंख्यानुपसादयेत् (बौ. श्रौ. २४।२०।७) इति वचनात् ।

त्रीणि काष्ठानीत्येवारब्धव्ये अग्नीनन्वादधातीति एतस्य कर्मणः संज्ञात्वख्यापनार्थम् । तच्चाभ्युदितमग्न्यन्वाधानमित्येवमादिषु संव्यवहारार्थम् । त्रीणि काष्ठानि गार्हपत्येऽभ्यादधाति तूष्णीमिति गम्यते मंत्रावचनात्, सूत्र-मौपमन्यवीपुत्रस्य (बौ. श्रौ. २०।१) इति भेदेन पक्षान्तरोपन्यासात् । केचिद् द्वैधकर्मान्तौपानुवाक्योक्तविधयो मूलकल्पप्रकरणोक्तैर्विधिभिर्विकल्प्यन्त इति ब्रुवते। अपरे विशेषोक्ता[३३] विशेषोक्तैर्विकल्प्यन्ते अविशेषोक्तैर्विशेषोक्ता[३४] अनुक्ताश्च शेषत्वेन सम्बध्यन्त इति । विशेषोक्तास्तावदिह शाखाच्छेदेन एको मन्त्रो द्वैधे (द्र. बौ. श्रौ. २०।१) पुरस्तात् प्रत्यञ्चमिति[३५] । अविशेषोक्ता-स्तावदग्न्यन्वाधानादयः अग्नीनन्वादधातीति इहोक्तम् । अङ्गुष्ठपर्वमात्राणि दैवतानि कृतानि (बौ. श्रौ. २४।२८।९) इत्यादि[३६] तत्र विशेषः। पूर्वार्धादव-दायेति (बौ. श्रौ. १।१४।१४) इहोक्तम् । व्यतिषज्यैवाङ्गुलीरवद्येदङ्गुष्ठप-र्वमात्राणि दैवतान्यवदानानि (बौ. श्रौ. २४।२८।८-९) इति तत्र । एवं प्रस्तरवेदिखननादिषु अनुक्तानामत्याक्रम्याश्राव्याह – समिधो यजेति (बौ. श्रौ. १। १६) इतीहोक्तमभिक्रामं जुहोति (बौ. श्रौ. २०।१३) इति तत्रोक्तम् ।

---

३२. 'यो वै दधाति' मु० मात्रे ।

३३. 'विशेषोक्ता' मु० मात्रे ।

३४. 'अविशेषोक्ता' सार्वत्रिकः पाठः, मु० विहाय ।

३५. 'विशेषो...मिति' मु० मात्रे ।

३६. 'उपस्थंकृत्वेत्यादि' कोशेषु, मु०विहाय।

सर्वेणाभिक्रामेत् (बौ. श्रौ. २०।१३) इत्यादिब्राह्मणोक्ता इहानुक्तास्तेऽप्युपसंग्राह्याश्छन्दसा ब्राह्मणेन (बौ. श्रौ.२४।१।१) इति वचनात् । यथोपवेषचर्मदयोर्लिङ्गादिना तयोर्विशेषनिश्चयः।

अग्न्यन्वाधानं याजमानमिति केचित् याजमाने समाम्नानात् । उपकल्पयते स इति प्रकृत्यान्वादधातीतिवचनात् स एवान्वाधत्ते इति गम्यते । योऽग्नीनन्वाधाय व्रतमुपैतीति व्रतेन समानकर्त्तृकत्वाच्च । व्रतं च निःसन्दिग्धं याजमानम् । आध्वर्यवमित्यन्ये इह समाम्नानात् । अथोपवसथीयेऽहन् (बौ. श्रौ. ३।१५।१) इत्यत्र चानाम्नानात्[३७] परस्मैपदात् ममाग्ने वर्चो विहवेषु (तै. सं. ४।७।१४।१) अस्त्वित्यध्वर्युरादधातीति शाखान्तरे दर्शनात् (द्र. का. श्रौ. २।१।२-३) । वेदिं विमायाग्नीनन्वादधातीति वेदिविमानादिसमानकर्त्तृकत्ववचनाच्चान्यतरस्मिन्नितरलिङ्गानुगमः कर्त्तव्यः । आचार्यस्योभयलिङ्गदर्शनादन्यतरानुगमे गौणत्वप्रसङ्गाद्विकल्पोऽभिप्रेत इति गम्यते ।

परिसमूहनं परितो जलसंयोगः । उपवसथस्य रूपमुपलेपनं पुष्पोपहारः कर्त्तव्यः । यमनियमेषु प्रयत्नः कर्त्तव्यः । अत्रैव परिसमूहनस्यान्तर्भावेपि पृथग्ग्रहणं परिसमूहनस्योपसमाहितेऽग्नौ अन्यत्रापि परिसमूहनपर्युक्षणपरिस्तरणनियमख्यापनार्थम् । उपवसथरूपापरिज्ञानाद्वा परिसमूहनाद्युपवसथरूपमिति । अथाश्रितस्य व्रतोपेतस्येति नोक्तमुभयथा दर्शनाद् व्रतोपायनीयमशित्वेतीह प्राप्नोति तस्य ब्राह्मणं प्रतिपाद्याश्नीयात् (बौ. श्रौ. २४।२१।१३) इति प्रस्तुत्याग्न्यान्वाधानवचनात्प्राप्नोति । नासन्द्यां शयीत (बौ. श्रौ. २४।२१।१६) इति वचनं न व्यवधायकमिति [३८]आरम्भे सङ्कल्पयितव्यं व्रतमिति तथान्यत्राप्युक्तमशनमग्न्यन्वाधानं व्रतोपायनमिति ।

अथ शब्दः पूर्वेषां व्यवच्छेदार्थः । तच्चैतदूर्ध्वं सन्नयतः । असंनयतो बर्हिः प्रतिपदेवेति विभागार्थम् । तथा सत्यग्न्यन्वाधानमुभयत्र सिद्धं भवति आतञ्चनं चास्य न भवति अर्थबलीयस्त्वात् । अस्येतिभेदनिर्देशादत ऊर्ध्वमाध्वर्यवमेवेति[३९] ज्ञापयति । व्रतोपेतस्य व्रतोपायनमव्रतनिवृत्तिसङ्कल्पो यस्य कृतपयस्वतीसमिदाधानस्येत्यर्थः । आभिमुख्येन पर्णशाखामाच्छैति गच्छति आप्तुं वा । आकारः प्रमादपाठ इति केचित् । आभिमुख्यार्थत्वादाच्छैतीत्याप्त्यर्थत्वादाभिमुख्येनाप्तुं गच्छतीत्यर्थः । बर्हिराच्छैतीत्यादिषुचोभयं[४०] विवक्षितम् । मर्यादार्थो वा, आ शाखाया गन्तव्यमिति। अर्थप्राप्तमिति छेदने दूरत्वेऽपि न प्रतिनिधिरिति । प्राङ्वोदङ्वेति वाशब्दद्वयमेकेन सिद्धे तुल्यविकल्पार्थम् । यत्र वेत्स्यन्नित्यनेनैव सिद्धे प्रागादिग्रहणं तदसम्भवेऽपि विकल्पार्थम् । अन्यत्र

---

३७. 'इत्यात्राम्नानात्' मु० ।
३८. 'विद्या°' पा०, वा० ।
३९. 'अस्येति चामेद°' मु०, म० ।
४०. 'नोमयं' गो०, मु० ।

लभमानोऽपि ईषत्प्राचीमुदीचीं वा गत्वा यथार्थं गच्छेदित्येवमर्थं च । तथाह –त्रीन् वा चतुरो वा प्राञ्चः (बौ. श्रौ. २०।२) इति । विदिर्लभार्थो मन्यतेः पृथगुपन्यासात् ।

प्राचीमुदीचीं वा वृक्षस्य प्रागग्रतो वा वाशब्दात् प्रागुदीची वेति ब्राह्मणे विस्पष्टमुक्तत्वात् (तै. ब्रा. ३।२।१।३) गम्यत इति अनयोरर्थवादेनाभेद-संस्तुतत्वात् तदभावाशंकानिवृत्त्यर्थम् । वा शब्दात्तयोरेवोपन्यासः । शम्युप-सङ्ग्रहार्थो वा वा शब्दः शाखान्तरे (द्र. का. श्रौ. ४।२।१) समाम्नातत्वात् । इहासमाम्नातमिति चेत् असिदग्रहणेन प्रदर्शितत्वात् न दोषः । बहुपर्णादिग्रहणं प्राचीनिन्दितापर्णादिनिवृत्त्यर्थम् । इषे त्वोर्जेत्वेतिच्छेदने विनियुक्तत्वात्प्रकाश-कत्वाच्च मन्त्राणामन्यथाऽसामर्थ्यात् । छिनद्मीति केचिदध्याहरन्ति (का. श्रौ. ४।२।२) तदयुक्तं पाठसामर्थ्याद्विनाशब्देन स्मर्त्तव्यम् । इमां प्राचीमुदीचीम् (तै. ब्रा. ३।७।४।८) इतिलिङ्गात्[४१] प्रागुदीच्यपि पक्षे[४२] प्रयोक्तव्यम् । विभज्य सर्वत्रेत्यपरे । वत्सानितिसम्भवापेक्ष एकशेषः । वायवस्थेत्यन्यायनिगदत्वादनूहः । प्रेरणं पृथक्करणम् । यजमानेक्षणं मनसा स्मरणं परोक्षेऽपीष्टत्वाच्चक्षुर्व्यापारे हि परोक्षनिवृत्तिः स्यात् । तत्र नित्यवत्पाठो[४३] बाध्येत । पूर्वपाठस्य प्रयोजनं केचित् प्राहुः मन्त्रे[४४] गवां प्राधान्यात् यजमानस्यासंस्पर्शनाद् गोपताविति शब्देन ऋषभ एवोच्यते । तत्र तासां ध्रुवत्वशासने एकमन्त्रताप्यस्तीति ।

शाखामित्येव सिद्धे एतामिति न पर्णशाखैव, शाखामात्रमिति । तत्र शाखान्तरे पठितं शम्याद्यस्तीति बोधयति । अग्रेणाहवनीयं पर्याहृत्य पूर्वया द्वारा प्रपाद्येति गार्हपत्यस्यैव शाला नेतरयोरिति,इतरस्याग्रेणाहवनीयागारमिति ब्रूयात् । अग्निष्ठे शकट इति वा शब्दाभावादेष मुख्यः कल्पः । उत्तरार्द्धे वा शालाया इत्यनुकल्पः । तथा च वक्ष्यति यद्यु वै नानो भवति (बौ. श्रौ. १।५।६) इति । उद्गूहतीत्युभयार्थः, न पर्णशाखार्थः एवेति । इति नु यदि संनयति, पाहीत्यत्रेति नास्ति क्वचिद्विना प्रयोगदर्शनात् उतेमनंनमुः (बौ. श्रौ. ७।४।३) इत्यथवो-भाभ्यां सम्बध्यते, एवं संनयत इत्यर्थः । पूर्वेणैव वा सम्बन्धः । नु शब्द एव-मित्यस्मिन्नर्थे । विध्यन्तरेऽपि दुग्धं लभमानस्येति मन्त्रनिवृत्त्यर्थम्, अर्थाभावे मन्त्रनिवृत्तिरिति[४५] । एतदेव ज्ञापयति अन्यत्रार्थाभावे निवृत्तिरिति । प्रयाजा-नुयाजाभावे जौहवाज्यादिनिवृत्तिः ख्यापिता भवति । असंनयतो बर्हिरारम्भ एव लवनं[४६] भवति । अथेत्यारभ्या एतस्मात् संनयतः व्रतोपायनानन्तरं बर्हिः

४१. 'लिङ्गात्' मु० ।
४२. 'प्रागुदीचीग्रहणपक्षे' गो०, ब० ।
४३. 'नित्यवत् आम्नातं' मु०, म० ।
४४. 'मन्त्रेण' मु०, म० ।
४५. '°भावे त्रा नि°' गो० ।
'°भावे मा नि°' मु० ।
४६. 'लवनं' नास्ति मु०, म० ।

प्रतिपत् । आतञ्चनाग्न्यन्वाधानयोर्यथोक्तम् ।

॥ **प्रथमोऽध्यायः** ॥

द्वितीयोऽध्यायः

अथ जघनेन गार्हपत्यं तिष्ठन्नसिदं वाश्वपर्शुं वादत्ते – देवस्य त्वा सवितुः प्रसवेऽश्विनोर्बाहुभ्यां पूष्णो हस्ताभ्यामाददे (**तै. ब्रा. ३।२।२।१**) **इति** ॥ **आदायाभिमन्त्रयते** – यज्ञस्य घोषदसि (**तै. सं. १।१।२।१**) **इति** ॥ **गार्हपत्ये प्रतितपति**– प्रत्युष्टं रक्षः प्रत्युष्टा अरातयः (**तै. सं. १।१।२।१**) **इति त्रिः** ॥ **अथाहवनीयमभिप्रैति** – प्रेयमगाद्धिषणा बर्हिरच्छ मनुना कृता स्वधया वितष्टा । त आवहन्ति कवयः पुरस्ताद् देवेभ्यो जुष्टम् (**तै. सं. १।१।२।१**) **इति** ॥ इह बर्हिरासदे (**तै. सं. १।१।२।१**) **इति वेदिं प्रत्यवेक्षते** ॥ **अथ तां दिशमेति यत्र बर्हिर्वेत्स्यन् मन्यते** ॥ **दर्भस्तम्बं परिगृह्णाति यावन्तमलं प्रस्तराय मन्यते** – देवानां परिषूतमसि (**तै. सं. १।१।२।१**) **इति** ॥ **अथैनमूर्ध्वमुन्मार्ष्टि** – वर्षवृद्धमसि (**तै. सं. १।१।२।१**) **इति** ॥ **असिदेनोपयच्छति** – देवबर्हिर्मा त्वान्वङ् मा तिर्यक् पर्व ते राध्यासम् (**तै. सं. १।१।२।१**) **इति** ॥ **आच्छिनत्ति** – **आच्छेत्ता ते मा रिषम्** (**तै. सं. १।१।२।१**) **इति** ॥ **आच्छेदनान्यभिमृशति** – देवबर्हिः शतवल्शं विरोह (**तै. सं. १।१।२।१**) **इति** ॥ सहस्रवल्शा वि वयं रुहेम (**तै. सं. १।१।२।२**) **इत्यात्मानं प्रत्यभिमृशते** ॥ **सर्वश एवैनं स्तम्बं लुनोति** ॥ **कृत्वा प्रस्तरं निदधाति** – पृथिव्याः सम्पृचः पाहि (**तै. सं. १।१।२।२**) **इति** ॥ **तूष्णीमत ऊर्ध्वमयुजो मुष्टीन् लुनोति** ॥ **त्रीन् वा पञ्च वा सप्त वा नव वैकादश वा यावतो वालं मन्यते** ॥ **अथ त्रिरन्वाहितं शुल्बं कृत्वापसलैरावेष्टयति** – अदित्यै रास्नासि (**तै. सं. १।१।२।२**) **इति** ॥ **तदुदीचीनाग्रं निधाय** । **तस्मिन् प्रस्तरमभिसम्भरति** – सुसंभृता त्वा सम्भरामि (**तै. सं. १।१।२।२**) **इति** ॥ **संनह्यति** – इन्द्राण्यै संनहनम् (**तै. सं. १।१।२।२**) **इति** ॥ **ग्रन्थिं करोति**– पूषा ते ग्रन्थिं ग्रथ्नातु (**तै. सं. १।१।२।२**) **इति** ॥ स ते

माऽऽस्थात् (तै. सं. १।१।२।२) इति **पश्चात्प्राञ्चमुपगूहति ।। अथैनदुद्यच्छते** – इन्द्रस्य त्वा बाहुभ्यामुद्यच्छे (तै. सं. १।१।२।२) इति ।। **शीर्षन्नधिनिधत्ते**–बृहस्पतेर्मूर्ध्ना हरामि (तै. सं. १।१।२।२) इति ।। **ऐति** – उर्वन्तरिक्षमन्विहि (तै. सं. १।१।२।२) इति ।। **एत्योत्तरेण गार्हपत्यमनधः सादयति** – देवंगममसि (तै. सं. १।१।२।२) इति ।। **तदुपरीव निदधाति यत्र गुप्तं मन्यते ।। तूष्णीं परिभोजनीयानि लुनोति ।। सकृदाच्छिन्नं पितृभ्य आच्छिनत्ति ।।**

अथ तथैव त्रिरन्वाहितं शुल्बं कृत्वैकविंशतिदारुमिध्मं संनह्यति– यत्कृष्णो रूपं कृत्वा प्राविशस्त्वं वनस्पतीन् ततस्त्वामेकविंशतिधा संभरामि सुसम्भृता (तै. ब्रा. ३।७।४।८) इति ।। **वेदं करोति वत्सज्ञुं पशुकामस्य मूतकार्यमन्नाद्यकामस्य त्रिवृतं तेजस्कामस्योर्ध्वाग्रं स्वर्गकामस्य ।। वेदिं करोति प्रागुत्तरात्परिग्राहात् ।। अथापराह्णे पिण्डपितृयज्ञेन चरति ।।**

भवस्वामिविवरणम्

अथेति शाखानिधानानन्तर्यार्थः सन्नयतः असन्नयतो व्रतानन्तर्यार्थः ।। असिदं वाश्वपर्शुं वेति वाशब्दौ समानविकल्पार्थौ शाखान्तराम्नानात्[1] मान वीहि पर्शुरिति स्वशाखाम्नानाच्चासिदस्य समानधर्मत्वं न स्यादिति तन्निवृत्त्यर्थम् । एतदेव ज्ञापयति शाखान्तरोक्तविधिसंग्रहोऽस्तीति । परिग्रहो दर्भस्तम्बस्यासिदादिना परिलेखनम् । त्रिः कर्मेति (बौ. श्रौ. २०।२) दर्शनात् मनसा परिग्रहेऽपि एतन्न स्यात् इह सकृदेव मन्त्रः कर्म च । यावन्तमलमिति प्रस्तरपरिमाणविकल्पार्थम्[2] । छेदनादिषूपस्पर्शनं धर्मशास्त्रादिति केचित् । अन्ये तुषनिरसनादिषु विधानादन्यत्रानियम इति । अपरे क्वचिद्विधानं वैदिकप्रायश्चित्तार्थं उपस्पर्शनं तु नित्यमेवेति[3] । अपरे यत्र विधानं तत्र नित्यमेवेति । एतस्मादेव लिङ्गात् अन्यत्र विकल्प इति ज्ञापकं च । शस्त्रकामे[4] आत्मानं प्रत्यवमृश्याथोदकं स्पृशेदिति आचार्यदर्शनमिति ब्रुवन् शालीकेर्नास्तीति वचनम् । आच्छेदनाभिमर्शनं सकृदाच्छिन्नानामिति केचित् । अनन्तरं सर्वश एवैनं स्तम्बं लुनोतीति वचनात् । अन्ये सर्वस्तम्बं छित्त्वेति आशासनस्याविशेषात् लुनोतिः

---

१. 'माग्नी शाखान्तरा' पा०, वा० । अन्यत्र नास्ति ।

२. 'प्रस्तर वि°' गो०, मु०, ब०, म०।

३. 'तु नित्य°' मु०, म० । 'तुषादिषु नित्य°' अन्यत्र।

४. 'वास्तुहोमे' मु०, म०।

स्वादिषु द्रष्टव्यः । कृत्वेत्यसन्देहार्थं बद्ध्वेत्यर्थः करोतेरनेकार्थत्वात् ।

तूष्णींशब्दस्य वागिन्द्रियव्यापारनिवृत्तिविषयत्वात् मन्त्रमात्रं निवर्तते । परिग्रहाद्यावृतः सर्वाः परिगृह्यन्ते । अयं चाभिप्रायः आधाने तूष्णीमग्निहोत्रे सर्वावृद्वचनात् । अन्ये तूष्णींग्रहणादावृतोऽपि निवृत्तिमिच्छन्ति । अत्र न शब्दार्थो न च लिङ्गं दृश्यते । अयुज इत्येतस्य विशेषणं त्रीन्वेत्यादि । अत ऊर्ध्वमिति प्रस्तरनिवृत्त्यर्थम् । सर्वत्र वावचनं पूर्वपूर्वापर्याप्तौ उत्तरोत्तरपरिग्रहार्थम् । यावतो वेत्येतेषामन्यतरपरिग्रहे वाशब्दः समर्थितः स्यात् । तस्मात्सादितव्यवशादेतैरपर्याप्तत्वे[५] उपर्युपरि संग्रहार्थम् । पूर्वं प्रदक्षिणं कृत्वा पश्चादपसव्यं मन्त्रेणावेष्टयति । अन्ये मन्त्रो निधानार्थम् इति तन्न सम्यक् तच्छब्देन व्यवायात् अदित्यै रास्नासीत्युदीचीनाग्रं निधायेत्येवं सिध्यति । तस्मिन्निति शुल्बस्याधिकरणत्वनिर्देशात् प्रस्तरं पूर्वं सम्भरतीति गम्यते । पाठक्रमाच्च संग्रहणात्समश्चैकीभावार्थत्वात् क्रमाच्चोपरि मुष्टिरिति गम्यते । मन्त्रविपर्यासः पाठक्रमादर्थक्रमस्य बलीयस्त्वादग्निहोत्रे दोहनहोमवत् तूष्णीं परिभोजनीयानीति यद्यपीहोक्तं तथापि लवनकाल एव द्रष्टव्यं न तु पुनर्निधाय[६] गत्वा । पुनस्तूष्णींग्रहणस्य प्रयोजनं पूर्वेषां याजुषपक्षेऽपि एषां तूष्णीमेवेति[७] । अन्ये इहावृन्निवृत्त्यर्थमिति । ततश्च पूर्वेषां तूष्णीं पक्षेऽव्यावृन्निवर्तते ।

अथ तथैवेति । अथ शब्दः पौर्णमास्यां बर्हिर्निधानानन्तर्यार्थः । तथैवेति सिद्धे त्रिरन्वाहितग्रहणं मन्त्रनिवृत्त्यर्थम् । एकविंशतिग्रहणं नित्यत्वात्सम्भरणस्य प्रकारान्तराभावाद् दाहप्रकारार्थो[८]वानित्यापरिमितपक्षे मन्त्रनिवृत्तिरसामर्थ्यादितरस्मिन् पक्षे[९] कृतार्थत्वात् । नैमित्तिकेषु त्रींस्तृचाननुब्रूयादित्येवमादिषु काम्यनैमित्तिकानां नित्यविकारादूहः । अपरिमितपक्षे पदलोपः । मन्त्रनिवृत्तौ च प्रकृतिवद्भावादूहसामर्थ्यादूहे च दोषश्रवणादपरिमितेऽप्युच्यमाने प्रकारस्याभावादप्रकृतिवत् स्यात् । प्रकृतौ चोपात्तेध्मसंख्याप्रकाशनाद् अत्र च यावन्त इध्मा उपात्तास्तत्संख्याभिधातव्या । याः पुरस्तात्प्रस्रवन्तीत्याच्छिद्रकादयो (तै. ब्रा. ३।७।४।१) मन्त्रा यथालिङ्गं प्रणीताप्रणयनादौ द्रष्टव्याः छन्दसा ब्राह्मणेनेति (बौ. श्रौ. २४।१।१) अथापि मन्त्र एवेति (बौ. श्रौ. २४।१।३) च परिभाषावशेनाप्राकरणिकार्था एव परिभाषा प्राकरणिकानां विशेषविनियोगवचनात्[१०] प्रकरणे चाम्नानाद् विकल्पः । विशेषवचनं नित्यार्थम्[११] । यथा यत्कृष्णो रूपं (तै. ब्रा. ३।७।४।८) त्रिवृत्पलाशे दर्भ (तै. ब्रा. ३।७।४।११) इत्येवमादीनां, न

५. '°स्तरित°' मु० ।
६. 'गुप्तं नि°' गो० । 'तु नि' मु० ।
७. 'एषां....पक्षे' नास्ति मु० ।
८. 'प्रकरणार्थो' मु० ।
९. 'मन्त्र...पक्षे' नास्ति मु० ।
१०. इतोऽग्रे 'प्राकरणिकत्वात्' इत्यधिकः गो० ।
११. 'निवृत्य' मु० ।

ह्यसति[१२] अविशेषे प्रकरणे आम्नानं युक्तम् । प्रकरणे आम्नातानां आहत्योक्तानां च नित्यत्वं इतरेषां च विकल्प इत्येष विशेषः । वेदार्थो मुष्टिर्बर्हिर्लवनकाल एव ग्रहीतव्यः परिभोजनीयेभ्यो वा । वत्सज्ञुं शयितवत्सजानुसदृशम् । मूतवत्कार्यं मूतकार्यं, धान्यनिधानार्थः तृणपुञ्जसन्निवेशविशेषो मूतः । त्रिवृतं त्रिशिरसमूर्ध्वाग्रं मूले बद्ध्वा छिन्नं, कल्पान्तरस्यानुपादानादित एव नित्यार्थेऽपि नित्य एव काम्यः खदिरादिष्विव । आचार्याभिप्रायश्च द्वैधे एषामेवाचार्यभेदेनाकामसम्बन्धेन वचनात् । वेदिकरणम् अथ वेदमादत्ते (बौ. श्रौ. १।१०।१५) इत्यारभ्य ब्रह्मन्नुत्तरमित्येतस्मात् (बौ. श्रौ. १।११।२६) प्राक् पुनर्हविरभिवासनोत्तरकालं समाम्नातानामामावास्येन वा पौर्णमासेन वेति विपर्यासेन समाम्नातम् । पूर्वोक्तस्य पूर्वं वेदिकरणं इतरदितरस्य यथा स्यादिति । अनन्तरं पिण्डपितृयज्ञस्याम्नानात्पुनरपि दोहोपक्रमादितरत्र चौषधानन्तरं समाम्नानात् शाखान्तरे चामावास्यायां पूर्वेद्युर्वेदिं करोतीति । अथापराह्णे पिण्डपितृयज्ञेन चरतीति । शाखान्तरे चामावास्यायामपराह्णे (तु.- का. श्रौ. ४।१।१) इतिवचनाद् वाक्यशेषे सोऽमावस्यायां प्रत्यागच्छदिति (तै. ब्रा. १।२।१०।१) चामावास्यायामपराह्ण इति गम्यते ॥

॥ द्वितीयोऽध्यायः ॥

तृतीयोऽध्यायः

अथैतस्यै शाखायै पर्णानि प्रच्छिद्याग्रेण गार्हपत्यं निवपति ॥ अथैनामधस्तात्परिवास्य जघनेन गार्हपत्यं स्थविमदुपवेषाय निदधाति ॥ अथास्याः प्रादेशमात्रं प्रमाय दर्भनाडीः प्रवेष्ट्य तत्त्रिवृच्छाखापवित्रं करोति – त्रिवृत्पलाशे दर्भ इयान् प्रादेशसम्मितः । यज्ञे पवित्रं पोतृतमं पयो हव्यं करोतु मे **(तै. ब्रा. ३।७।४।११) इति ॥ अथ सायं हुतेऽग्निहोत्र उत्तरेण गार्हपत्यं तृणानि संस्तीर्य तेषु चतुष्टयं संसादयति दोहनं पवित्रं सान्नाय्यतपन्यौ स्थाल्याविति ॥ अथैनान्यद्भिः प्रोक्षति** – शुन्धध्वं दैव्याय कर्मणे देवयज्यायै **(तै. सं. १।१।३।१) इति त्रिः ॥ अथ जघनेन गार्हपत्यमुपविश्योपवेषेणोदीचोऽङ्गारान्निरूहति** – मातरिश्वनो घर्मोऽसि **(तै. सं. १।१।३।१) इति ॥ तेषु सान्नाय्यतपनीमधिश्रयति** – द्यौरसि पृथिव्यसि विश्वधाया असि परमेण धाम्ना । दृंहस्व मा ह्वाः **(तै. सं. १।१।३।१) इति ॥**

---

१२. '°नामनम्यांस इति' मु°, म° । रज्ज्वादीनां

तस्यां प्राचीनाग्रं शाखापवित्रं निदधाति – वसूनां पवित्रमसि शतधारं वसूनां पवित्रमसि सहस्रधारं **(तै. सं. १।१।३।१) इति ।। तदन्वारभ्य वाचंयम आस्ते ।। अथ गा आयतीः प्रतीक्षते** – एता आचरन्ति मधुमद्दुहानाः प्रजावतीर्यशसो विश्वरूपाः । बह्वी-र्भवन्तीरुपजायमाना इह व इन्द्रो रमयतु गावः **(तै. ब्रा. ३।७।४।१४-१५) इति ।। महेन्द्र इति वा यदि महेन्द्रयाजी भवति ।। अथाह** – उपसृष्टां मे प्रब्रूतात् **(श. ब्रा. १।७।१।१०) इति ।। उपसृष्टां प्राहुः ।। दोह्यमानामनुमन्त्रयते** – हुत स्तोको हुतो द्रप्सोऽग्नये बृहते नाकाय स्वाहा द्यावापृथिवीभ्याम् **(तै. सं. १।१।३।१) इति ।। अथ पुरस्तात्प्रत्यगानयन्तं पृच्छति** कामधुक्षः **(तै. ब्रा. ३।७।४।१६) इति ।। अमूमितीतरः प्रत्याह ।। तामनुमन्त्रयते** –सा विश्वव्यचाः **(तै. सं. १।१।३।१) इति ।। तृतीयमानयन्तं पृच्छति** –कामधुक्षः **(तै. सं. ३।७।४।१६) इति ।। अमूमित्येवेतरः प्रत्याह ।। तामनुमन्त्रयते** –सा विश्वकर्मा **(तै. सं. १।१।३।१) इति ।।**

तिसृषु दुग्धासु वाचं विसृजते – बहु दुग्धीन्द्राय देवेभ्यो हव्यमाप्यायतां पुनः । वत्सेभ्यो मनुष्येभ्यः पुनर्दोहाय कल्पताम् **(तै. ब्रा. ३।७।४।१७) इति ।। महेन्द्रायेति वा यदि महेन्द्रयाजी भवति ।। विसृष्टवागनन्वारभ्य तूष्णीमुत्तरां दोहयित्वा ।। दोहनेऽप आनीय संक्षाल-नमानयति** – संपृच्यध्वमृतावरीरुर्मिणीर्मधुमत्तमा । मन्द्रा धनस्य सातय **(तै. सं. १।१।३।१) इति ।। अथैनत् तप्त्वोदगुद्वास्य शीती-कृत्वा तिरःपवित्रं दध्नातनक्ति** – सोमेन त्वातनच्मीन्द्राय दधि **(तै. सं. १।१।३।१) इति ।। महेन्द्रायेति वा यदि महेन्द्रयाजी भवति ।। यावता मूर्च्छयिष्यन्मन्यते तावदानयति ।।**

अग्निहोत्रोच्छेषणमभ्यातनक्ति – यज्ञस्य सन्ततिरसि यज्ञस्य त्वा सन्ततिमनुसन्तनोमि **(तै. ब्रा. ३।७।४।१७) इति ।। अथैन-दुदन्वता कंसेन वा चमसेन वापिदधाति** – अदस्तमसि विष्णवे त्वा यज्ञायापिदधाम्यहम् ।। अद्भिररिक्तेन पात्रेण याः पूताः परिशेरते **(तै. ब्रा. ३।७।४।१७) इति ।। तदुपरीव निदधाति यत्र गुप्तं मन्यते** – विष्णो हव्यं रक्षस्व **(तै.सं. १।१।३।१) इति ।। एतस्मिन् काले दर्भैः प्रातर्दोहाय वत्सानपाकरोति तूष्णीम् ।।**

भवस्वामि-विवरणम्

एतस्या इति पर्णशाखाया मुख्यत्वख्यापनार्थम् । पर्णानि सत्सरुकाणि द्रष्टव्यानि पर्णत्सरुकाणामितिविनियोगे सत्सरुदर्शनात् । एनामिति शाखायाः प्राधान्यार्थम् । प्रयोजिका शाखा अप्रयोजक उपवेष इति ख्यापितं भवति । परिवास्य मूलतः छित्त्वा स्थविमत् स्थूलम्[१] उपवेषाय निदधाति । अस्या इति पर्णशाखायाः प्रकृतत्वात् अन्यस्या अपि ग्रहणं यथा स्यादिति सामान्यवचनम् । प्रादेशमात्रं मीत्वा प्रादेशमात्रमिति न शाखापरिमाणं, प्रादेशमात्रं दर्भनाडीः प्रवेष्टयेति सम्बन्धः । शाखाया अधिकरणत्वेन श्रवणात्त्रिवृत्पलाश इति त्रिवृत्-पलाशशाखायामिति च । उपवेषणमपास्य शेषस्यैकदेशं प्रादेशमात्रं दर्भैस्त्रिवृतं करोति । छित्त्वा ग्रहणे मध्यस्य विनियोगावचनात् समत्वे चाधारत्वं गौणं स्यात् । दर्भगुणाभ्यां शाखया सह त्रिवृतं करोति ।

चतुष्टयग्रहणं प्रदर्शनार्थं रज्वादीनां प्रोक्षणलिङ्गमन्त्रे दर्शनादिति केचित् नियमार्थमित्यपरे । लिङ्गप्राप्तस्य विशेषानुक्रमणं सादनक्रमनियमार्थम् । तान्येव-मेव द्वन्द्वमिति परिभाषितत्वादिहापि तथा सादनीयानीति चतुष्टयं नित्यार्थम्[२] । प्रोक्षणस्य प्राधान्यात्संख्याप्रोक्षणेन सम्बध्यते । मन्त्रः सकृदेवाभ्यासकार्याभावात् । गोरमणं प्रति परार्थत्वादनूहशङ्कानिवृत्त्यर्थं महेन्द्र इति वा यदि महेन्द्रयाजी भवतीति तस्य सम्प्रदानत्वाद् रमणमात्मार्थमेवेति प्राधान्यादिन्द्रस्य नैमित्तिका-दूहितः । यदि शब्दाद् गतश्रियोऽपि सम्वत्सरमिन्द्रेज्यास्तीति बोधयति । वा-शब्दादगतश्रियोऽपि सम्वत्सरादूर्ध्वमनियम इति । दोह्यमानामिति प्रकृतिशब्देना-भेदेन विकारावगमात् द्रप्सा एवोच्यन्ते अन्यस्य कर्मणोऽश्रुतत्वात् । गोरेव हि कर्मत्वे स्तोकानामनुमन्त्रणमिति दुर्गमं स्यात् ब्राह्मणे च मन्त्रस्य स्तोकहोमा-र्थत्वदर्शनात् आनयन्तं स्थालीं प्रापयन्तं स्थाल्यां सिञ्चन्तमित्यर्थः आहराप आनयेति (बौ. श्रौ. १।९।२) भेदेन निर्देशादाहरणादन्यो नयत्यर्थो यथोक्त इति गम्यते । तथा चाप्रमत्तः सन्ततमानय दोहनेऽप आनीय संक्षालनमानयति (बौ. श्रौ. १।१।२५) तावदानयतीति (बौ. श्रौ. १।१।२७) च कामधुक्ष इत्येतावान् मन्त्रः । अमूमिति च नामवचनमात्रं[३] महेन्द्रायेत्यवचनात् अच्छिद्रकाणां समस्त-पाठात् ब्राह्मणे चामुमिति नाम गृह्णातीति (तै. ब्रा. ३।२।३।७) वचनात् प्रतीकेन मन्त्रोपदेशे सति[४] विशेषविधानशक्यत्वात्प्रश्नप्रतिवचनयोश्च समाप्त-त्वात्[५] । अन्ये उभयोर्मन्त्रयोः प्रतीकग्रहणमित्याहुः । महेन्द्रायेति वचनं (तै. सं. २।५।४।४) इतरेषां प्रदर्शनत्वात्तेषु वचनमिन्द्रशब्दस्य पठितत्वादिह[६] वचन-

---

१. 'स्थूलम्' नास्ति गो०, पा० ।
२. 'तान्येव°....र्थम्' नास्ति म० ।
३. 'नाम न वचन°' पा०, वा० ।
४. 'सति' नास्ति पा०, मु०, म० ।
५. 'विधाना...त्वात्' नास्ति मु० ।
६. 'प्रतित°' गो०। 'प्रतीक°' पा०,वा०।

मुपपद्यते[७] । अभिधानवैचित्र्यात् असमस्तपाठाद् ब्राह्मणे च मन्त्रस्य रूपादेव प्राप्तत्वान्नामग्रहणमेव विधीयते । भद्रमेवासां कर्माविष्करोतीति (तै. ब्रा. ३।२।३।७) प्रतीकपक्ष एव उपपद्यते । प्रैषाभ्यासे वक्तव्येऽवचप्रयोजन-मपद्येकद्विग्रहे[८] निवृत्त्यर्थं प्रश्नाद्युपक्रमश्च प्रैषस्य निवृत्त्यर्थम् इति केचित् । अन्येषां प्रश्नाद्यावृत्तिवचनं बहुत्वपक्षे प्रदर्शनार्थम्[९] । प्रैषाभ्यासवचनं चैकत्वपक्षे प्रश्नाद्यनभ्यासार्थमिति बहु दुग्धीति सकृदेव त्रित्ववचनस्य मन्त्रान्तरविषयत्वात्[१०] त्रिर्वा प्रत्येकमनुक्रान्ताभिसम्बन्धात् । बहु दुग्धीति चैकवचनस्य गोविषयस्यैव-मर्थत्वात् तिसृषु दुग्धास्विति च इतरथाथ वाचं विसृजत इत्येवावक्ष्यत् तेनास्य विकल्पः । ब्राह्मण उक्तत्वादिहावचनं प्रत्यक्षविहितेनानारभ्याधीतस्यानुमानिकस्य विकल्पस्य न्याय्यत्वाद् विकृतौ निवेशे प्राप्ते आचार्यस्य वचनात् श्रुत्यन्तर-मनुमीयते नह्येकस्मात् प्रमाणादाचार्योऽब्रवीदिति । बहु दुग्धीति प्रैषासम्भवात् त्रिरित्यवचनाच्च सकृदेव मन्त्र इत्यपरम् । मन्त्रो विकृतौ न प्रवर्तते पुनराप्या-यनप्रयोजनाभावात् उत्तरवाक्ये[११] च पुनः शब्दस्य पुनरुपादानत्वात् । हव्यमिति स्वार्थिकत्वात् तद्धितस्य प्रकृत्यन्तरस्य प्रतीकोपादादेक एव मन्त्र इत्यपरे एत-स्मिन्दर्शनेऽभ्यसितव्यो ब्राह्मणवचनाल् । तूष्णींग्रहणं वागिन्द्रियव्यापारनिवृत्तौ आवृत्प्रसङ्गेऽनन्वारभ्येत्यावृन्निवृत्त्यर्थम् । षडवमा (बौ. श्रौ. २४।२३।१०) इति न परिसंख्यार्थम् । एवमपरिमितानामितीदमुपपद्यते[१२] । चतुर्थे स्रुवे तृतीये स्रुवे (बौ. श्रौ. २०।४) इति स्रुवन्नित्यवत्कृत्वा संख्याविकल्पवचनात् स्रुवेणातञ्चनं तयोः स्रुवनियमः । इह तु पक्षान्तरमपि सम्भवति येन केनचित् सकृदेव यावता मूर्च्छयिष्यन्निति इह वचनात् ।

आपः प्रोक्षणीशेषाः तिरःपवित्रमतिनीता आपो धारयेति (तै. ब्रा. ३।७।४।१४) लिङ्गाद् धारणस्यान्याप्रयोजनादिह वचनात् इत्येके । तदुपपन्नं, इह प्रोक्षणीनां मन्त्रानाम्नानात् देवेन सवित्रा (तै.ब्रा.३।७।४।१४) इत्यसम्भवः । अवचनाच्च इहस्थानां च इहस्थानामाप्तिलिङ्गान्मन्त्रानाम्नानात्[१३] च पुरोडाशीय प्रोक्षणीषु स्थानाच्च लिङ्गं बलीयः । अयं चाभिप्रायः आचार्यस्येति गम्यते अति-शिष्टाः प्रोक्षणीर्निधायेति (बौ.श्रौ.१।६।६) वचनात् आहरन्त्येताः प्रोक्षणीरभि-पूर्येति (बौ. श्रौ. १।११।३०) धारणं देवेन सवित्रोत्पूता (तै.ब्रा. ३।७।४।१४) इति वचनं तत्रोपपद्यते । तस्मात्तत्र युक्तो मन्त्रः प्रैषवचनाच्च याजमानमेवं च मन्त्रार्थवाद उपपन्नो भवति, तस्मादुदकमात्रस्य ग्रहणम् । अद्भिररिक्तेन इत्युप-

७. '°दिहपाठादवचन' सार्वत्रिकः, मु० विहाय ।
८. '°द्येत गो विग्र°' पा० ।
९. इतोऽग्रे 'प्रैषाभ्यासस्य' गो०, म०, ब०।
१०. 'मन्त्रोत्तर°' गो० ।
११. 'उरादेकत्वे' गो० । 'उरादेमिप्रायत्वे' पा०, बा० ।
१२. '°मितार्थवादउप' मु०, म० ।
१३. 'इहसस्थात्रापिलि°' गो० ।

पद्यते, इमौ पर्णं चेति (तै. ब्रा. २।७।४।१५) पवित्रमपिधाने निदध्यात् । कमण्डलुभिरित्यादौ पूता इत्युपपन्नं भवतीति अनियमः । प्रोक्षणीशेष पक्षे हव्यं हि रक्षसीत्यागम्यपेक्षमपि[१४] सम्भवतीति ।

अपाकरणं वत्सानां शाखाया विनियुक्तत्वात् आख्यान्तरप्रतिपत्तौ दोषाभिधानाभावात् अन्यश्चाभावात् पर्णशाखया वत्सानपाकरोतीति[१५] च कृतार्थत्वात् मन्त्राणां च तत्सम्बद्धत्वात् प्रकृतौ च कृत्स्नविधानाच्छाखामाच्छिनत्तीति चैकत्वस्य विवक्षितत्वात् साधारणत्वेऽपि तूष्णीं दर्भैरित्युक्तम् । दर्भैरिति वचनमुत्प्रेक्ष्यम् । अशनवचनमशनपरिग्रहार्थं ब्राह्मणोक्तपरिग्रहार्थं वा । एतदेव युक्ततरं दृश्यते । अशनानशने (बौ. श्रौ. २०।४) द्वैधसूत्रमौपमन्यवस्येत्युक्तत्वाद् द्वयोरुपन्यासेन लघीयसा[१६] सिद्धे त्रयाणामुपन्यासादनशनमेवाभिप्राय इति गम्यते ॥

॥ तृतीयोऽध्यायः ॥

---

१४. '°गमव्यपे°' म०।

१५. '°खया च वत्सा°' मु०।

१६. 'बलीयसा' गो०।

ĀPASTAMBA ŚRAUTASŪTRA

with

The Commentary of Rudradatta

Edited by
Radhey Shyam Shastri

INTRODUCTION

The great Sanskrit scholar of Germany, Richard Garbe (1857-1927) prepared the *editio princeps* of this work which was published by the Asiatic Society, Calcutta, in 1882 and 1885. (The 3rd volume was published in 1902 which contains only the Sūtra, as the commentary of Rudradatta has come, so far, to light only upto the 15th Praśna).[1] This may be regarded a critical edition, for the editor used many MSS., (See his Preface) both of the Sūtra and the commentary, although he has not recorded the variant readings of the commentary.

Another edition of this work was published in 1909 at Kumbhakoṇam which runs only upto the 7th Praśna. This being in the Grantha script was accessible only to a limited number of scholars. Hence for over a century Garbe's edition has re-mained the basis of all studies regarding this Sūtra and thus it has rendered a great service to the Vedic studies.

The Grantha edition does not mention the MSS. used by the editor. Though, on the title page it says नानादेशानीतप्राचीन-तालपत्रकोशानुसारेण श्रौतविद्भिः पण्डितवरैः सम्यक् परिशोध्य, it is almost similar to Garbe's edition which gives one the impression that the editor has followed Garbe.

A work entitled दर्शपूर्णमासप्रकाशः was published by आनन्दाश्रम, पुणे in 1924. It also contains Praśnas 1- 4 with the commentary of Rudradatta (named Dīpikā). Evidently, the editor has

1. All the three vols. were reprinted under my guidance by Munshiram Manoharlal, Delhi, 1983.

based his text on Garbe's edition, so I do not consider it an independent edition.

The Mysore edition of this Sūtra with the Bhāṣya of Dhūrtasvāmin cites from the Dīpikā from 1 to 8 Praśnas in footnotes. These are taken from Garbe. For Praśnas 9-10, this edition gives the complete text of the Dīpikā. The editor says in the Introduction that for this he has also used a ms. of the Dipikā (No. C 1370). I possess a xerox copy of this ms. which contains 1 -15 Praśnas along with the Sūtra-text.

Rudradatta was a native of Maharashtra (which I will show in the detailed Introduction). Garbe was fortunate in having a MS. of the Dīpikā which, in his own words, is described as "An ancient, excellent, and accurately corrected MS." It is due to this MS. that Garbe could prepare an excellent edition. I have collected about ten MSS. of each Praśna and I am sorry to say that none of these is accurate. Still, with their collective aid, the text presented by Garbe can be improved. So I have taken Garbe's text as tentatively accepted one and tried to improve it with the help of the other MSS. Today there is known a large number of the mss. of the Dīpikā and it is neither practicable nor necessary to collate them all.

Garbe's edition requires to be revised in the following directions :

1. There are some wrong readings.
2. At some places the punctuation is wrong which shows that there Garbe could not understand the text properly.
3. No references are given.
4. Sometimes the division of the Sūtras is contradictory to the commentary.
5. In a few cases, the sūtra-text also requires revision.

In the following pages, I present a specimen of the revised edition. A description of all the five points is given below.

1. Wrong readings corrected
(page and line are of Garbe's edition)

Page	Line	Garbe's reading	Revised reading
1	5	ध्याये	ध्यायेत्

	8	°मध्यस्थित°	°मध्यक्षित°
	12	सुविवक्तारः	सुविवेक्तारः
3	5	स्व आयतने	स्व एवायतने
	5	परिगृह्णामि	परिगृह्णाति
	6	कर्मविधि°	मन्त्रविधि°
	7	इति	इति च
4	6	तत्र प्रणयनप्रसङ्गः	तत्राप्रणयनप्रसङ्गः
	7	ब्रवीदिति	वादीदिति
5	1f.b.	यदाभ्यास°[1]	पदाभ्यास°
6	5	यस्य	या
	10	ऋजुकरोति	ऋजूकरोति
	10	°नुलोममनुमार्ष्टि	°नुलोमं मार्ष्टि
9	5 f.b.	अध्वर्योरायतनं	see footnote in the text
10	10	प्रतितप्स्यति	प्रतितपति
11	6	°ऽनेन	See footnote in the text

Sometimes, I have adopted a correct reading without mentioning the mss. which contain it. It was done to expedite the work. So, whenever a reading different from Garbe's is found, it must be taken for granted that it is based on MSS. In the above list पदाभ्यास, या, ऋजूकरोति, °नुलोमं मार्ष्टि, प्रतितपति are such readings. Nowhere have I emended the text. The emendations have been suggested in the footnotes. In the given specimen, I have suggested two for which see the above mentioned footnotes.

At page 8, line3, Garbe conjectures प्रतियोगिकेन for प्रतियोगित्वेन (see his Vol. I, P. 469). But प्रतियोगित्वेन, which is found in all the MSS., is the correct reading. प्रतियोगिकेन has no sense here. It shows that Garbe was not good at the terminology of the Navya-nyāya system in 1882 when he was only 25 years old.

There are some cases where even though Garbe's reading is correct, yet I have adopted another reading because it is supported by more MSS. or due to some other obvious grounds. Such cases are listed below :

Page	Line	Garbe's edition	Revised edition
1	4	श्रीवत्सवक्षसे	श्रीवत्सलक्ष्मणे

1. It cannot be a misprint; for a number of MSS., even the Grantha edition, has this reading.

	6	मुनिं स्तुमः	ऋषिं नुमः
	7	°ऽप्यन्यथा°	°ष्वन्यथा°
2	5 f.b.	वाक्यानुवन्दितौ	वाक्यानूदितौ
4	8	°स्यैवायमनुवादः	°स्यैवार्थस्यानुवादः
6	1	प्रतिषेधः	प्रतिषेधस्तु
11	1	मन्यत इति	मन्येत इति

2. Wrong punctuation corrected

Page	Line	Garbe's reading	Revised reading
1	5 f.b.	अत्र भगवान्	अत्रभगवान्
2	2	प्रयुज्यते । वृद्धैः	प्रयुज्यते वृद्धैः ।
	8	°र्शनात् । अमा.....वाच्यम्।।	°र्शनात् अमा....वाच्यम्,
4	4	°दुक्तमिदम् । यद्दर्श°	°दुक्तमिदं यद्दर्श°
	5	प्रत्यवशिष्यते न्यायत	प्रत्यवशिष्यते । न्यायत
6	6	भेत्तव्यम् । या	भेत्तव्यं या
8	4	सांनाय्यदेवता । निगमे	सांनाय्यदेवतानिगमे
11	8	दर्शिता । अथो	दर्शिता–अथो
	9	भवतीति तस्यै°	भवतीति । तस्यै°
	7 f.b.	°यीष्यते तथै°	°यीष्यते, तथै°

3. References

In the first three Kaṇḍikās which cover only 13 pages of Garbe's edition, I have given 70 references, whereas Garbe gives none.

4. Sūtra-division

There is only one case in the given specimen. In the 3rd Kaṇḍikā, Garbe takes देवस्य त्वा सवितुः प्रसव इत्यसिदमश्वपर्शुं वादत्ते तूष्णीमनडुत्पर्शुम् ।२। as one Sūtra. But Rudradatta in the commentary writes गतौ (योगौ अर्थौ वा). I think it is necessary that the Sūtra-division must be in conformity with the commentary. Accordingly I have divided this sūtra like this : देवस्य त्वा सवितुः प्रसव इत्यसिदमश्वपर्शुं वादत्ते ।।२।। तूष्णीमनडुत्पर्शुम् ।।३।। . This has resulted in increasing the number of the following sūtras by one, thus causing the concordances and indices based on Garbe's edition slightly wrong. But this is unavoidable.

5. Sūtra-text

I have preferred व्याहृतिभिर् to व्याहृतीभिर् in 1.1.7 for व्याहृतिभिर् is found at 12 and व्याहृतीभिर् at 7 places in my source material. Though both the forms are available in the Vedic language, yet the majority always favours the *Hrasva*-form. In addition, I have recorded the following variants.

1.1.4	जपति ।।४।। for जपित्वा
1.3.5	पर्शू for पर्शुम्
1.3.13	इति सव्यहस्तेन संयच्छति for इति संयच्छति
1.3.16	लुनाति for लुनोति

Naturally some misprints have been corrected. They are :

Page	Line	Incorrect	Correct
2	11	एवशब्दो	एव शब्दो
3	10	बिलम्बिष्ट	विलम्बिष्ट
11	5 f.b.	यदप्यस्याविशेषणं	यदप्यस्या विशेषणं

A special feature of this edition is worth mentioning. Āpastamba gives only the Pratīka of the Mantras of the तैसं. I have given in footnotes the remaining part of the Mantra. Thus this edition will help to know the full Mantra to be used at a particular rite.

The text is based on the following materials :

1) The Sūtra

Printed editions

गा– Garbe's edition with the Dīpikā.

चि– Chinnaswami's edition with the Bhāṣya of Dhūrtasvāmin, Baroda.

मै.धू.–Mysore edition with Dhūrtasvāmibhāṣya and Rāmāṇḍāra Vṛtti.

द– Darśapūrṇamāsa-prakāśa, Pune.

कु– Kumbhakoṇam-edition with the Dīpikā (in Grantha script).

Manuscripts

वै.म.–A complete ms. of आपस्तम्बकल्पसूत्र from वैदिक संशोधन मंडल, पुणे.

वा सा अ इ फ ब[१] सं मै– These 8 mss.(described below) contain the Sūtra-text also along with the Dīpikā.

2) Rudradatta's commentary called Sūtradīpikā or Dīpikā

Printed editions

गा– Garbe
कु– Kumbhakoṇam

Manuscripts

वा– प्राज्ञपाठशाला मंडल, वाई (महाराष्ट्र) प्रश्न 1-15
सा– साङ्गवेदविद्यालय, काशी । प्रश्न 1, 7, 8, 9, 10-13 (3 mss.), 14 (2 mss.)
अ– राजस्थान प्राच्य विद्या प्रतिष्ठान, अलवर । प्रश्न 1-5, 8-15
इ– भारत इतिहास संशोधक मंडल, पुणे । प्रश्न 1-15
फ– फर्ग्युसन कालिज, पुणे । प्रश्न 1-15
ब१– M. S. University, Baroda प्रश्न 1-15 (प्रश्न 8-9 partly missing)
ब२– M. S. University, Baroda प्रश्न 1-6 and a part of 7
ब३– M. S. University, Baroda प्रश्न 1-4, 8-9
वै– वैदिक संशोधन मंडल, पुणे । प्रश्न 1-7
भ१– Bhandarkar Oriental Research Institute, Poona. प्रश्न 1-9
भ२– Bhandarkar Oriental Research Institute, Poona. प्रश्न 1-8
भ३– Bhandarkar Oriental Research Institute, Poona. प्रश्न 5
सं– संपूर्णानन्द संस्कृत विश्वविद्यालय, काशी । प्रश्न 1-15
मै– Oriental Research Institute, Mysore. प्रश्न 1-15
त– Sarasvatī-Mahal, Tanjore. In the catalogue of this excellent library, the beginning and ending portions of a MS. of Dīpikā are given. I have compared just the five Maṅgala-ślokas from this. Garbe used this MS. for Praśnas 1-3 and 8-15.

All these MSS. are in Devanagari script. Details of the MSS. will be given in the detailed introduction to the forthcoming edition.

I express my sincere thanks to all those who have helped me in procuring the MSS. or otherwise. Their names will also appear in the detailed introduction. Suggestions to improve this edition are most earnestly invited.[1]

---

1. Where no work is mentioned, citations are from the Āpastamba Śrauta Sūtra itself. The abbreviations of the Vedic works are wellknown to scholars.

आपस्तम्बीयं श्रौतसूत्रम्

रुद्रदत्तवृत्तियुतम्

प्रथमः प्रश्नः

अथातो दर्शपूर्णमासौ व्याख्यास्यामः ।।१।।

शुक्लाम्बरधरं देवं शशिवर्णं चतुर्भुजम् ।
प्रसन्नवदनं ध्यायेत्सर्वविघ्नोपशान्तये[१] ।।
आज्ञा श्रुतिस्मृती यस्य यस्य यज्ञाः सभाजनम्[२] ।
नमः परस्मै विश्वस्मात्तस्मै श्रीवत्सलक्ष्मणे[३] ।।
आदिमं ब्रह्मणः कोशमध्यक्षितपरावरम्[४] ।
अपास्तरोषपाप्मानमापस्तम्बमृषिं नुमः[५] ।।
आपस्तम्बीयसूत्रार्थेष्वन्यथाज्ञानसंशयान्[६] ।
सूत्रदीपिकया वृत्त्या रुद्रदत्तः परास्यति ।।
सन्तु[७] ये सुविवेक्तारः[८] सन्तः स्युर्गुणसाक्षिणः[९] ।
रत्नं रत्नमिति ग्राह्यं मूल्यं किं तस्य गृह्यते ।।

अत्रभगवानापस्तम्बः समस्तलोकहितकाङ्क्षी विध्यर्थवादमन्त्रात्मकविविधवेदभागव्याकीर्णं विभक्तानेकशाखाव्यासक्तं च विश्वस्य वैतानिकस्य कर्मणो याजुर्वेदिकं प्रयोगं व्याचिख्यासुस्तत्र सर्वप्रथमभाविनोऽग्न्याधेयस्य सेष्टिकत्वात्सर्वेष्टीनां च दर्शपूर्णमासप्रकृतित्वात् समाम्नाये च दर्शपूर्णमासमन्त्राणामेव प्राथम्यात्तावेवाग्रे व्याख्यास्यन्नधिकारं दर्शयति 'अथात' इति । अथातःशब्दोऽयं प्रकरणारम्भे प्रायः प्रयुज्यते वृद्धैः । क्वचिदानन्तर्येऽपि, यथा इमे भृगवो व्याख्याताः (२४.६.९) अथातोऽङ्गिरसाम् (२४.६.१०) इत्यादौ । न पुनरिहानन्तर्यार्थः, वृत्तस्य कस्यचिदनन्तरस्यानुपलम्भात् । न दृश्यतेऽस्मिंश्चन्द्रमा इति विपरीतलक्षणया दर्श इत्यमावास्योच्यते । न त्वियमन्वर्थसंज्ञेति, चन्द्रदर्शनस्य सर्वतिथिसाधारण्यात् । न च सूर्येण संगतो दृश्यत इति विशेष्टव्यं सूर्यसंगतेरमावास्याशब्दप्रवृत्तिहेतोर्दर्शनात् अमा सह वसतोऽस्यां चन्द्रार्काविति वाच्यम्, अतितेजस्विसूर्यमण्डलान्तर्विलीनः क्षीणकलश्चन्द्रमाः सिद्धैरेव दृश्यते

नास्मद्विधैरिति । तत्रापि सिद्धदर्शनस्याविशेषकत्वादस्मद्दर्शनपरिसंख्यापर एव शब्दोऽभ्युपगन्तव्य इति स एवार्थश्छद्मनोक्तः स्यात् । न चासौ प्राञ्जलः विवक्षिततिरोधानात् सूत्रकृतैव विपरीतलक्षणया विवरणाच्च यथा यदहर्न दृश्यते तदहरमावास्या (२४.२.२४) इति । तस्माद्यथोक्त एवार्थः शोभते । मासश्चन्द्रः यदाहुर्नैरुक्ताः मासो मानात्कालश्चन्द्रश्चेति[१०] । स पूर्यते यस्मिन् तदहः पूर्णमासः । दर्शश्च पूर्णमासश्च दर्शपूर्णमासौ । इह च दर्शपूर्णमासाख्यकालचोदितानामाग्नेयादिप्रधानानां यौ विद्वद्वाक्यानूदितौ[११] समुदायौ य एवं विद्वान् पौर्णमासीं......य एवं विद्वानमावास्याम् (तैसं १.६.९) इति, तयोरपि तत्तत्कालसंबन्धेन दर्शपूर्णमासाविति नामनी । तत्र पूर्णमासस्य प्रयोगतः प्रथमत्वेऽपि दर्शशब्दस्याल्पाच्तरत्वात्पूर्वनिपातः । तौ व्याख्यास्यामः । श्रुतौ संक्षिप्तयोः व्याकरणेन शाखान्तरोपसंहारादिना च विस्पष्टीकरणं व्याख्यानम् ।

१. अस्मात् श्लोकात्पूर्वमधिकः पाठ इत्थम्–

गा– श्रीगणेशाय नमः । ओम्

सं ब$_{१}$ वा– श्रीगणेशाय नमः । श्रीमार्तंडभैरवाय नमः ।

सा– श्रीमहागणपतये नमः ।

मै भ$_{१}$ फ इ– श्रीगणेशाय नमः ।

भ$_{२}$ – श्रीगणेशाय नमः । श्री विश्वेश्वराय नमः । श्री कालभैरवाय नमः ।

अ ब$_{२}$ ब$_{३}$ वै–अयं श्लोको नास्ति ।

त –अस्य श्लोकस्य स्थाने निम्नलिखितः श्लोक उपलभ्यते–

स्वं स्वं मनोरथमवाप्तुमपोढविघ्नं
यस्य प्रसादमनवाप्य न शक्नुवन्ति ।
पद्मासनप्रभृतयः प्रथमेऽपि देवास्
तद्वस्तु हस्तिमुखमस्तु मयि प्रसन्नम् ।।

सर्वे कोशाः – ध्यायेत् । गा-ध्याये ।

ध्यै-धातुः परस्मैपदी, अतः 'ध्याये' न साधु ।

कदाचित् मुद्रणकाले अक्षरपातोऽयम् ।

२. सं वा सा इ फ ब$_{१}$ मै – सभाजनाः ।

३. गा कु – श्रीवत्सवक्षसे ।

अस्मात् श्लोकात्पूर्वमधिकः पाठः –

अ– श्रीगणेशाय नमः । श्रीसरस्वत्यै नमः ।

ब$_{२}$–श्रीगणेशाय नमः ।

ब$_{३}$–श्रीवेदव्यासाय नमः ।

वै– श्रीगणेशाय नमः । श्रीगुरुदेव । श्री आपस्तंबाय नमः ।

४. आदिमं श्रेष्ठं, ब्रह्मणः वेदस्य कोशं निधिम्, अध्यक्षितं प्रत्यक्षितं परावरं येन सः अध्यक्षितपरावरम् । अयं शुद्धः पाठः वा ब१ मै कोशेषु उपलभ्यते ।

गा कु – कोशमध्यस्थित॰

इ सं सा भ१– कोशं मध्यक्षिति॰

फ– कोशं मध्यक्षितं

ब२ ब३– कोशं मध्यः क्षिति॰

वै– कोशमध्यक्षिति॰

त– आदिमं ब्राह्मणं क्षेममध्यस्थित॰

भ२ अ– अयं श्लोको नास्ति ।

५. त– अपास्ताशेष॰ ।

भ१–ऋषिं नुमः ।

गा कु – मुनिं स्तुमः ।

मै सं वा सा इ फ ब१ ब२ ब३ वै – ऋषिं मुनिं

६. गा कु – ॰सूत्रार्थेऽप्यन्यथा॰

ब२ ब३– अथापस्तम्बसूत्रार्थविपर्याज्ञानसंशयान्

वै– अथापस्तम्बसूत्रार्थेष्वन्यथाज्ञानसंश्रयान्

त– अस्यापस्तम्बसूत्रस्य दुर्ज्ञानिज्ञानसंशयान्

मै सं वा सा अ इ फ ब१ भ१ भ२ – यथास्वीकृतम्

७. मै सा अ ब२ ब३ – सन्ति

८. गा कु भ२ – सुविवक्तारः

मै सं वा सा अ इ फ ब१ ब२ ब३ वै भ१ – सुविवेक्तारः

९. सा अ – स्युर्गुणतोषिणः

१०. यास्कीयनिरुक्ते (४.२७) तु 'मासा मानात्' एतावदेव लभ्यते । परन्तु सर्वेषु कोशेषु यथामुद्रितपाठ एव लभ्यते ।

११. इत्थं कु अ

वै भ१ ॰नुदितौ

ब२ ब३ ॰नुमितौ

सं गा वा इ फ ब१ ॰नुवन्दितौ

मै सा ॰नुवदितौ

प्रातरग्निहोत्रं हुत्वाऽन्यमाहवनीयं प्रणीयाग्नीनन्वादधाति ।।२।।

अन्वाधानं नाम अग्नौ काष्ठाधानं, तच्च कर्माङ्गत्वेन सुरथादि-

गुणविशिष्टानामग्नीनां ग्रहणार्थं तद्द्वारेण देवतापरिग्रहार्थं च । कुतः? अग्निं गृह्णामि सुरथं यो मयोभूः (तैब्रा ३.७.४.३), स्व [१२]एवायतने देवताः परिगृह्णाति[१३] (तैसं १.६.७) इति [१४]मन्त्रविधिवाक्यशेषाभ्यामग्निं गृह्णाति[१५] देवताश्च[१६] परिगृह्णाति[१७], स्व आयतने (तैब्रा ३.७.४.३-५) इति च[१८] मन्त्रलिङ्गात् । तथा ममाग्ने वर्चो विहवेष्वस्त्विति पूर्वमग्निं गृह्णाति, तूष्णीमितरौ (भा.४.१.४,५) इति भारद्वाजवचनाच्च । प्रातरग्निहोत्रं हुत्वा इत्यनुवाद आनन्तर्यार्थः यथा औपवसथ्येऽह्नि प्रातरग्निहोत्रं हुत्वा प्रागेवान्येभ्यः कर्मभ्योऽन्वादध्यात् मा विलम्बिष्ट मा चाहुतेऽन्वादध्यादिति । अविलम्बश्च ब्राह्मणे प्रशस्यते यो वै देवताः पूर्वः परिगृह्णाति (तैसं १.६.७) इति । मन्त्रवर्णश्च भवति तान्देवान्परिगृह्णामि पूर्वः (तैब्रा ३.७.४.३) इति । अर्थादन्यत्वे सिद्धे अन्यमाहवनीयं प्रणीयेति किमर्थम्? दर्शपूर्णमासावारभमाणस्य चतुर्होत्रर्थाग्निव्युदासार्थमिति केचित् । तदयुक्तं, सर्वदर्शपूर्णमासप्रयोगसाधारणस्यैव तन्त्रस्याधिकारात् । तत्र नामैतद्वक्तव्यं यत्र तयोरारम्भोऽभिधायिष्यते, वक्ष्यन्ते च तद्वैशेषिका धर्मास्तत्रैव दर्शपूर्णमासावारप्स्यमान (५.२४.७) इत्यादिना । तस्मान्न तदर्थं वचनम् । किमर्थं तर्हि? माऽग्निहोत्रार्थोऽग्निरन्वाधायीति । कः प्रसङ्गः? अस्ति परमतेन । यथाह भारद्वाजः य एवैषोऽग्निः[१९] अग्निहोत्राय प्रणीतस्तं गृह्णीयादित्याश्मरथ्योऽन्यं प्रणीयेत्यालेखनः (भा ४.३.१) इति । दक्षिणाग्नेरपि आहार्यस्याधानक्रमेणार्थसिद्धा स्वयोनित उत्पत्तिः ।

१२. गा कु अ ब$_{२}$ ब$_{३}$ वै भ$_{१}$ भ$_{२}$ – 'एव' नास्ति

१३. सं गा कु इ ब$_{२}$ ब$_{३}$ वै भ$_{१}$ – परिगृह्णामि

१४. गा कु सा वै – कर्मविधि°; मै – मंत्रकर्मविधि°

१५. सा ब$_{२}$ ब$_{३}$ वै भ$_{१}$ भ$_{२}$ – गृह्णामि

१६. सा ब$_{२}$ ब$_{३}$ वै भ$_{१}$ – 'च' नास्ति
मै सं वा इ फ ब$_{१}$ – 'ताः पूर्वः' इति चकारात्परमधिकः पाठः

१७. सं वा सा इ फ ब$_{२}$ ब$_{३}$ वै भ$_{१}$ मै – परिगृह्णामि
भ$_{२}$ – 'देवताश्च परिगृह्णाति' इति नास्ति
अ – 'परिगृह्णाति स्व आयतने इति च मन्त्रलिङ्गात्' इति नास्ति

१८. सं गा कु वा फ ब$_{१}$ – 'च' नास्ति

१९. भारद्वाजसूत्रे 'अग्निः' नास्ति परन्तु 'फ' कोशं विहाय सर्वेषु अस्ति ।

न गतश्रियोऽन्यमग्निं प्रणयति ।।३।।

अनुसंधास्यति स्वयमेव गतश्रीशब्दार्थम् । तस्यान्यं न प्रणयेत् ।

[२०]नन्विदमपार्थकं वचनं, नित्यो गतश्रियो ध्रियत (६.२.१२) इत्यनेनैव सिद्धत्वात् । सत्यमत्रापार्थकं, वरुणप्रघासेषु तु[२१] दक्षिणविहारार्थं[२२] भविष्यतीत्येके । सम्यक् तावदुक्तमिदं[२३] यद् दर्शपूर्णमासौ व्याख्यास्यामः (१.१.१) इत्यधिकृत्य वरुणप्रघासा[२४] व्याख्यायन्त[२५] इति पर्यनुयोगः[२६] प्रत्यवशिष्यते[२७]। न्यायत एव च[२८] तत्राप्रणयनप्रसङ्गः[२९] । तस्मादनन्तरेणैव प्रणयनानुवादेन गतश्रियोऽप्यन्वाधास्यतोऽन्यः प्रणेतव्य इति मा कश्चिद् वादीदिति[३०] सिद्धस्यैवार्थस्यानुवादः[३१] स्पष्टत्वाय[३२] कथनमिति[३३] । नन्वेवमपि 'न गतश्रियः प्रणयति' इत्येतावद्वक्तव्यं, किमन्यग्रहणेनाग्निग्रहणेन वा । इदं तावदग्रे विदांकुर्वन्तु तत्रभवन्तः यन्नातिसूक्ष्मेक्षिकया[३४] शैल्या शब्ददरिद्रः सूत्रकारः । किं तर्हि? व्यक्ताभिर्वचनव्यक्तिभिरर्थान् आचष्टे[३५] इति । तदलमनेन[३६] आक्षेपक्लेशेन ।

२०. सा अ इ ब$_{२}$ ब$_{३}$ वै भ$_{१}$ भ$_{२}$ सं मै – नन्वेतद°

२१. वा इ फ ब$_{१}$ सं - तद् । अ – नास्ति

२२. वा फ ब$_{१}$ – °रार्थे

२३. अ – °दिदमुक्तं

२४. ब$_{२}$ ब$_{३}$ – °प्रघासो

२५. ब$_{२}$ ब$_{३}$ – व्याख्यायत । कु – व्याख्यास्यन्त

२६. अ ब$_{२}$ ब$_{३}$ वै भ$_{१}$ भ$_{२}$ – 'पर्यनुयोगः' नास्ति । पर्यनुयोगः = दूषणार्थः प्रश्नः

२७. वा इ फ ब$_{१}$ ब$_{२}$ ब$_{३}$ वै भ$_{२}$ सं – प्रत्यवसिष्यते । प्रत्यवशिष्यते एव साधु, अर्थस्तु समाधीयते इति ।

२८. अ ब$_{२}$ ब$_{३}$ वै भ$_{१}$ भ$_{२}$ – च न्यायत एव

२९. गा कु अ ब$_{२}$ ब$_{३}$ वै भ$_{१}$ भ$_{२}$ – तत्र प्रणयनप्रसंगः

३०. गा कु वा अ इ फ ब$_{१}$ भ$_{१}$ भ$_{२}$ सं – ब्रवीदिति

३१. गा अ – सिद्धस्यैवायमनुवादः । कु – सिद्धस्यैवानुवादः । सा ब$_{२}$ ब$_{३}$ वै भ$_{१}$ भ$_{२}$ मै – सिद्धस्यैवार्थस्य

३२. सा ब$_{२}$ ब$_{३}$ वै भ$_{१}$ भ$_{२}$ मै – नास्ति

३३. अ – नास्ति

३४. सा – सूक्ष्मेहिकया

३५. गा कु अ ब$_{२}$ वै भ$_{२}$ – व्याचष्टे

३६. कु – 'अनेन' नास्ति

देवा गातुविदो गातुं यज्ञाय विन्दत । मनसस्पतिना देवेन

वाताद्यज्ञः प्रयुज्यताम् (तैब्रा ३.७.४.१) इति जपित्वा[३७] ममाग्ने वर्चो विहवेष्वस्तु[३८] (तैसं ४.७.१४.१) इत्याहवनीयमुपसमिन्द्धे। उत्तरया[३९] गार्हपत्यमुत्तरया[४०] ऽन्वाहार्यपचनम् ॥४॥

अन्वाधानाधिकारात्तस्याङ्गं जपः। तेन प्रायणीयादौ निवर्तते। उपसमिन्द्धे काष्ठैर्दीपयति। तत्र त्रीणि त्रीणि काष्ठान्यादधीतेति बौधायनः[४१]। समिध आदधातीति कात्यायनः[४२]।

३७.चि – जपति ।४। धूर्तस्वामिनाऽपि 'जपति' एव व्याख्यातं, परंतु बहुतरकोशेषु 'जपित्वा' इत्येव पाठः।

३८.वयं त्वेन्धानास्तनुवं पुषेम। मह्यं नमन्तां प्रदिशश्चतस्रस्त्वयाऽध्यक्षेण पृतना जयेम॥ इति मन्त्रशेषः।

३९.मम देवा विहवे सन्तु सर्व इन्द्रावन्तो मरुतो विष्णुरग्निः। ममान्तरिक्षमुरु गोपमस्तु मह्यं वातः पवतां कामे अस्मिन्॥

४०.मयि देवा द्रविणमा यजन्तां मय्याशीरस्तु मयि देवहूतिः। दैव्या होतारा वनिषन्त पूर्वेऽरिष्टाः स्याम तनुवा सुवीराः॥

४१. त्रीणि काष्ठानि गार्हपत्येऽभ्यादधाति त्रीण्यन्वाहार्यपचने त्रीण्याहवनीये (बौ १. १.)।

४२. इत्याहवनीये समिधमादधाति (का २.१.३.), तूष्णीं द्वितीयाम् (४), एवमितरयोरग्न्योः (५)।

तिसृभिस्तिसृभिर्वा ॥५॥

विहव्यानुवाकस्य[४३] दशर्चस्य तिसृभिस्तिसृभिर्ऋग्भिस्त्रीनेतानग्नीन्सकृत्सकृदुपसमिन्द्धे।

४३. तैसं (४. ७. १४.)

उत्तमां तु जपेदाहवनीये वाऽऽदध्यात् ॥६॥

तदा तूत्तमां दशमीं जपेत्। तया पुनराहवनीये काष्ठानि वा आदध्यात्।

[४४]व्याहृतिभिरन्वाधानमेके समामनन्ति ॥७॥

एकैकया व्याहृत्या तानेवाग्नीन् गार्हपत्याद्याहवनीयान्तानेकैकमुपसमिन्द्धे। कुत एतत्? वाजसनेयिनां तथाम्नानात्, महाव्याहृतिभिर्वा प्राक्संस्थम् (का २.१.६) इति कात्यायनवचनात्, आधाने च तस्य तस्याग्नेस्तत्तद्व्याहृतिसंबन्ध-

प्रसिद्धेः, स्वयमातृण्णासु समस्तोपदिष्टानामपि विभागप्रदर्शनाच्च । सभ्यावसथ्यावप्यत्र तूष्णीमुपसमिन्धनीयौ; तत्तु याजमाने दर्शयिष्यामः ।

४४. व्याहृतीभिरिति पाठभेदः

संनयतः पलाशशाखां शमीशाखां वाऽऽहरति बहुपर्णां बहुशाखामप्रतिशुष्काग्रामसुषिराम् ।।८।।

सांनाय्ये[४५] नाम दार्शिके दधिपयसी[४६], ताभ्यां प्रवृत्तेज्यः संनयन्नित्युच्यते ।

४५. ब$_{२}$ ब$_{३}$ वै भ$_{२}$ – सांनाय्यं ४६. अ ब$_{२}$ ब$_{३}$ वै भ$_{१}$ भ$_{२}$ दधिश्रृत

यं कामयेतापशुः स्यादित्यपर्णां तस्मै शुष्काग्रामाहरेदपशुरेव भवति । यं कामयेत पशुमान्त्स्यादिति बहुपर्णां तस्मै बहुशाखामाहरेत् पशुमन्तमेवैनं करोति (तैब्रा ३.२.१.२) इति विज्ञायते ।।९।।

यं कामयेतापशुः स्यादित्यगुणाया वर्जनार्थं न त्वध्वर्युकामवशात्तस्या एव ग्रहणार्थम् । कुतः? यजमानपरिक्रीतस्यर्त्विजस्तदहिते प्रवर्तनायोगात्, यं कामयेतापशुः स्यादिति पराचीं तस्य[४७] इत्युक्तम् (२४.१४.१६), पदाभ्यासप्रतिषेधस्तु (२४.१४.१७) इति सूत्रकारवचनाच्च । यत्र प्रतिपादनीयेऽर्थे ब्राह्मणं प्रदर्शयति तत्र 'विज्ञायते' इत्याहेत्यनुसंधातव्यम् ।

४७. तैसं (१. ७. १. ३.)

सा या प्राच्युदीची प्रागुदीची वा भवति इषे त्वोर्जे त्वा (तैसं १.१.१.१) इति तामाच्छिनत्ति ।।१०।।

सा एवंगुणा आहार्या शाखा या वृक्षस्य प्रागादिषु दिक्षु प्रवृत्ता भवति तामाच्छिनत्तीत्यर्थः । भवत्यन्तेन वाक्यं भेत्तव्यं या प्राची सा भवतीति वान्वयः।

अपि वा 'इषे त्वा' इत्याच्छिनत्ति 'ऊर्जे त्वा' इति संनमयत्यनुमार्ष्टि वा ।।११।।

संनमयति ऋजूकरोति वक्रत्वे, इतरथा अनुलोमं मार्ष्टि ।

इति प्रथमा कण्डिका ।

इमां प्राचीमुदीचीमिषमूर्जमभिसंस्कृताम् । बहुपर्णा-मशुष्काग्रां हरामि पशुपामहम् (तैब्रा. ३.७.४.८) इत्याहरति ॥१॥

प्रागुदीचीलिङ्गत्वेऽपि मन्त्रस्य प्राच्युदीच्योरपि शाखयोरनिवृत्तिः, शाखा-जात्यभिप्रायेण तत्तदभिधानोपपत्तेः ।

वायव. स्थोपायव स्थ (तैसं १.१.१.) इति तया षडवरार्ध्यान् वत्सानपाकरोति ॥२॥

अर्धशब्दोऽत्र स्थानवाची यथा आऽस्यार्धं वव्राज (तैब्रा. २.३.१०.३), त्रिर्दक्षिणार्ध्यम् (तैसं २.५.११.५) इत्यादौ । येषामवरे स्थाने षट्संख्या भवति ते षडवरार्ध्याः । तानपाकरोति मातृभ्यः पृथक्करोति । मातृसंगतानां वत्सानां युगपद्दुरपाकरणीयत्वात् प्रतिवत्सं मन्त्रावृत्तिः । बहुवचनं तु मन्त्रगत-मुपरवमन्त्रवत्सर्वापेक्षं द्रष्टव्यम् ।

दर्भैर्दर्भपुञ्जीलैर्वा ॥३॥

पुञ्जीलं स्तम्बः ।

देवो वः सविता प्रार्पयतु (तैसं १.१.१)[1] इति शाखया गोचराय गाः प्रस्थापयति ॥४॥

गावो यत्र चरन्ति तस्मै देशाय यथासमाम्नातेनाघशंसान्तेन मन्त्रेण गाः सर्वा निष्कासयति । वत्सविनाकृतानां गवां युगपच्छक्यनिष्कासनत्वात् नावृत्ति-र्मन्त्रस्य । यत्र तु न शक्यते तत्रावृत्तिः ।

१. श्रेष्ठतमाय कर्मण आप्यायध्वमघ्निया देवभागमूर्जस्वतीः पयस्वतीः प्रजावतीरनमीवा अयक्ष्मा मा वः स्तेन ईशत माघशंसः। इति मन्त्रशेषः।

प्रस्थितानामेकां शाखयोपस्पृशति दर्भैर्दर्भपुञ्जीलैर्वा ॥५॥

गतः । अथ देवो व इत्यादेः प्रस्थापनमन्त्रस्यैव शाखान्तरीयौ कौचित् पाठविकारौ दर्शयति ।

आप्यायध्वमघ्निया इन्द्राय देवभागमित्येके समामनन्ति, महेन्द्रायेत्येके ॥६॥

आप्यायध्वमघ्निया देवभागमिति यथासमाम्नातेन पाठेन द्विप्रकारोऽयं पाठो विकल्पते । अथानयोः पाठयोः सर्वत्र तुल्यवद्विकल्पे प्राप्ते व्यवस्थासिद्ध्यर्थं सामान्येनेन्द्रमहेन्द्रशब्दयोर्देवतापरयोः प्रयोगव्यवस्थामाह ।

इन्द्रं निगमेषूपलक्षयेदिन्द्रयाजिनो महेन्द्रं महेन्द्रयाजिनः ॥७॥

निगम्यन्ते येषु हविषः प्रतियोगित्वेन रूपेण देवतास्ते मन्त्रा निगमाः । तेषु

सांनाय्यदेवतानिगमे इन्द्रयाजिनो यजमानस्येन्द्रं निर्दिशेत् महेन्द्रयाजिनो महेन्द्रमित्यर्थः । एतेन चानन्तरोक्तौ प्रयोगविकल्पावन्ये च कामधुक्षः (१.१३.३)[२] इत्यादयो निगमा व्याख्याता भवन्ति । एतदेवाभिप्रेत्य निगमेष्विति बहुवचनं कृतमिति वेदितव्यम् ।

२. तैब्रा (३. ७. ४. १६.)

शुद्धा अपः सुप्रपाणे पिबन्तीः शतमिन्द्राय शरदो दुहानाः । रुद्रस्य हेतिः परि वो वृणक्तु[३] इति प्रस्थिता अनुमन्त्रयते ।।८।।

अनुपूर्वोऽभिपूर्वश्च मन्त्रयतिस्तदभिसंधाय मन्त्रोच्चारणे प्रयुज्यते । अभिपूर्वस्तु तस्मिन्नेवाभिमुख्याधिक इत्यपरम् । अत्र केचित् शतमिन्द्रायेति निगमे महेन्द्रयाजिनो महेन्द्रोपलक्षणं निषेधन्ति । तत्तु न मृष्यामहे पूर्वसूत्रविरोधात् । न चास्यानिगमत्वं शङ्कनीयम्, इन्द्राय दुहाना इति दोहदेवतासंबन्धस्य प्रयोगसमवायिनोऽभिधानात् । तथा च शतमिन्द्रायेति प्रकृत्याह भारद्वाजः महेन्द्राय इति वा यदि महेन्द्रयाजी भवति (भा. १.२.१९) इति ।

३. मन्त्रोऽयं भारद्वाज-सत्याषाढ-मानव-वाराहसूत्रेष्वपि इत्यमेव पठ्यते । वैखानससूत्रे च 'शुद्धा अपः' इति प्रतीकमात्रं दृश्यते । तत्र प्रथमः पादः ऋ (६. २८. ७); अथ (४. २१. ७.), (७. ७५. १.); मैसं(४. १. १.); तैब्रा(२. ८. ८. १२.) एषु ग्रन्थेषु लभ्यते । तृतीयपादश्च तैसं (१. १. १.); मैसं (४. १. १.) तैब्रा (३. २. १. ५.) एषु । द्वितीयपादस्य मूलं त्वद्यापि मृग्यमेव । उपलब्धसंहिता-ब्राह्मणेषु न दृश्यते ।

ध्रुवा अस्मिन् गोपतौ स्यात बह्वीः (तैसं १.१.१) इति यजमानस्य गृहानभिपर्यावर्तते ।।९।।

अभिपर्यावर्तते अभिमुखः प्रतिनिवर्तते ।

यजमानस्य पशून् पाहि (तैसं १.१.१) इत्यग्निष्ठेऽनस्यग्न्यगारे वा पुरस्तात्प्रतीचीं शाखामुपगूहति पश्चात्प्राचीं वा ।।१०।।

अग्निसमीपस्थमनोऽग्निष्ठं, यद्वक्ष्यति— शकटमवस्थितं भवति (१.७.६) इति । तस्मिन् अग्न्यगारे वा पुरस्तात्प्रतिपद्य [४]प्रत्यगग्रतामुपगूहति पश्चाद्वा प्रतिपद्य [५]प्रागग्रतामित्यर्थः । पुरस्ताद्भागेऽनसः प्रत्यगग्रां पश्चाद्भागेऽनसो वा प्रागग्रामित्यन्ये । शाखानिधानं भाव्युपयोगार्थं न वत्सापाकरणशेषः, तेन पशावपि भवत्येव ।

४. वा ब$_{१}$ -प्रत्यगायता°; ब$_{२}$ ब$_{३}$ - प्रत्यगग्रां ता°
५. वा सा इ फ ब$_{१}$ सं – प्रागायता° ; ब$_{२}$ ब$_{३}$ प्रागग्रभूतां°

अथेदानीमुत्तरोत्तरेषु अनुष्ठेयेषु ऋत्विजामप्रमादार्थं कर्मानुसंधानप्रशंसां ब्राह्मणोक्तामुदाहरति–

यो वा अध्वर्योर्गृहान् वेद गृहवान् भवति । आ चतुर्थात् कर्मणोऽभिसमीक्षेतेदं करिष्यामीदं करिष्यामीति । एते वा अध्वर्योर्गृहाः । य एवं वेद गृहवान् भवति[६] इति विज्ञायते ।।११।।

योऽध्वर्युरध्वर्योर्गृहान् वेद स गृहवान् भवति । के ते अध्वर्योर्गृहाः? अग्नीनाधास्यामि, शाखामाहरिष्यामि, इत्येवम् आ चतुर्थात्कर्मणः अभिसमीक्ष्य येऽनुसन्धीयन्ते पदार्थास्तेऽध्वर्युगृहाः । य एवं वेद, य एतेऽध्वर्युगृहा इति वेद सोऽपि गृहवान् भवतीत्यर्थः । तत्र तु वेदनस्य परार्थत्वात् फलवचनं प्ररोचनार्थं, यथा यो वा अध्वर्योः प्रतिष्ठां वेद (तैसं ३.१.२), यो वा अध्वर्योः स्वं वेद (तैसं ३.१.२), यो वा अध्वर्योरायतनं वेद[७] इत्यादौ । ततश्चैवं न शङ्कितव्यं यजमानस्यैवेदमेवंविदुषः फलमिति । चतुर्थग्रहणं यावच्छक्यस्योपलक्षणम्, अनुसंधानाधिक्ये गुणाधिक्यात् । तथाध्वर्युग्रहणमपि सर्वर्त्विजामुपलक्षणमुपयोगसाम्यात् ।

६. अनुपलब्धमूलमिदम् ।

७. मयोपयुक्तेषु त्रयोदशसु कोशेषु द्वयोश्च मुद्रितपुस्तकयोरयमेव पाठ उपलभ्यते । उपलब्धवैदिकवाङ्मये तु इदं वाक्यं नोपलब्धम् । तैसं (६. ६. १०. २.) इत्यत्र ''यो वा अंशोरायतनं वेद'' इति वाक्यं दृश्यते । अतः ''यो वा अध्वर्योरायतनं वेद'' इति वाक्यं लेखकप्रमादादागतं, लुप्तायां वा कस्यांचित् शाखायां स्यात् ।

इति द्वितीया कण्डिका । इति प्रथमः पटलः ।

उत्तरेण गार्हपत्यमसिदोऽश्वपर्शुरनडुत्पर्शुर्वा निहिता ।।१।।

असिदो दात्रम् । पर्शुः पार्श्वास्थि ।

देवस्य त्वा सवितुः प्रसवे[१]
इत्यसिदमश्वपर्शुं वाऽऽदत्ते[२] ।।२।।
तूष्णीमनडुत्पर्शुम् ।।३।।

गतौ ।

१. अश्विनोर्बाहुभ्यां पूष्णो हस्ताभ्यामाददे इति मन्त्रशेषः ।

२. तैब्रा (३. २. २. १.)

यज्ञस्य घोषदसि (तैसं १.१.२) इति गार्हपत्यमभिमन्त्र्य प्रत्युष्टं रक्षः प्रत्युष्टा अरातयः (तैसं १.१.२) इत्याहवनीये गार्हपत्ये वाऽसिदं प्रतितपति ।।४।।

यदाप्याहवनीये प्रतितपति तदाप्यभिमन्त्रणं गार्हपत्यस्यैव, प्रतितपन एव विकल्पवचनात् ।

न पर्शुम्[३] ।।५।।

प्रतितपतीति शेषः । अत एव प्रतिषेधाज्जानीमो यदेकत्रानेकसाधनविकल्पेषु मुख्ये कृतो विधिः सर्वार्थो भवतीति ।

३. पर्शू – इति बहुषु कोशेषु

प्रेयमगाद् (तैसं १.१.२)[४] इत्युक्त्वा उर्वन्तरिक्षमन्विहि (तैसं१.१.२) इति प्राचीमुदीचीं वा दिशमभिप्रव्रज्य यतः कुतश्चिद्दर्भमयं बर्हिराहरति ।।६।।

प्रथमं विहारात् प्राचीमुदीचीं वा दिशमभिप्रव्रज्य ततो यतः कुतश्चिद् दिशो दर्भमयं बर्हिराहरति यतो लभ्यते । बौधायनस्त्वाह – आहवनीयादेवाग्रे त्रीन्वा चतुरो वा प्राचः प्रक्रमान्प्रक्रम्याथ तां दिशमभिप्रव्रजेद्यत्र बर्हिर्वेत्स्यन्मन्येत (बौ २०.२) इति । प्रेयमगादित्यपि गमनमन्त्र एव तल्लिङ्गत्वात्, यौ गमनौ (१.५.१) इत्युत्तरत्रानुवादाच्च । किमर्था तर्हि 'उक्त्वा' इति अधिकोक्तिः? उच्यते । मन्त्रसमाम्नाये हि द्वितीयो मन्त्रः प्रत्यागमनक्रमे पठितो न गमनक्रमे । कल्पान्तरकारैश्च तौ उभयत्र व्यवस्थया विकल्पेन च विनियुक्तौ । आचार्यस्तु उभयोरुभयत्र समुच्चयं मन्यते । तेन यत्नं कृतवानेतत्प्रथममुक्त्वा ततोऽनेन[५] प्रव्रजतीति । अथवा यतः कुतश्च बर्हिराहरणेऽपि पुरस्ताद्बर्हिरासद इति मन्त्रार्थवशेन पुरस्तादाहरणगुणसिद्धिर्ब्राह्मणे दर्शिता– अथो यदेतदुक्त्वा यतः कुतश्चाहरति तत्प्राच्या एव दिशो भवति (तैब्रा ३.२.२.३) इति । तस्यैवार्थमनुकरोत्याचार्यः प्रेयमगादित्युक्त्वा यतः कुतश्चाहरतीति । स चायं मन्त्रः स्त्रीलिङ्गादसिदे नीयमाने निवर्तते इति केचित् । तदयुक्तं, तूष्णीमनडुत्पर्शुम् (सू. ३) न पर्शुम्[६] (सू. ५) इति पर्श्वसिदयोरभिप्रेतविशेषवचनादवचनाच्चात्र विशेषस्य । न च स्त्रीलिङ्गविरोधः धिषणाभिधानात्, यथोक्तं ब्राह्मणे विद्या वै धिषणा विद्ययैवैनदच्छैति (तैब्रा ३.२.२.२) इति । यदपि पर्शुविधानबला-

द्धिषणाशब्दो गुणवृत्त्या पर्श्वभिधायीष्यते, तथैवेष्यतामसिदेऽपि । न च तत्रासिदे वैलिङ्ग्यं दोषाय, धिषणात्वेन तस्योपचारात् । असिदाकृतिविवक्षया, व्यत्ययेन वा स्त्रीलिङ्गोपपत्तेः । यदप्यस्या विशेषणं मनुना कृतेत्यादि, तदप्यविशिष्ट-मेवोभयोः । तस्मादनिवृत्तिरुभयत्रापि मन्त्रस्य ।

४. धिषणा बर्हिरच्छ मनुना कृता स्वधया वितष्टा त आवहन्ति कवयः पुरस्ताद् देवेभ्यो जुष्टमिह बर्हिरासदे इति मन्त्रशेषः ।

५. त्रयोदशसु कोशेषु द्वयोश्च मुद्रितपुस्तकयोरयमेव पाठः। ''ततोऽन्येन'' इति पाठः समीचीनः स्यात् । द्र. - तालवृन्तवासिप्रयोगः – प्रेयमगा.....सद इत्युक्त्वा (असिदं कमंडलुं चादाय) उर्वन्तरिक्षमन्विहीति गच्छति ।

६. पर्शू इति पाठभेदः ।

देवानां परिषूतमसि[७] (तैसं १.१.२) इति दर्भान् परिषौति ।।७।।

परिषौति यावता पर्याप्तं तावत्परिगृह्णाति ।

७. वर्षवृद्धमसि – इति मन्त्रशेषः

विष्णोः स्तूपोऽसि (तैसं १.१.११) इत्यभिप्रेतानामेकं स्तम्बमुत्सृजति ।।८।।

तेषां लाव्यत्वेनाभिप्रेतानां मध्ये स्तम्बं त्वेकमुत्सृजति यथा न लूयते तथा बहिष्करोतीत्यर्थः ।

एकं वा स्तम्बं परिषूय तं सर्वं दाति ।।९।।

एकमूलप्रभवो दर्भसमूहः स्तम्बः । तावत्सर्वं छिनत्ति न तु किंचिदुत्सृजति, अन्ये त्वपरिषूता एव लूयन्त इत्यर्थः ।

अतिसृष्टो गवां भागः (मैसं १.१.४) इति वैकां द्वे तिस्रो वा नाडीरुत्सृजति ।।१०।।

नाडी शलाका ।

इदं देवानाम् (तैसं १.१.४) इति परिषूतानभिमृशति । इदं पशूनाम्[८] इत्यतिसृष्टान् ।।११।।

अनुत्सर्गपक्षेऽपि भवत्येव परिषूतस्तम्बाभिमर्शनं बर्हिःसंस्कारत्वात् ।

८. सौत्रोऽयं मन्त्रः । सत्याषाढसूत्रेऽप्यस्ति (१.२, पृ. ८२), वैखानससूत्रेऽपि (३.४, पृ. ३४)

देवस्य त्वा सवितुः प्रसवेऽश्विनोर्बाहुभ्यां पूष्णो हस्ताभ्यां बर्हिर्देवसदनमारभे[९] इति विशाखेषु दर्भानारभते ।१२।

विशाखाः प्रकाण्डादूर्ध्वभागाः यतः शलाकाः पृथग्भवन्ति, तेष्वारभते आलभते स्पृशतीति यावत् ।

९. भारद्वाजसत्याषाढसूत्रयोरपि मन्त्रोऽयम् । मूलं त्वस्य (मैसं १.१.२.) । एतावांस्तु विशेषः – तत्र 'आरभे' इत्यस्य स्थाने 'दामि'

देवबर्हिर्मा त्वाऽन्वङ्मा तिर्यक् (तैसं १.१.२) इति[१०] संयच्छति ।।१३।।

संयच्छति लवनानुगुणं सव्यमुष्टिना गृह्णाति ।

१०. चि - इति सव्यहस्तेन संयच्छति

पर्व ते राध्यासम् (तैसं १.१.२) इत्यसिदमधिनिदधाति ।।१४।।

पर्वणि निदधाति । यत्परुषि दिनं तद्देवानाम् (तैब्रा १.६.८.६) इति श्रुतेः । पर्व ते राध्यासम् - इति मन्त्रवर्णाच्च ।

आच्छेत्ता ते मा रिषम् (तैसं १.१.२)इत्याच्छिनत्ति ।।१५।।

गतः ।

संनखं मुष्टिं लुनोति[११] ।।१६।।

संनखं संगताङ्गुल्यङ्गुष्ठनखं तावत्प्रमाणमित्यर्थः । लुनोति लुनाति विकरणव्यत्ययः ।

११. चि –लुनाति

स प्रस्तरः ।।१७।।

सोऽयं प्रथमलूनो मुष्टिः प्रस्तरः समाख्यायते ।

कुल्मिमात्रोऽरत्निः प्रादेश ऊर्वस्थि जान्वस्थि स्रुग्दण्ड इति वा तिर्यक्प्रमाणानि ।।१८।।

कुल्मिर्गोवालः, अरत्निर्हस्तस्य पूर्वभागः[१२], प्रादेशः प्रदेशिन्यङ्गुष्ठयोरायामः, स चात्र सामर्थ्यात्संनखवन्मण्डलीकृतः संनिवेशो गृह्यते । अरत्नि प्रादेश इति पठतां विसर्जनीयः प्रमादभ्रष्टः । ऊरोरस्थि ऊर्वस्थि । तिर्यक्प्रमाणानि स्थौल्यप्रमाणानि[१३] । तानि च संनखप्रमाणेन विकल्पन्ते ।

१२. अरत्नेर्मध्यभागस्य स्थौल्यं ग्राह्यम् ।

१३. अरत्निप्रादेशादिशब्दाः सामान्यतः दैर्घ्यवाचकाः । किन्तु अत्र सूत्रकाराणां टीकाकाराणां च स्थौल्यग्रहणमेव इष्टम् । द्र. (बौ २४.२५.), (हि १.२ - पृ. ८३), (भा १.३. १५–१८) । धूर्तस्वामी च "तिर्यक्प्रमाणानि स्थौल्यस्य, न तु दीर्घत्वस्य" इति स्पष्टमेव दीर्घत्वं खण्डयामास ।

इति तृतीया कण्डिका ।

SATYĀṢĀḌHA -ŚRAUTA-SŪTRA

Edited by
P. D. Navathe

INTRODUCTION

1. The Sūtra of Satyāṣāḍha-Hiraṇyakeśin, which belongs to the Taittirīya recension of the Black Yajurveda, is, like the Sūtras of Bodhāyana and Āpastamba, a complete Kalpasūtra as it embraces all its aspects, viz., the Śrauta (Praśnas I-XVIII & XXI-XXIV), the Gṛhya (Praśnas XIX & XX), the Śulba (Praśna XXV), the Dharma (Praśnas XXVI & XXVII), and also the Pitṛmedha (Praśnas XXVIII & XXIX). This Sūtra was entirely published at Poona in the Ānandāśrama-Saṁskṛta-Granthāvali by Pt. Kāśīnāthśāstrī Agashe and others in 10 volumes in 1907-32 with the commentaries of Mahādeva (on Praśnas I-VI, XI-XVIII and XXI-XXIX), of Gopīnāthabhaṭṭa (on Praśnas VII-X) and of Mātṛdatta (on Praśnas XIX and XX). The Khaṇḍas and Paṭalas in a Praśna are numbered continuously, the latter being a larger division consisting of a certain number of Khaṇḍas. The Sūtras in a Khaṇḍa are not numbered. This is the only available complete edition of the work.

In connection with this edition Dr. C. G. Kashikar[1] remarks that it cannot be regarded as a critical edition, there is ample scope for improvement. Similarly J. Gonda[2] observes that it is uncritical and full of mistakes. Thus the views expressed by these veteran Indologists clearly indicate that a critical edition of this Sūtra is a desideratum.

---

1. *A Survey of the Śrauta Sūtras* (MM. Dr. P. V. Kane Sanskrit Prize Endowment Lectures), *Jr. of the University of Bombay*, Sept. 1966, Vol. XXXV (New Series) Part 2, Arts Number (No. 41), Bombay 1966, pp. 60-61.
2. *A History of Indian Literature*, Vol. I, Fasc. 2, the Ritual Sūtras, Wiesbaden, 1977, p. 521, Foot note 60.

2. The work of preparing the critical edition of the bare text of the Satyāṣāḍha-Śrauta-Sūtra was started by my late friend and colleague Dr. V. V. Bhide towards the end of 1977. Accordingly he had collated various Mss. of the Sūtra, which are indicated later on, and had prepared the press-copy of the first six Praśnas which cover the pre-soma Śrauta rites. However, owing to his unfortunate and premature death on 4.10.1985 the responsibility of editing this Sūtra has now been entrusted to me. I have duly checked the script of the press-copy of Dr. Bhide and have presented it with the necessary corrections. However, it was not possible for me to go through the original Mss. used by Dr. Bhide.

3. Dr. Bhide[3] has discussed the problem regarding the proper title which is to be used for this Sūtra. He considers whether the Hiraṇyakeśi-Sūtra and the Satyāṣāḍha-Sūtra are two different Sūtra-texts or they are the names of one and the same work. While examining the evidence of the Caraṇavyūha and the Sūtra-literature, the colophons in the commentaries on the Sūtra and the practice followed by the Western scholars he argues : "Thus it seems that the name of the recension is Hiraṇyakeśī. Sometimes the name of this recension is associated with the name Satyāṣāḍha, the author of the Sūtra-text. Hence in the tarpaṇa (libation of water to the ancestors), according to the BaudhDS 2.5.14 the sage Satyāṣāḍha belonging to the Hiraṇyakeśi-recension is mentioned"[4]. He finally concludes :"Thus it is again clear that Satyāṣāḍha is the name of the author and that Hiraṇyakeśi-Sūtra is the correct name of the Sūtra-text"[5].

However, this cannot be regarded as a sound view as it indirectly implies that Satyāṣāḍha-Sūtra is not a correct name. Hence Dr. Bhide's insistence on the name Hiraṇyakeśi-Sūtra appears to be quite out of place. The earliest reference to the name of the Sūtrakāra as cited by him is from the BaudhDS : *Satyāṣāḍhaṁ hiraṇyakeśinaṁ tarpayāmi* which is rendered by him as "I satisfy Satyāṣāḍha belonging to the Hiraṇyakeśi recension". However, this

---

3. *The Cāturmāsya Sacrifices* (with special reference to the Hiraṇyakeśi Śrautasūtra) Publications of the Centre of Advanced Study in Sanskrit, Class B No. 5, University of Poona, Pune 1979, pp. 1-4.

4. *Ibid.* p. 2.

5. *Ibid.* p.4.

rendering is not proper; it is to be corrected as :"I satiate Satyāṣāḍha, the golden-haired one". In this passage Satyāṣāḍha is the proper name of the Sūtrakāra and Hiraṇyakeśin is its distinctive epithet or attribute. This latter does not indicate the name of the recension as Dr. Bhide understans. The name of the school was obviously derived from this attribute. Bearing in mind this Sūtra-tradition the commentator Gopīnāthabhaṭṭa,[6] while paying his homage to the Sūtrakāra, uses the expression *jātarūpaśiroruham* which is a paraphrase of hiraṇyakeśinam. So the title Satyāṣāḍha-sūtra which is associated with the name of the author is equally correct as Hiraṇyakeśi-Sūtra, which latter has become current due to the exclusiveness of the epithet. The commentators Mahādeva and Gopīnāthabhaṭṭa, in their colophons, use the expression Satyāṣāḍha-Hiraṇyakeśi-Sūtra as the name of the Sūtra.

The plan of the present project is to bring out a critical edition of the bare text of the Śrauta portion of the Sūtra of Satyāṣāḍha Hiraṇyakeśin which comprises Praśnas I -XVIII and XXI -XXIV as stated before. In this proposed edition the term Satyāṣāḍha-Śrauta-Sūtra will be used as the title of the work. The attribute Hiraṇyakeśin will be dropped in order to avoid a lengthy title.

4. The text of the Satyāṣāḍha-Śrauta-Sūtra can be improved with the help of two types of aids as indicated below :

a) Dr. Kashikar[7] has pointed out the close relationship existing between the Satyāṣāḍha-Sūtra on the one hand and the Bhāradvāja Śrauta Sūtra and the Āpastamba Śrauta Sūtra on the other. Many sūtras of Āpastamba are found to be verbally identical with those of Satyāṣāḍha. Sometimes injunctions of Satyāṣāḍha agree with those of Bharadvāja more closely than with those of Āpastamba. Dr. Bhide[8] has also discussed in detail the topic of relationship in connection with the chapter on the Cāturmāsya sacrifices in these Sūtras. Thus a careful comparison with these two Sūtra-texts is going to be of great advantage for improving the text

---

6. सत्याषाढं मुनिश्रेष्ठं जातरूपशिरोरुहम् । --नत्वा --।। सत्याषाढविरचितं श्रौतसूत्रं, तृतीयो भागः, आनन्दाश्रमसंस्कृतग्रन्थावलिः, ग्रन्थाङ्क ५३, १९०८, पृ. ५४९.
7. *A Survey of the Śrautasūtras*, p. 60.
8. *The Cāturmāsya Sacrifices*, pp. 115-128.

of the Satyāṣāḍha-Śrauta-Sūtra.

b) It will be noticed from the critical apparatus that barring one or two exceptions, most of the Mss. on which the text of the printed edition is based are local as they belong to Poona or Wai. Existence of Mss. of the Sūtra in Grantha characters deposited at Mysore and Adyar pointed to the fact that the followers of this Sūtra were spread futher southward beyond the borders of Maharashtra. Devanāgarī transcripts of these Mss which are utilised for the present edition, though corrupt, often yield good readings which are preferable to those in the printed edition.

5. The Mss utilised for constituting the text of the Satyāṣāḍha-Śrauta-Sūtra are :

1) A - Adyar Library Ms
2) B_1 - Oriental Institute Baroda No. 509
3) B_2 - Oriental Institute Baroda No. 2583
4) BH_1 - Bhandarkar Or. Res. Institute Poona, Limaye collection No. 173
5) Bh_2 - " " No. 38
6) Bh_3 - Bhandarkar Or. Res. Institute Poona No. 15/1866-68
7) M_1 - Or. Res. Institute Mysore No. SP-3639 in Grantha script (Devanāgari transcript deposited in the CASS University of Poona).
8) M_2 - Or. Res. Institute Mysore No. B-148 in Telugu script (Devanāgari transcript deposited in the CASS University of Poona).
9) M_3 - Or. Res. Institute Mysore No. A-347 in Grantha script (Devanāgarī transcript deposited in the CASS University of Poona).
10) V_1 - Vaidika Saṁśodhana Maṇḍala Poona No. 4820
11) V_2 - Vaidika Saṁśodhana Maṇḍala Poona No. 1054-56
12) Ān Ānandāśrama edition

6. The following portion comprising the first two Paṭalas of

the Satyāṣāḍha-Śrauta-Sūtra is given here as a specimen of the proposed edition of this work. The first Paṭala comprising Khaṇḍas 1-3 contains the Paribhāṣās or general rules and the second Paṭala comprising Khaṇḍas 4-7 contains the *Anvādhāna, Vatsāpākaraṇa* and *Idhmābarhirāharaṇa*, the commencing rites of the New- and Full-moon Sacrifices.

सत्याषाढश्रौतसूत्रम्

प्रथमः प्रश्नः

।। श्रीगणेशाय नमः[1] ।।

यज्ञं व्याख्यास्यामः ।।१।। स त्रिभिर्वेदैर्विधीयत ऋग्वेदेन यजुर्वेदेन सामवेदेन[2] ।।२।। सर्वैर्ज्योतिष्टोमः ।।३।। ऋग्वेदयजुर्वेदाभ्यां दर्शपूर्णमासौ ।।४।। यजुर्वेदेनाग्निहोत्रम् ।।५।। विधिलक्षणानि कर्माणि ।।६।। मन्त्रब्राह्मणयोर्वेद[3]नामधेयम् ।।७।। कर्मविधानं ब्राह्मणानि ।।८।। तच्छेषोऽर्थवादः । निन्दा प्रशंसा परकृतिः[4] पुराकल्पश्च ।।९।। अतोऽन्ये मन्त्राः[5] ।।१०।। लौकिकाः प्रयुज्यमाना अमन्त्रा यथा पुत्रस्य नामधेयं दुन्दुभिशब्दश्च ।।११।। यज्ञकर्मार्था मन्त्राः ।।१२।। रूपविप्रतिषेधाल्लौकिकेषु यथा गृह्णामि ते सुप्रजास्त्वाय हस्तम्, इमां खनाम्योषधीं, वह वपां जातवेदः पितृभ्यः इति ।।१३।। यथोपदिष्टं ब्राह्मणवन्तो यथारूपमितरे ।।१४।। शेषस्य विनिधानम् ।।१५।। [6]पारिप्लवार्था दाशतय्यः ।।१६।। उत्तरयोः पवमानयोः स्तोमाभ्यासे सामानि ।।१७।। तूष्णीकेषु प्राकृतेषु यजुः ।।१८।। वेदः कर्मनामधेयेन श्रूयमाणस्तदर्थो[7] यथा वाजपेयो[8] याज्यापुरोनु[9]वाक्याश्च ।।१९।। उपाꣳशु यजुर्वेदेन क्रियते ।।२०।। अन्यत्र प्रवरसंवादाश्रावणसंप्रैषेभ्यः ।।२१।। उच्चैरितराभ्याम् ।।२२।। सर्वैरुपाꣳशु ।।२३।। ।।१।।

---

1. After this Bh_2 has हिरण्यकेशीसूत्रप्रारंभः and Bh_3 has अथ हिरण्यकेशीसूत्रे प्रथमप्रश्ने दर्शपूर्णमासारंभः ।।
2. A सामवेदेन च.
3. Bh_3 °वेदे नाम°
4. Bh_3 प्रकृतिः
5. Bh_3 मन्त्रान्
6. M_1 प्रधानपरि°
7. Bh_3 V_1 V_2 °माणास्तदर्थाः; Bh_1 Bh_2 °स्तदर्थाः°
8. A Bh_2 °पेयेः°
9. Bh_3 V_2 याज्यानु°

ज्योतिष्टोमे[10] प्रागग्नीषोमीयात्[11] ।। १ ।। यावताऽर्थो[12]ऽप वृज्यते स एकमन्त्रः ।।२।। आदिप्रदिष्टा मन्त्रा भवन्ति ।।३।। उत्तरस्याऽदिना पूर्वस्यान्तं विद्यात् ।।४।। मन्त्रान्तेन[13] कर्म संनिपातयेत्[14] ।।५।। क्रियमाणे हौत्रा[15]ण्युच्यन्ते ।।६।। एकमन्त्राणि कर्माणि ।।७।। समभ्युच्चीयेरन् हौत्रा[16]ण्यन्यत्र याज्यानुवाक्याभ्यः ।।८।। यत्रैकस्मिन् द्रव्ये[17] विचेष्टापृथक्त्वेनार्थो निष्पद्यते सकृदेव तत्र मन्त्रं ब्रूयाद्यथा प्रोक्षणे[18] यूपच्छेदने च ।।९।। द्रव्य[19]पृथक्त्वेऽभ्यावर्तत यथा[20]ऽऽज्यग्रहणे लवने स्तरणे च ।।१०।। अर्थपृथक्त्वात् कण्डूयन् मन्त्रोऽभ्यावर्तते ।।११।। परार्थान्येकेन क्रियेरन् यथा कपालेनोपवपति यजमानेन संमितौदुम्बरी भवतीति[21] ।।१२।। यजुर्वेदेनाध्वर्युः करोति ।।१३।। ऋग्वेदेन होता ।।१४।। सामवेदेनोद्गाता।।१५।। सर्वैर्ब्रह्मा ।।१६।। वचनलक्षणा[22] इतरे[23] ।।१७।। असंभवाद्वा यथाऽश्वमेधे पशुकर्मसु ।।१८।। आहवनीय आहुतयो जुह्वा[24] हूयन्ते ।।१९।। उत्तरतउपचारो विहारः ।।२०।। //२//

प्राङ्[25]न्यायान्युदङ्न्यायानि[26] वा प्रदक्षिणं यज्ञे[27] कर्माणि करोति ।।१।। न यज्ञाङ्गेनाऽत्मानमन्यं वाऽभिपरिहरति[28]।।२।। न[29] विहारा[30]दपपर्यावर्तते ।।३।। अन्तराणि यज्ञाङ्गानि बाह्याः कर्तारः ।।४।। प्राचीनावीती पित्र्याणि करोति ।।५।। यज्ञोपवीती दर्शपूर्णमासयोरग्निहोत्रे च ।।६।। अनियमोऽन्यत्र ।।७।। चोदनासंयोगात् प्रधानान्येककालानि ।।८।। तेषां विभवन्ति तन्त्र[31]मङ्गान्यविभवन्त्या-

10. Bh_3 °ष्टोमेन.
11. M_1 प्रागग्निष्टोमवपायाः.
12. Bh_2 Ān यावदर्थो.
13. Bh_3 मंत्रांते कर्म.
14. M_1 संपात°
15. Bh_1 Bh_3 होत्रा°
16. Bh_1 होत्रा°
17. M_1 द्रव्येऽपि चेष्टा°; A द्रव्ये चेष्टा°
18. Thus A Bh_1 Bh_2; Bh_3 प्रोक्षे.
19. Bh_3 om. द्रव्य
20. A om. यथा.
21. M_1 भवति
22. M_1 °लक्षणादितरे.
23. Here A adds : अथोदाहरणानि संज्ञया हौत्रं यजुर्वेदस्थमपि होता करोति.
24. M_1 om. जुह्वा.
25. Bh_3 प्राङ्न्यायोदङ्°
26. A M_3 °न्यायानि दैवानि कर्माणि.
27. A यज्ञेषु.
28. M_3 °हरति दक्षिणान्यायानि पित्र्याणि.
29. A. om. न.......प्राचीनावीती.
30. Thus M_1; cf. ĀpŚS 24. 2.11,12; Bh_1 Bh_2 Bh_3 M_2 विहारदुप°
31. M_2 तन्त्रमन्यान्यभिपर्यावर्तन्ते; A om. तन्त्र---वर्तन्ते.

वर्तन्ते ।।९।। नानाकालेषु पृथक् ।।१०।। यः प्रधानस्य कालः सोऽङ्गानाᳫं स देशः स कर्ता सोऽग्निः ।।११।। आधानप्रभृति यावज्जीवं पात्राणि धार्यन्ते ।।१२।। तेषां प्रतितन्त्रᳫं सᳫंस्कारोऽभ्यावर्तते ।।१३।। सर्वकामौ दर्शपूर्णमासौ ।।१४।। तौ समानविधानौ ।।१५।। निर्देशाद् व्यवतिष्ठेते ।।१६।। ताभ्यां यावज्जीवं यजते[32] ।।१७।। त्रिᳫंशतं वा वर्षाणि ।।१८।। एक[33]स्मिन् प्रयोगे सर्वान् कामान् कामयेत प्रयोगपृथक्त्वे वैकैकम् ।।१९।। पूर्वा पौर्णमास्युत्तराऽमावास्या ।।२०।। पौर्णमास्यां पौर्णमास्या यजते[34] ऽमावास्यायाममावास्यया ।।२१।। आग्नेयोऽष्टाकपाल उपाᳫंशुयाजश्चाग्नीषोमीयो वैष्णवः प्राजापत्यो वाऽग्नीषोमीय[35]श्चैकादशकपालः पौर्णमास्यां[36] प्रधानानि ।।२२।। नासोमयाजिनो ब्राह्मणस्याग्नीषोमीयः पुरोडाशो विद्यत[37] इत्येकेषाम्।।२३।। आग्नेयोऽष्टाकपाल ऐन्द्राग्न एकादशकपालो द्वादशकपालो[38] वाऽमावास्यायामसंनयतः ।।२४।। आग्नेयः सांनाय्यं च संनयतः[39] ।।२५।। तदङ्गमितरे होमाः ।।२६।। पूर्वां पौर्णमासीमुपवसेत्[40] संपूर्णां वा ।।२७।। पूर्वाममावास्याम् ।।२८।। यदहर्वा न दृश्यते [41] ।।२९।। //३//

।। इति सत्याषाढश्रौतसूत्रे प्रथमप्रश्ने[42] प्रथमः पटलः ।।१।।

प्रातरग्निहोत्रᳫं हुत्वाऽनुगमयित्वाऽऽग्निहोत्रिकमपोद्धृत्य वोदित आदित्ये गार्हपत्यादाहवनीयमुद्धृत्य ममाग्ने वर्च इत्यन्वादधाति ।।१।। उत्तरया गार्हपत्यमुत्तरया[1] दक्षिणाग्निम् ।।२।। सर्वाभिर्वाऽऽहवनीयम् ।।३।। अवशिष्टा विकल्पार्थाः[2] ।।४।।व्याहृति[3]भिरन्वादधातीत्येकेषाम् ।।५।। अग्निं गृह्णामि सुरथं यो मयोभूर्य उद्यन्तमारोहति सूर्यमह्ने ।

32. A यजेत 33. A M_3 om. एकस्मिन् प्रयोगे; B_2 Bh_3 V_1 V_2 M_1 एकप्रयोगे.
34. A यजेत
35. A °षोमीय एकादश°
36. AM_3 om. पौर्णमास्यां प्रधानानि
37. AM_3 विद्यते पौर्णमास्यामेतानि प्रधानान्याग्नेयो°
38. AM_3 om. द्वादशकपालो वा.
39. AM_3 °नयतोङ्ग°
40. AM_1 M_3 Bh_1 Bh_2 V_1 °वसति.
41. AM_3 दृश्यते तां वा.
42. M_1 om. प्रथमप्रश्ने.
1. AM_3 °यान्वाहार्यपचनमुत्तरया सभ्यमुत्तरयावसथ्यमव°
2. A °ल्पार्थाभिर्वा विहव्याभिः
3. ABh_2 °व्याहृतीभिः

आदित्यं ज्योतिषां ज्योतिरुत्तमꣳ श्वो यज्ञाय रमतां देवताभ्यः ॥ वसून् रुद्रानादित्यानिन्द्रेण सह देवताः । ताः पूर्वः परिगृह्णामि स्व आयतने मनीषया ॥ इमामूर्जं पञ्चदशीं ये प्रविष्टास्तान् देवान् परिगृह्णामि पूर्वः । अग्निर्हव्यवाडिह ताना[4]वहतु पौर्णमासꣳ हविरिदमेषां मयी**ति पौर्णमास्या**मामावास्यꣳ हविरिदमेषां **मयीत्यमावास्यायामिति तिसृभिराहवनीयम्** ॥६॥ अन्तराऽग्नी पशवो देवसꣳसदमागमन्[5]। तान् पूर्वः परिगृह्णामि स्व आयतने मनीषये**त्यन्तराऽग्नी तिष्ठञ्जपति** ॥७॥ इह[6] प्रजा विश्वरूपा रमन्तामग्निं गृहपतिमभिसंवसानाः । ताः पूर्वः[7] परिगृह्णामि स्व आयतने मनीषया ॥ इह पशवो विश्वरूपा रमन्तामग्निं गृहपतिमभिसंवसानाः[8] । तान् पूर्वः परिगृह्णामि स्व आयतने मनीषये**ति द्वाभ्यां गार्हपत्यम्** ॥८॥ अयं पितृणामग्निरवाड्ढव्या पितृभ्य आ । तं पूर्वः परिगृह्णाम्यविषं नः पितुं करदि**ति दक्षिणाग्निम्** ॥९॥ अजस्रं त्वाꣳ सभापाला विजयभागꣳ समिन्धताम् । अग्ने दीदाय[9] मे सभ्य विजित्यै शरदः **शतमिति सभ्यम्** ॥१०॥ अन्नमावसथीयमभिहराणि शरदः शतम् । आवसथे श्रियं मन्त्रमहिर्बुध्नियो नियच्छत्वि**त्यावसथ्यमिति वैताभिः**[10] ॥११॥ **पलाशशाखाꣳ**[11] **शमीशाखां वाऽऽहरति प्राचीमुदीचीं प्रागुदीचीं वा**[12]**ऽहीनां बहुपर्णा**[13]**-मशुष्काग्राम्** ॥१२॥ **यं कामयेतापशुः स्यादित्यपर्णां तस्मै शुष्काग्राम्** ॥१३॥ **यं कामयेत पशुमान् स्यादिति बहुपर्णां तस्मै बहुशाखामा**[14]**हरेत् पशुमन्तमेवैनं करोतीति विज्ञायते** ॥१४॥ इषे त्वे**ति शाखामाच्छिनत्त्यूर्जे त्वेति संनमयत्यनुमार्ष्टि वा** ॥१५॥ **अपि**[15] वेषे त्वोर्जे त्वे**त्याच्छिनत्ति** ॥१६॥ इमां प्राचीमुदीचीमिषमूर्जमभिसꣳस्कृताम् । बहुपर्णा-

---

4. M_2 तान् वहतु.
5. M_1 °मागन्.
6. M_2 °ह वा प्रजा.
7. M_2 पूर्वाः
8. Bh_3 संवसानः
9. M_2 दीधाय.
10. Bh_1 चैताभिः
11. M_1 M_2 पालाश °
12. M2 वा बहु°
13. AM3 वा बहुपर्णां बहुशाखासुषिरामप्रतिशु°
14. Thus AM_3; cf. ĀpŚS 1.1.9. Ān Bh_3 M_2 °शाखामशुष्काग्रामिषे.
15. Thus AM_3; cf. ĀpŚS 1.1.10; the other MSS om. this sūtra.

मशुष्काग्राꣳ हरामि पशुपामहमित्याहरति ।।१७।। वायवः स्थेति[16] तया षड् वत्सानपाकरोति ।।१८।। ।।४।।

दर्भैर्वा ।।१।। सदर्भ[17]येत्येकेषाम्[18] ।।२।। अपाकृतानामेकꣳ शाखयोपस्पृशति ।।३।। देवो व[19] इति गोचरमभि मातृः प्रस्थापयति ।।४।। इन्द्रं निगमेषूपलक्षयेदिन्द्रयाजिनो महेन्द्रं महेन्द्रयाजिनः ।।५।। प्रस्थितानामेकाꣳ शाखयोपस्पृशति दर्भैर्दर्भपुञ्जीलैर्वा[20] ।।६।। शुद्धा अपः सुप्रपाणे पिबन्तीः[21] शतमिन्द्राय शरदो दुहानाः। रुद्रस्य हेतिः परि वो वृणाक्त्विवति प्रस्थिता अनुमन्त्रयते ।।७।। ध्रुवा [22]अस्मिन्निति यजमानस्य गृहानभि पर्यावर्तते ।।८।। यजमानस्य पशून् पाहीत्यग्निष्ठेऽनस्यग्न्यगारे वा पुरस्तात् प्रतीचीꣳ शाखामु[23]पगूहति ।।९।। [24]पश्चात् प्राचीमित्येकेषाम्[25] ।।१०।। देवस्य त्वेत्यश्वपर्शुमसिदं[26] वाऽऽदत्ते ।।११।। यज्ञस्य घोषदसीति गार्हपत्यमुपतिष्ठते ।।१२।। प्रत्युष्टमित्याहवनीये गार्हपत्ये वा निष्टपति ।।१३।। प्रेयमगा[27]दुर्वन्तरिक्षं प्रेहीत्यन्यतरेण प्राचीनमुदीचीनं वा[28]ऽभिप्रव्रज्य यतः कुत[29]श्चिद् दर्भमयं[30] बर्हिराहरति ।।१४।। विष्णोः स्तूपोऽसीत्यभिप्रेतानामेकꣳ स्तम्बमुत्सृजति ।।१५।। इन्द्रस्य परिषूतमसी[31]त्यन्यं परिषौति देवानामिति वा ।।१६।। तꣳ सर्वं दाति ।।१७।। अपि वा पशूनां त्वा भागमुत्सृजामीति परिषूतस्यैकां द्वे वा दर्भनाड्या[32]वुत्सृजति ।।१८।। इदं देवानामिति परिषूतमभिमृशतीदं पशूनामि[33]त्युत्सृष्टम् ।।१९।। अवसृष्टो गवां भाग इति वा ।।२०।। देवस्य त्वा सवितुः प्रसवेऽश्विनोर् बाहुभ्यां पूष्णो हस्ताभ्यां बर्हिर्देवसदनमारभ इति विशाखेष्वभिपद्यते

16. A स्योपायवः स्येति.
17. AM_3 °र्भमयैरित्ये°
18. M_2 °त्येषामेकां शा°
19. AM_1 वस्सविता प्रार्पयत्विति; M_2 om. देवो व इति.
20. Thus AM_3; the other MSS om. दर्भै--- लैर्वा.
21. M_1 पिबन्ति.
22. A अस्मिन् गोपतौ स्यात बर्हिरिति.
23. AM_1 M_2 °मवगूहति.
24. M_2 पश्चिमात् प्रतीचीमि °
25. AM_3 °षां सावित्रेणाश्व°
26. Bh_3 °मसीदं.
27. AM_3 °गाद्धिषणोर्वन्तरिक्षमित्य°
28. AM_3 °वातिप्र°; M_1 वाभियुज्य.
29. A कुतश्च दर्भ°
30. M_1 दर्भं बहिरा°
31. AM_3 °सीति परि°
32. M_2 °नाड्या व्युत्सृ°
33. AM_3 °मित्यतिसृ°

।।२१।। देवेभ्यस्त्वोर्ध्वबर्हिर्भ्य **इत्यूर्ध्वमुन्मार्ष्टि** ।।२२।। देव बर्हिर्मा त्वाऽन्वङ् मा तिर्यगि**त्यसिदं निदधाति** ।।२३।। माऽधो मोपरि परुस्त ऋध्यासमि**ति वा** ।।२४।। //५//

या जाता ओषधयो देवेभ्यस्त्रियुगं पुरा । तासां पर्व राध्यासं परिस्तरमाहरन्नि**त्यभिमन्त्र्या**च्छेत्ता ते मा रिषमि**त्याच्छिनत्ति** ।।१।। **संनखं**[34] **मुष्टिं दाति**[35] ।।२।। **स प्रस्तरः** ।।३।। **स्रुग्दण्डमात्र-मुर्वस्थिकुल्मिमात्रं वा** ।।४।। **एतेनैव कल्पेनेतरान् दाति** ।।५।। **यदन्यत् परिषवणादुत्सर्जनाच्च** ।।६।। **सर्वं यथार्थं लुत्वा**[36] देव बर्हिः शतवल्शं विरोहे[37]**त्यालवानभिमृशति** ।।७।। [38]सहस्रवल्शा वि वयं रुहेमे-**त्यात्मानं प्रत्यभिमृशति** ।।८।। **अयुजो युजो**[39] **वा मुष्टीन् निधनानि वा लुनोति**[40] ।।९।। अदित्यै रास्नाऽसीति[41] **प्रदक्षिणं शुल्बमावेष्टयति** ।।१०।। अयुपिता योनिरि**ति प्रतिदधाति**[42] ।।११।। **त्रिधातु पञ्च-धातु**[43] **वा** ।।१२।। धातौ धातौ मन्त्रमावर्तयति ।।१३।। पृथिव्याः संपृचः पाही**ति प्रागग्रमुदगग्रं वा शुल्बं निदधाति** ।।१४।। अपरिमितानां परिमिताः संनह्ये सुकृताय कम्[44] । एनो मा[45] निगां कतमच्चनाहं पुनरुत्थाय बहुला भवन्त्वि**त्यभिमन्त्र्य** सुसंभृता[46] त्वे**ति शुल्बे निधनानि संभरति** ।।१५।। अलुभितो योनिरि**त्युत्तमे निधने प्रस्तरमादधाति** ।।१६।। इन्द्राण्यै संनहनमि**ति संनह्यति** ।।१७।। पूषा त **इति प्रदक्षिणं ग्रन्थिमावेष्ट्य**[47] स त **इति पुरस्तात् प्रत्यञ्चमुपकर्षति पश्चा-द्वा**[48] **प्राञ्चम्** ।।१८।। आपस्त्वामश्विनौ त्वामृषयः सप्त मामृजुः । बर्हिः सूर्यस्य[49] रश्मिभिरुषसां केतुमारभ **इत्यारभते** ।।१९।। इन्द्रस्य त्वा बाहुभ्या[50]मुद्यच्छ **इत्युद्यच्छते** ।।२०।। बृहस्पतेरि**ति शीर्षन्नधि निधाय हरति** ।।२१।। **यौ गमनौ तौ प्रत्यायनौ** ।।२२।। अदित्याः

---

34. M_3 असन्नखं; Bh_3 सनखं
35. A लुनोति; M_2 ददाति
36. A लुनोति; M_1M_2 लुनाति
37. Ān in foot-note °हेत्युलपान°
38. M_2 om. sūtra 8.
39. Bh_3 om. युजो.
40. M_1 लुनाति.
41. Bh_3 °सीति दक्षिणं.
42. Ān प्रतिनिद°
43. Bh_3 पञ्चधातौ मन्त्र°.
44. M_1 कः
45. M_1 मानुगां; M_2 मानिनां.
46. M_2 °तास्त्वेति; Ān °ता त्वा संभरामीति.
47. Ān in foot-note °वेष्टयति.
48. AM_3 पश्चात् प्राञ्चं वा.
49. Bh_3 सूत्रस्य
50. AM_3 °भ्यामित्यु °

सद आसीदेति **परिधिदेशेऽन्तर्वेद्यनधः सादयति** ॥२३॥ देवंगम-मसीत्यासन्नमभिमन्त्रयते ॥२४॥ अदित्यास्त्वा पृष्ठे सादयामीति **गार्हपत्यदेश उपरि** [51]**निदधाति** ॥२५॥ ॥६॥

पालाशं खादिरं वैकविꣳशतिदारुमिध्मꣳ संनह्यति ॥१॥ **पञ्चदश सामिधेन्यर्थानि** ॥२॥ **त्रयः परिधयो नियतवृक्षाः सत्वक्काः** ॥३॥ **आर्द्रा भवन्ति ते हि सरसा इति विज्ञायते** ॥४॥ **स्थविष्ठो मध्यमोऽणीयान् द्राघीयान् दक्षिणार्ध्योऽणिष्ठो ह्रसिष्ठ उत्तरार्ध्यः** ॥५॥ **द्वे आघारसमिधावनूयाजसमिदेकविꣳ**[52]**शीति** ॥६॥ **समूलानाममूलानां वा दर्भाणाम**[53]**युग्धातु शुल्बं कृत्वा प्रागग्रमुदगग्रं वा निदधाति** ॥७॥ यत् कृष्णो रूपं कृत्वा प्राविशस्त्वं वनस्पतीन् । ततस्त्वामेकविꣳशतिधा संभरामि सुसंभृता ॥ त्रीन् परिधीꣳस्तिस्रः समिधो यज्ञायुरनुसंचरान् । उपवेषं मेक्षणं धृष्टिं संभरामि सुसंभृतेति **शुल्ब इध्मꣳ संभरति**[54] ॥८॥ कृष्णोऽस्यारवरेष्ठो देव पुरश्चर[55] सध्यासं त्वेति **संनह्यति** ॥९॥ पूषा त **इति प्रदक्षिणं ग्रन्थिमावेष्ट्यैते**[56] **नैव कल्पेन यथा बर्हिषि विप्रतिपाद्य वा तेनैव मन्त्रेण बर्हिषा सह निदधाति** ॥१०॥ वेदोऽसि येन त्वं देव वेद देवेभ्यो वेदोऽभवस्तेन[57] मह्यं वेदो भूया **इति दर्भाणां वेदं करोति वत्सुज्ञुं मूतकार्यं पड्क्तिकार्यं त्रिवृतं वा** ॥११॥ **वत्सज्ञुं पशुकामस्य मूतकार्यमन्नाद्यकामस्य पड्क्तिकार्यं प्रजाकामस्य त्रिवृतं ब्रह्मवर्चसकामस्य** ॥१२॥ **त्रिवृच्छिरसं ब्रुवते** ॥१३॥ **शुल्बात्**[58] **प्रादेशे परिवासयति** ॥१४॥ **इध्मप्रव्रश्चनानि वेदपरिवासनानि च सह निदधाति** ॥१५॥ ॥७॥

॥[59]इति सत्याषाढश्रौतसूत्रे प्रथमप्रश्ने द्वितीयः पटलः ॥

---

51. AM$_3$ उपरि द°
52. M$_3$ °विंशति स°; M$_1$ M$_2$ °विंशी स°
53. Bh$_3$ °मायुग्धातु
54. M$_2$ संहरति.
55. M$_2$ °श्चर संत्विति.
56. A Ān °वेष्ट्य तेनैव
57. AM$_1$ भव तेन; M$_2$ भवति तेन.
58. Thus AM$_3$; also cf. ĀpŚS 1.6.6; AM$_3$ तस्मात्; Ān तृणात्
59. M$_1$ M$_2$ M$_3$ om इति...पटलः

MĀNAVA ŚRAUTASŪTRA

Edited by
C. G. Kashikar

INTRODUCTION

It is proposed to prepare a revised critical edition of the Mānava Śrautasūtra. Friedrich Knauer undertook for the first time a critical edition of that text. He published five parts of the text in 1901-03 at St. Pétersbourg. Unfortunately he could not publish the complete text. J. M. van Gelder took up the work and published in 1921 the sixth part covering the Agnicayana. It however remained to prepare and publish a critical edition of the entire text of that Śrautasūtra. Gelder pursued her work and published the complete text together with some Pariśiṣṭas (New Delhi 1961).

A reprint of this edition was issued in 1985 by Shri Sat Guru Publications of Delhi. In my studies of the Śrautasūtras I had suggested corrections and emendations to the text of the Mānava Śrautasūtra. These were published in my "Survey of the Śrautasūtras" (*Journal of the University of Bombay,* Sept. 1966, Vol. XXXV New Series part 2 Arts number No. 41) and also elsewhere. At the request of the Delhi Publishers, I prepared a revised list of such corrections and emendations which was appended to the Reprint (pages 1-6). In my Introductory remarks to that Appendix I had stated that "a further critical and comparative study of the Sūtra-text may necessitate additional corrections and emendations" and that " the present edition together with the appendix should be regarded as a partially improved text". Meanwhile my revised edition of the Vārāha Śrautasūtra—another Sūtra-text belonging to the Maitrāyaṇī recension—was published (Pune 1988).

In 1987 it was proposed that I should undertake the work of preparing a revised edition of the Mānāva Śrautasūtra. I appreciated the idea since it afforded to me an opportunity of further prosecuting my study of the Maitrāyaṇī recension in general and the Mānava Śrautasūtra in particular.

J. M. van Gelder had based her critical edition on a number of manuscripts. My efforts to collect unused manuscripts succeeded to some extent. I procured eleven manuscripts - a collection obtained from the Janorkar family of Nashik and deposited in the library of the Vaidika Saṁśodhana Maṇḍala, Pune. Three of these cover Prāksoma, three contain a fraction of it, two cover the Agniṣṭoma, one Iṣṭikalpa, one gives the text of Cayana, Vājapeya and Dvādaśāha, and one covers the Rājasūya book. From the Baroda Oriental Institute I procured three manuscripts — one covering the Prāksoma, another giving a fraction of it, and the third one covering a part of Agniṣṭoma. This last manuscript is the oldest one of all the manuscripts discovered so far; it was written in Saṁvat 1491 at Karpaṭavāṇijya (modern kapadvanj) in Gujarat. My manuscripts lack the portions covering Prāyaścitta and Pravargya.

A comparison of variants recorded from the manuscripts procured by me with those recorded by Gelder in her edition shows that the manuscripts procured by me belong to the same groups of manuscripts which were utilised by Gelder. One important discovery however was that I could procure a transcript of a Manuscript from the collection of the Prājña Pāṭhaśālā, Wai (Satara) which covered five Adhyāyas of the Rājasūya chapter and which provided very important correct readings.

The manuscripts procured from the Vaidika Saṁśodhana Maṇḍala have been generally designated as P. When necessary, individual manuscripts of this group have been denoted by numbers (P1, P2 etc.). The manuscripts from the Oriental Institute Baroda bear the general disignation B. When necessary, individual manuscripts have been denoted by numbers (B1, B2 etc.). The transcript from Prājña Pāṭhaśālā,Wai has been designated as W. Many of the minor variants in B and P are identical with those in Gelder's manuscripts. These have been ignored. When none of the manuscripts gave the correct reading, the variants found in manuscripts have necessarily been recorded. For the Prāksoma, Gelder procured several manuscripts, two (M1, C1) out of which, being old ones, give the correct readings. My manuscripts do not include any one which corresponds to those. Therefore, with regard to the text of Prāksoma, I have relied on Gelder's M1 and C1, and have recorded in foot-notes the variant found in my manuscripts. In many cases Gelder has retained into bracket the reading found in other manuscripts but absent in M1 and C1. I have dropped them since they do not represent the original text. Even in Prāksoma I could improve the Sūtra-text to a certain extent. In the subsequent books, particularly in the five Adhyāyas of the Rājasūya book, I have improved the text to a large extent.

Another point concerning the better presentation of text is the proper punctuation of the sūtras. I found that the sūtras often need to be marked in a different way so as to facilitate the easy and correct understanding of the text. In many cases a sūtra marked in Gelder's edition needed to be divided into two or more sūtras. In a few cases the sūtra was found to be wrongly separated. As a result of the different punctuation, the numbers of sūtras in a Khaṇḍa are often changed. Such change might create difficulty in referring to the word-index or concordnace. Such an excuse however need not deter one from presenting a Vedic text in an improved form.

Sequence of the text

A more important point about the revision of the Sūtra-text is its extent and sequence. Gelder has divided her Sūtra-edition in eleven parts, each part generally being subdivided into Adhyāyas, Khaṇḍas and sūtras. Gelder has taken up the extent and sequence from the manuscript M2 which is quite modern (written in 1864 A. D.) The tenth and eleventh parts comprise several Pariśiṣṭas mostly belonging to the Mānava Gṛhyasūtra. Gelder is well aware of this. She however allowed them to be included in the edition because certain manuscripts contained them. Really speaking, there is no place for Gṛhya Pariśiṣṭas in a Śrautasūtra. All of them therefore require to be dropped out.

About the Anugrāhika chapter (8th part) Gelder has said : "The anugrāhika brings additions to the Śrauta ritual, but also sections that do not belong to it. Now it contains a sūtra, 8.18.1, that refers to the aśvamedha, (that is only treated of afterwards in the rājasūya 9.2,) and that thereupon refers to the puruṣamedha that is nowhere dealt with in the Mānava-śrautasūtra. This confirms a supposition that the anugrāhika has been a later addition or a combination of additions" (Preface, p. 5). Thus Anugrāhika cannot be a part of the original Śrautasūtra. It is a Pariśiṣṭa to the Śrautasūtra, hence deserves to be excluded from the Śrautasūtra proper. It may, however, be appended as a Pariśiṣṭa. It is to be noted that while the Śrautasūtra has a fourfold division, the Anugrāhika has a threefold one, indicating that it was not a part of any book (*vibhāga*).

Gelder has said; " As told above, the sequence of the eleven parts is given as in M2. But other mss have other sequences. The original one must have been different from that in M2, but cannot be reconstructed with such a certainty that a change in the text was recommendable. Moreover the given sequence has long been in use and also Bloomfield's Concordance follows it " (p. 3). When one is sure that a particular sequence is not the original one, it becomes imperative to seek the original one, and adopt it in spite of the fact that Bloomfield adopted the sequence in the first printed text. Now that the sequence from a particular manuscript is before scholars in a printed form, it is possible and also essential to try to arrive at the original one. The Pariśiṣṭas and the Anugrāhika cannnot have formed part of the original Sūtra-text as seen above. So the problem of the remaining eight parts (excluding 8,9 and 11) requires to be solved. The manuscripts procured by me do not render any conspicuous help in this regard. We have therefore to see whether the information recorded by Gelder provides any clue to arrive at the original sequence.

Six manuscripts including M2 mention the sequence as Prāksoma, Agniṣṭoma, Iṣṭikalpa, Vājapeya and Cayana. They conclude by saying *ete pañca vibhāgāḥ*. Many of these manuscripts are modern and written at Nashik. Now the sequence noted in the Colophons of the manuscripts C2 and Ç4 is : Prāksoma, Iṣṭikalpa, Agniṣṭoma, Rājasūya and Cayana. The difference between these two groups is that while in the first group Agniṣṭoma, is the second, in the second group Iṣṭikalpa stands as the second. Again the fourth book is Vājapeya in the first group, while it is the Rājasūya in the second. The manuscript C2 in the second group is an old one, and it seems to have been copied from C4 which must obviously be still older. The manuscripts M1 and

C1 mentioned above are also old. M1 was written at Ahmedabad. The manuscripts C2 and C4 might have very likely been written in Gujarat. Thus it may be said that there were two traditions of the Mānava School—one in Gujarat and the other in the adjoining districts of Maharashtra and that the Gujarat tradition is an older one and better preserved.

The common feature about the sequence of the Sūtra-text according to the two groups is that the Sūtra-text comprises five books and that the opening and concluding books are respectively the Prāksoma and Cayana. Iṣṭikalpa is the third book according to the first group and second according to the second group of C2 and C4. Gelder's view that " the Iṣṭikalpa should not have been originally the second of the five parts" (p.5) is acceptable. The reasons given by her for that purpose do not however seem to be convincing. The Iṣṭikalpa comprises two Adhyāyas. The second Adhyāya presupposes the Rājasūya, Cayana and Aśvamedha which in fact form the subsequent parts of the Sūtra-text. Gelder surmises that in view of this discrepancy the second Adhyāya might have been added later. The fact about the references to the subsequent topics need not however be regarded as a discrepancy. The Sūtrakāra who was fully aware of the detailed rituals prescribed in his recension would deal even with the subsquent portion in order to make his section on the Iṣṭis complete. Futher the position of Gonāmika rite is not uniform in the manucsript-tradition. Following some manuscript, Gelder has placed the Gonāmika at the end of the Rājasūya book. This tradition is not trustworthy. Its position within the Iṣṭikalpa as found in certain manuscripts is the correct one. Gelder concludes that in view of the discrepancies the sequence in the Iṣṭikalpa was uncertain and that additions might have been made to it. Obviously the section of Iṣṭikalpa is of a miscellaneous character. Since the matter presented in it is traced to the Maitrāyaṇī Saṁhitā and since it is fixed within the frame of five books, one need not be suspicious about its genuine character. In the Saṁhitā, Adhvara comes next to the Darśa-Pūrṇamāsa. The tradition holding the Iṣṭikalpa as the third book may therefore be regarded as sound.

The fourth book is named Vājapeya according to the first group and Rājasūya according to the second. Here Vājapeya and

Rājasūya are the names of books each of which covers certain other sacrifices also. Thus the Vājapeya covers Dvādaśāha and Gavām Ayana, and the Rājasūya covers Aśvamedha, Ekāhas, and Sattras. This is confirmed by the position of the portions dealing with those sacrifices in the manuscripts. If the Gujarat tradition is adopted, the fourth book, namely, Rājasūya will cover Rājasūya, Aśvamedha, Ekāhas, Ahīnas and Sattras. The fifth book Cayana will include Cayana, Vājapeya, Dvādaśāha and Gavām Ayana. This arrangement will fully accord with the relevant order adopted by Gelder following the manuscript M2. A glance at Gelder's order of contents shows that Cayana is followed by Vājapeya, Dvādaśāha and Gavām Ayana, which should mean that the latter three form part of the book Cayana. This agrees with the Gujarat tradition. It may be noted that the Maitrāyaṇī Saṁhitā does not contain mantra-brāhmaṇa for Dvādaśāha Gavām Ayana, Ekāha, Ahīnas and Sattras. For Aśvamedha, it records only the mantras. The author of Mānava Śrautasūtra was free to choose his own order in laying down the procedure of these sacrifices. He chose to place Dvādaśāha and Gavām Ayana together in the book of Cayana. The Vārāha school which covers under the term "Vājapeyādikam" Dvādaśāha, Gavām Ayana, Ekādaśinī, Sautrāmaṇī, Rājasūya and Aśvamedha may be said to be following the Maharashtra tradition.

Two topics remain to be considered, namely, Prāyaścittas and Pravargyakalpa. The Mānava Śrautasūtra has recorded together in one Adhyāya all Prāyaścittas for Darśa-Pūrnamāsa, Agnihotra, Soma, Sattra and Cayana. The Pravargyakalpa also consists of one Adhyāya. In Gelder's edition these two topics are placed as two parts (third and fourth) after Agniṣṭoma. It seems none of the five books originally included these two topics because each of these has a threefold division; it omitted the first book division. The compilation of all Prāyaścittas together seems to be a later idea. As for the Pravargya, the Yajurveda-sūtras have generally placed it at the end. It may be that some follower of Manu, perhaps belonging to the next generation, composed the sūtras of these topics for the purpose of preserving the tradition and appended them to the last book. The Anugrāhika might have been composed by one or more authors at a still later date. It therefore deserves to be treated as an Appendix. In the Vārāha school it has the position of one of the Pariśiṣṭas.

Consequently the sequence of the Mānava Śrautasūtra will in my opinion be as follows :

Book	*Title*	*Topics*	*Adhyāya*
I	Prāksoma		
		Darśapūṇamāsau	1-4
		Agnyādheyam	5
		Agnihotram	6. 1-3
		Āgrayaṇam	6.4
		Punarādheyam	6.5
		Cāṭurmāsyāni	7
		Nirūḍhapaśuḥ	8
II	Agniṣṭoma		1-5
III	Iṣṭikalpa		
		Kāmyā Iṣṭayaḥ	1
		Kāmyā Iṣṭayaḥ	2. 1-7
		Hautraṃ	2. 8-9
		Kāmyāḥ Paśavaḥ	2.10
		Kaukilī Sautrāmaṇī	2. 11
		Paśvaikādaśinī	2. 12-13
		Caturhotāraḥ	2.14
		Gonāmikaḥ	2.15-16
		Brahmatvam	2.17-18
IV	Rājasūya		
		Rājasūyaḥ	1
		Aśvamedhaḥ	2
		Ekāhāḥ	3
		Ahīnāḥ	4
		Sattrāṇi	5
V	Cayana		
		Agnicayanam	1-2
		Vājapeyaḥ	3
		Dvādaśāhaḥ and Gavām Ayanam	4
		Prāyaścittāni	5
		Pravargyakalpaḥ	6

Appendix Anugrāhikaḥ

The total number of Adhyāyas would be 8+5+2+5+6 = 26.

The History of the Manava school

In the Introduction to my edition of the Vārāha Śrautasūtra (Pune, 1988), I have discussed the character of the Maitrāyaṇī Saṁhitā, its relation to the Mānava and the Vārāha Śrautasūtras and also the history of the Maitrāyaṇīyas (p. XLIV ff.) "Since the last few centuries the Maitrāyaṇīyas have been living in Gujarat and the districts of Dhulia and Jalgaon in Maharashtra—the region which is known in history by the name Bāglāṇ. The name Bāglāṇ is related to the royal dynasty of Baguls who originally hailed from Kanauj in Uttar Pradesh and were known as Rathods. History tells us that a Bagul chief Nānadeva claiming descent from the Rathods established in the fourteenth century A. D. his kingdom in Bāglāṇ protected by seven hill-forts, prominent among them being Mayuragiri (Mulher) and Sālagiri (Salher). It is likely that he settled and patronised Maitrāyaṇī Vaidikas in his kingdom. The dynasty ruled over Bāglāṇ for eleven generations, that is to say, up to the seventeenth century A. D., during which period the Maitrāyaṇīyas enjoyed royal patronage. There is evidence to show that the Bāglāṇ rulers had made grants to the Maitrāyaṇiyas" (p. LXXII).

As the epigraphical records indicate, grants were made to the Maitrāyaṇīya Pandits by royal families in different regions like Sambalpur (Orissa), Saurashtra, Śūrpāraka etc. One cannot say whether the grants were made to the Pandits by special invitations or whether there were colonies of the Maitrāyaṇīyas in those regions. The manuscripts which were procured for preparing the editions of the Maitrāyaṇī Saṁhitā and the Mānava Śrauta and Gṛhya Sūtras belonged to the region known as Bāglāṇ. This means that in historical times Maitrāyaṇīyas lived only in this region. In Patañjali's time the Kālāpakas or Maitrāyaṇīyas lived in Punjab in large numbers. There is no trace of this recension now in that region. Nor do we come across any Maitrāyaṇīya settlement in the regions known from epigraphical records. From the fact that the royal family of the Bāguls brought with them the Maitrāyaṇīya families from Kanauj to Bāglāṇ, it becomes evident that the Maitrāyaṇīyas were originally included among the five Gauḍa sects. A verse from the Sahyādrikhaṇḍa of the Skandapurāṇa supports this fact. After being settled in Bāglāṇ they were enumerated among the five Dravida sects. Ultimately the Maitrāyaṇīyas were confined only to this region. The districts of Gujarat and northern Maharashtra preserved the Maitrāyaṇīya tradition. The credit of preserving on the surface of the earth the literature and religious practices of the Maitrāyaṇīyas thus goes to the rulers who colonised the Vaidikas in Bāglāṇ and patronised them and also to the Vaidikas who came down and maintained the tradition. The lovers of Vedic lore have to be grateful to them.

The generations of Maitrāyaṇīyas living in Bāglāṇ were divided into two branches by reason of the different spoken languages, namely, Gujarati and Marathi. Naturally their Maitrāyaṇīya traditions developed along rather different lines. Already during their migration to Bāglāṇ which might have taken a long time, the Maitrāyaṇīyas might have suffered from heavy odds resulting in the damage to their religious traditions. During migration and also in Bāglāṇ their tradition of domestic rites might have been adequately preserved. On the other hand, the tradition of sacrificial rituals was declining from the Sūtra-period itself, hence there is no wonder that the Śrautasūtra-text had begun to suffer from an insecure tradition. Since the ritual-tradition was on a decline, the preservation of Śrautasūtra-text in a written form must also have suffered. It seems the tradition in northern Maharashtra suffered more than in Gujarat. All the manuscripts, which exist, are copied in fractions. Such a practice might have been responsible for the loose and defective sequence of the Sūtra-text.

The damage done to the Maitrāyaṇīya recension as a whole is quite obvious. The Maitrāyaṇī Saṁhitā itself suffered from insecure tradition (cf VārŚS, Intro. pp. XLIV ff). There must have been a Pada-text for the Saṁhitā which is now totally lost. A mantra-Saṁhitā serially collecting only the mantra-portions out of the mixed mantra-brāhmaṇa portions was formulated probably for avoiding the strain on memory of the Vedic students. One is at a loss to know the age of that compilation. In recent times even a Padapāṭha was newly devised for priestly purpose. While the Padapāṭha in the Gujarat tradition was based on the mantra-portions only, that in the Maharashtra tradition was based on the

Saṁhitā-text as it is irrespective of whether it was mantra or brāhmaṇa. In selecting only the mantra-portions for the Padapāṭha, the Gujarat tradition followed the Śukla Yajurveda tradition in which the mantras form an independent collection. The Maharashtra tradition followed the Kṛṣṇa Yajurveda Taittirīya tradition in which the Saṁhitā consisting of both the mantras and the brāhmaṇa is provided with a Padapāṭha. Both Padapāṭhas are defective; the Gujarat Padapāṭha may be said to be less defective. This clearly indicates the distinction between the two tradtions.

Since the Maitrāyaṇīya tradition was restricted to the Bāglāṇ (i.e. Gujarat and northern Maharashtra), and since the Gujarat tradition seems to be better preserved, the sequence found in the Gujarat tradition may reasonably be preferred with the exception of the Iṣṭikalpa. Even for the constitution of the text, that tradition would claim preference. A history of the various Vedic schools has not so far been written, even though an attempt in that direction was made by L. Renou. Such a history, if written, will form a source of the cultural history of India.

In regard to the comparative chronology, the relationship between the Mānava and Āpastamba has been discussed. The old view is that Āpastamba was under the influence of Mānava. Further study has pointed to the indebtendness of the Mānava to Āpastamba. The problem needs closer attention.

* * *

I request scholars interested in Śrauta literature to express their views on the sequence of the Mānava Śrautasūtra proposed here.

।। श्रीगणेशाय नमः ।।

।। मानवश्रौतसूत्रम् ।।

प्रथमो विभागः

दर्शपूर्णमासौ

उत्तरतउपचारो विहारः ।।१।। अन्तराणि यज्ञाङ्गानि कर्तुः ।।२।। चत्वारिचत्वारि कर्माणि प्रसंपश्यन् कुर्यादा चतुर्थात् कर्मणः ।।३।। मन्त्रान्तेन कर्मादिं संनिपातयेत् ।।४।। आदिनोत्तरस्य पूर्वस्यान्तं विद्यात् ।।५।। यज्ञोपवीती दक्षिणाचारः प्राङ्न्यायं[१] कर्मोपांशु यजुर्वेदेन कुर्यात् ।।६।। दर्शपूर्णमासयोर्धर्माः साधारणाः ।।७।। निर्देशाद् व्यवतिष्ठेरन् ।।८।। चत्वार ऋत्विजोऽध्वर्युर्होता ब्रह्माग्नीध्रः ।।९।। अनादेशेऽध्वर्युः कुर्यात् ।।१०।। उपवत्स्यदशने[२] भुक्ते गार्हपत्यादाहवनीयं ज्वलन्तं प्रणयति ।।११।।

देवा गातुविदो गातुं वित्त्वा गातुं यज्ञाय विन्दत ।
मनसस्पतिना देवेन वाताद्यज्ञं प्रयुज्यताम् ।।

इति जपित्वा व्रतोपेतस्य शाखामच्छैति पर्णशाखां शमीशाखां वा प्राचीमुदीचीं वाहानां[३] बहुशाखां बहुपर्णामशुष्काग्रामसुषिराम् ।।१२।। इषे त्वा इति छिनत्ति ।।१३।। ऊर्जे त्वा इत्यनुमार्ष्टि ।।१४।। सुभूताय इति संनमयति ।।१५।। वायवः स्थ इति शाखया वत्सानपाकरोति त्रीन् यजुषा तूष्णीं त्रीन् ।।१६।। अपाकृतानामेकं शाखया तूष्णीमुपस्पृशति ।।१७।। दर्भपिञ्जूलैः सह शाखया देवो वः सविता प्रार्पयतु इति गाः प्रार्पयति ।।१८।। आप्यायध्वमघ्न्या देवेभ्या इन्द्राय भागम् इतीन्द्र-

---

१. B, P, G प्राङ्न्याय्यं.
२. B, P, G उपवत्स्वशने
३. B, P वाहनां, G वाहनां,

याजिनः । महेन्द्राय इति **महेन्द्रयाजिनः** ।।१९।।

शुद्धा अपः सुप्रपाणे पिबन्तीः शतमिन्द्राय शरदो दुहानाः ।
रुद्रस्य हेतिः परि वो वृणक्तु ।।

इति व्रजन्तीरनुमन्त्रयते ।।२०।। ध्रुवा अस्मिन् गोपतौ स्यात बह्वीः **इति यजमानस्य गृहानभिपर्यावर्तते । यजमानं वा प्रेक्षमाणो जपति** ।।२१।। **अग्निष्ठेऽनस्यग्न्यगारे वा** यजमानस्य पशून् पाहि **इति प्रत्यगग्रां शाखामुपकर्षति** ।।२२।। **उत्तरतो गार्हपत्यस्य** देवस्य त्वा सवितुः प्रसवे **इत्यसिलमादत्ते** ।।२३।। गोषदसि **इति गार्हपत्यमुपतिष्ठते** ।।२४।। उर्वन्तरिक्षँ वीहि **इति व्रजति** ।।२५।। प्रत्युष्टँ रक्षः **इत्याहवनीये निष्टपति** ।।२६।। प्रेयमगाद् **इति जपति** ।।२७।। **प्रागुदग्वाभिप्रव्रज्य बर्हिरच्छैति** ।।२८।। देवानां परिषूतमसि **इति दर्भान् प्रस्तराय परिषुवति** ।।२९।। विष्णोः स्तुपः **इति दर्भस्तम्बमभिमृशति** ।।३०।। अतिसृष्टो गवां भागः **इत्येकान्तमतिसृजति** ।।३१।। **शेषं प्रस्तराय** ।।३२।। माधो मोपरि परुस्त ऋध्यासम् **इति जपति** ।।३३।। देवस्य त्वा सवितुः प्रसवे **इति विशाखानि प्रति लुनाति संनखं**[४] **मुष्टिम्** ।।३४।। पृथिव्याः संपृचस्पाहि **इति तृणमन्तर्धाय प्रस्तरं सादयति** ।।३५।। **अकल्माषान् दर्भान् लुनाति प्रभूतानप्रधूनयन्** ।।३६।। आच्छेत्ता ते मार्षम्[५] **इति जपति** ।।३७।। अतस्त्वं बर्हिः शतवलिशँ[६] विरोह **इत्यालवानभिमृशति** ।।३८।। सहस्रवलिशा[७] वि वयँ रुहेम **इत्यात्मानं प्रत्यभिमृशति** ।।३९।। अयुपिता योनिः **इति शुल्बं प्रतिदधात्ययुग्धातु प्रदक्षिणम्** ।।४०।। अदित्या रास्नासि **इति शुल्बमनुलोमं त्रिरनुमार्ष्टि** ।।४१।। **यथालूनममुतो वा** सुसंभृता[८] त्वा संभरामि **इति शुल्बे बर्हिस्त्रिः संभरति** ।।४२।। अयुपिता योनिः **इति प्रस्तरम्** ।।४३।। इन्द्राण्याः संनहनम् **इत्यन्तौ समायम्य** पूषा ते ग्रन्थिम् **इति प्रदक्षिणमावेष्टयति** ।।४४।। स ते मास्थात् **इति पश्चात्प्राञ्चमुपकर्षति** ।।४५।। आपस्त्वामश्विनौ त्वामृषयः सप्त मामृजुः । बर्हिः सूर्यस्य रश्मिभिरुषसां केतुमारभे ।। **इत्यारभते** ।।४६।। इन्द्रस्य त्वा

---

४. B, P सनखं
५. P, G मा रिषम्
६. Thus B,P: G °वल्शों
७. Thus B,P; G °वल्शा
८. B, G सुसंभृते

बाहुभ्यामुद्यच्छे **इत्युद्यच्छते ।।४७।।** बृहस्पतेर्मूर्ध्ना **हरामि इति मूर्धन्यादधाति ।।४८।।** उर्वन्तरिक्षँ वीहि **इत्येति ।।४९।।** अदित्यास्त्वा पृष्ठे सादयामि **इति पश्चादपरस्य सादयत्यनोऽधो वा ।।५०।।** बर्हिरसि देवंगमम् **इत्युपर्यादधाति ।।५१।। समूलैर्दर्भैः पालाशं खादिरं रोहितकं[९] वाष्टादशदारुमिध्मँ संनह्यति त्रींश्च परिधीन्यो यज्ञियो वृक्षस्तस्य ।। ५२।। स्थविष्ठो मध्यमो द्राघीयान् दक्षिणोऽणीयान् ह्रसिष्ठ उत्तरः ।। ५३।। उपरीध्ममादधाति ।।५४।।** ।।१।।

चन्द्रादर्शनेऽमावास्यायामिध्माबर्हिः संनह्यापराह्णे पिण्डपितृयज्ञेन चरन्ति प्राग्दक्षिणाचाराः ।।१।। प्राचीनाववीत्युत्तरतः पश्चाद्दक्षिणाग्नेः सँस्तीर्य पात्राणि प्रयुनक्ति पवित्रं कृष्णाजिनमुलूखलं मुसलँ शूर्पमुदकीमायवनं[१] दर्वीं स्फ्यमेकैकं दक्षिणंदक्षिणम् ।।२।। दक्षिणतोऽग्निष्ठमारुह्योदक्यामेकपवित्रमवधाय[२] पूरयित्वा बिलं निमार्ष्टि ।।३।। कृष्णाजिने पत्न्यवहन्ति परापावमविवेचम्[३] ।।४।। सकृत् फलीकरोति ।।५।। दक्षिणाग्नावुदकीमधिश्रित्य पवित्रान्तर्हितेऽप आनीय तण्डुलानोप्य मेक्षणेन प्रसव्यं पर्यायुवञ्जीवतण्डुलँ श्रपयति ।।६।। घृतेनानुत्पूतेन नवनीतेन वोत्पूतेन शृतमभिघार्य दक्षिणत उद्वासयति ।।७।। दक्षिणतःपुरस्ताद्दक्षिणाग्नेस्त्रिषु प्रक्रमेष्वपरिमिते वावकाशे स्फ्येन सकृत्परमुद्धत्यावसिञ्चति ।।८।।

अपयन्त्वसुराः पितृरूपा ये रूपाणि प्रतिमुच्याचरन्ति ।

परापुरो निपुरो ये हरन्त्यग्निष्टानस्मात्प्रणुनोत्तु लोकात् ।।

इत्यग्निं प्रणयति ।।९।। अग्रेणोद्धतमवोक्षिते सादयति ।।१०।। समूलेष्वन्यानुपसँयम्य त्रिः कर्षूमग्निं च प्रसव्यमुद्धावं त्रिः परिस्तीर्य कर्ष्वामुद्धवानास्तृणाति ।।११।। प्रतिपरिक्रम्य सव्यमन्वेकैकमाहरत्यायवनं दर्वींमोदनमाञ्जनमभ्यञ्जनमूर्णास्तुकमुदकुम्भम् ।।१२।। एत पितरो मनोजवा आगन्त पितरो मनोजवाः **इत्यावाहयति ।।१३।। परिश्रयेद्यद्यादित्यः सकाशे स्यात् ।।१४।।** परेतन पितरः सोम्यासः **इत्युदकुम्भेनाग्निं प्रसव्यं त्रिः परिषिञ्चन्पर्येति ।।१५।।** अया विष्ठा **इत्येतया निधायं[४] निधायं[४] त्रिरपरिषिञ्चन् प्रतिपर्येति ।।१६।।** शुन्धन्तां

---

९. P 1, 2, 3 रौहीतकं
१. Thus B,P; G उदङ्की°
२. G °द्योदङ्क्या°
३. B, P, G °मविवेचयन्
४. B, P निधाय निधाय

पितरः, शुन्धन्तां पितामहाः, शुन्धन्तां प्रपितामहाः **इति मूलदेशे बर्हिष-स्त्रीदनुकाञ्जलीन्निनयति** ।।१७।। **मेक्षणेनोपहत्य** सोमाय पितृमते स्वधा नमः **इति जुहोति** ।।१८।। अग्नये कव्यवाहनाय स्वधा नमः **इत्यसँसक्तां दक्षिणार्धपूर्वार्धे द्वितीयाँ हुत्वा मेक्षणमन्वध्यस्यति कञ्चुकानि पवित्रं च** ।।१९।। **दर्व्योद्धृत्योद्धवेषु पिण्डान्निदधाति । पितुर्नाम्ना** असावेतत्ते ये चात्र त्वानु तस्मै ते स्वधा **इति प्रथमम् । पितामहस्य नाम्ना स्थवीयाँसं मध्यमम् । प्रपितामहस्य नाम्ना स्थविष्ठं दक्षिणम्** ।।२०।। **द्वयोरपरयोर्नामिनी**[५] **गृह्णन् मूलदेशे लेपं निमार्ष्टि** ।।२१।। **लुप्यते जीवत्पितुः पिण्डनिधानं जीवत्पितामहस्य वा** ।।२२।। **न जीवन्तमतिदद्यात् । यदि दद्याद्येभ्य एव पिता दद्यात्तेभ्यो दद्यात्** ।। २३।। **यदि बन्धुनाम न विदितं**[६] स्वधा पितृभ्यः पृथिवीषद्भ्यः[७] **इति प्रथमं पिण्डं निदध्यात्** । स्वधा पितृभ्योऽन्तरिक्षसद्भ्यः **इति द्वितीयम् । स्वधा** पितृभ्यो दिविषद्भ्यः **इति तृतीयम्** ।।२४।। यात्र पितरः स्वधा तया यूयं मादयध्वम् **इति दक्षिणां दिशमन्वीक्षमाणो जपति** ।।२५।। येह[८] पितर ऊर्क्तस्यै वयं ज्योग्जीवन्तो भूयास्म **इत्युक्त्वावर्तते** ।। २६।। **आ तमितोरास्ते दक्षिणाग्निमन्वीक्षमाणः** ।।२७।। **व्यूष्मसु पिण्डेषु** अमीमदन्त पितरः **इति प्रतिपर्यावर्तते** ।।२८।। **वासस ऊर्णां दशां वाभ्युक्ष्य पिण्डदेशे निदधाति** ।।२९।। **लोमोत्तरवयसश्छित्त्वा वाससो वा दशाम्** अतो नोऽन्यत् पितरो मा योष्ट **इति निदध्यात्** ।।३०।। आङ्क्ष्वासौ[९] **इत्याञ्जनस्य प्रतिपिण्डं लेपं निमार्ष्टि** अभ्यङ्-क्ष्वासौ **इत्यभ्यञ्जनस्य** ।।३१।। मार्जयन्तां पितरः, मार्जयन्तां पिता-महाः, मार्जयन्तां प्रपितामहाः **इति प्रतिपिण्डं त्रीनुदकाञ्जलीन्निनयति** ।।३२।।

आधत्त पितरो गर्भं कुमारं पुष्करस्रजम् ।
यथा पुमान् भवेदिह तथा कृणुतोष्मपाः ।।

इति मध्यमं पिण्डं पत्नी प्राश्नीयात् ।।३३।। **अग्नावितरावादध्याद् ब्राह्मणो वा भक्षयेदप्सु वा गमयेत्** ।।३४।। **उद्धवाननुप्रहृत्य** वीरं नो दत्त पितरः इत्युदकीमवजिघ्रेत्[१०] ।।३५।। **अप उपस्पृश्य** नमो वः

५. Thus B, P; G द्वयोः परयो°
६. B, P विंदेत
७. B, P पृथिवीस°
८. B, P येहि
९. B, P अंक्ष्वासौ
१०. Thus B, P, G इत्युदंकी

पितरः **इति नमस्करोति ।।३६।।** एषा युष्माकं पितरः **इति दिशमनुदिशति ।** इमा अस्माकम् **इतीतराः ।।३७।।** जीवा वो जीवन्त इह सन्तः स्याम **इति जपति ।।३८।।** परेतन पितरः सोम्यासः **इति प्रवाहयति ।।३९।।** प्रजापते न त्वत् **इत्येतयोपोत्तिष्ठति ।।४०।।** अक्षन्नमीमदन्त **इति पुनरेति ।।४१।। मनस्वतीर्जपन्** अग्ने तमद्य **इत्येतया गार्हपत्यमुपतिष्ठते ।।४२।। अभ्युक्ष्य पात्राणि द्वेद्वे प्रतिपरिहरति ।।४३।। अप्यनाहिताग्निना कार्यः ।।४४।।** *।।२।।*

वेदं करोति वत्सज्ञुं प्रसव्यमावेष्ट्य तूलैर्दक्षिणोत्तरिणम् ।।१।। तूलेषु शुल्बं प्रतिनिधाय त्रिरावेष्ट्य संनह्यत्युत्तरमुत्तरं प्रदक्षिणम् ।।२।। प्रादेशमात्रे शुल्बात् परिवास्योत्करे मूलानि गमयति । तूलानि निदधाति ।।३।। वेदं कृत्वा वेदिं करोति पूर्वेद्युरमावास्यायामोत्तरस्मात् परिग्राहात् ।।४।। अन्तर्वेदि शाखायाः पलाशानि विशात्य मूलतः परिवास्य तस्यान्तर्वेदि न्यस्येत्[1] **।।५।। उपवेषं च कुर्यात्तेन च कपालान्युपदधाति ।।६।। दर्भमयं पवित्रं त्रिगुणरज्जु**[2] **शाखायामनुलोममवसृजेद् ग्रन्थिमकुर्वन् ।।७।।**

एता आचरन्तीर्मधुमद्दुहानाः प्रजावरीर्यशसे विश्वरूपाः ।
बह्वीर्भवन्तीरुपजायमाना इह वो महेन्द्रो रमयतु गावः ।
इह व इन्द्रो रमयतु गावः

इत्यायतीरनुमन्त्रयते ।।८।। यवाग्वैतां रात्रीं यजमानोऽग्निहोत्रं जुहोति। तस्याः पिण्डं निदध्यात् ।।९।। परिस्तृणाति पूर्वमग्निमपरौ च ।।१०।। उत्तरतो गार्हपत्यस्य सँस्तीर्णे द्वेद्वे प्रयुनक्ति कुम्भ्यौ शाखापवित्रं निदाने दोहनं प्रोक्षणीम् ।।११।। बर्हिषः पवित्रे कुरुते प्रादेशमात्रे समे अछिन्नप्रान्ते[3] **।।१२।। ओषध्या** वैष्णवे स्थः **इति छिनत्ति ।।१३।।** विष्णोर्मनसा पूते स्थः **इत्यद्भिस्त्रिरनुमार्ष्टि ।।१४।। अपः स्रुच्यासिच्योत्तानौ पाणी कृत्वाङ्गुष्ठेनोपमध्यमया चादाय** देवो वः सवितोत्पुनातु **इत्येतया पच्छोऽप उत्पुनाति ।। १५ ।।** शुन्धध्वम् **इति पात्राणि प्रोक्षति ।।१६।। दोहनं निदाने गोदुहे प्रदाय** उपसृष्टां मे प्रब्रूताद्विहारं च गां चोपसृष्टामन्तरेण मा संचारिषुः **इति ब्रूयात्**

---

१. B, P न्यसेत्
२. B, P त्रिगुणा रज्जुः
३. B, P, G अच्छिन्नप्रान्ते

।।१७।। उपसृजामि **इत्युक्ते** पोषाय त्वा **इति वत्समवसृज्यमानमनुमन्त्रयते** ।।१८।।

अयक्ष्मा वः प्रजया सँसृजामि रायस्पोषेण बहुला भवन्तीः ।

इति संगछमानाम् ।।१९।। अदित्या रास्नासि **इति निदीयमानाम्** ।।२०।। उपसीदामि **इत्युक्ते**

ऊर्जं पयः पिन्वमाना घृतं च जीवा जीवन्तीरुप वः[४] सदेम[४] ।।

इति जपति ।।२१।। वसूनां पवित्रमसि **इति शाखापवित्रमादत्ते** । द्यौरसि पृथिव्यसि **इत्युखाम्** ।।२२।। मातरिश्वनो घर्मः **इत्यधिश्रयति**। **पवित्रमवदधाति** ।।२३।। **अन्वारभ्य वाचँ यछति** ।।२४।। **प्राक्सायं पवित्रमादधाति । तिर्यक् प्रातः** ।।२५।।

उत्सं दुहन्ति कलशं चतुर्बिलमिडां धेनुं मधुमतीँ स्वस्तये ।

तदिन्द्राग्नी पिन्वतां सूनृतावत्तद्यजमानममृतत्वे दधातु ।।

इति धाराघोषं जपति ।।२६।। **दुग्ध्वानयति कुम्भ्याम्** ।।२७।। द्यौश्चेमँ यज्ञं पृथिवी च संदुहातां धाता सोमेन सह वातेन वायुर्यजमानाय द्रविणं दधातु **इत्यासिच्यमाने जपति** ।।२८।। कामधुक्षः **इति पृछति** । अमूम्[५] **इतीतरः** ।।२९।। सा विश्वायुरस्त्वसौ **इति गोर्नाम गृह्णाति** । सा विश्वभूः **इति द्वितीयस्याम्** । सा विश्वकर्मा **इति तृतीयस्याम्** ।।३०।। **समानं दोहनम्** ।।३१।। **तिसृषु दुग्धासु** बहु दुग्धीन्द्राय देवेभ्यो हविः **इति त्रिरुक्त्वा वाचँ विसृजते** । महेन्द्राय **इति वा** ।।३२।। **विसृष्टवागनन्वारभ्य तूष्णीमुत्तरास्तिस्रो दोहयति** ।।३३।। हुतः स्तोकः **इति सर्वासु दुग्धासु जपति** ।।३४।।

संपृच्यध्वमृतावरीरूर्मिणा मधुमत्तमाः ।

पृञ्चतीः पयसा पयो मन्द्रा[६] धनस्य सातये ।।

इति दोहनसंक्षालनं कुम्भ्यामानयति ।।३५।। दृँह गा दृँह गोपतिं[७] मा[७] वो यज्ञपती[८] रिषत्[८] **इत्युदगुद्वासयति वर्त्म कुर्वन्** ।।३६।। **शीतीभूतमग्निहोत्रोच्छेषेण दध्ना** इन्द्राय त्वा भागँ सोमेनातनच्मि **इत्यातनक्ति** । महेन्द्राय **इति वा** ।।३७।। अदस्तमसि विष्णवे त्वा **इति यवाग्वाः पिण्डमवदधाति** ।।३८।। विष्णो हव्यँ रक्षस्व **इत्युपर्यादधाति** ।।३९।।

---

४. B, P वासदेम
५. B, P, 1, 2, 3 अमुम्
६. B, P मेंद्रा
७. P गोपतिर्मा
८. B, P यज्ञपतीर्षम्

आपो जागृत इति सोदकेनापिदधाति दारुपात्रेणायस्पात्रेण वा । यदि मृन्मयँ स्यात्तृणं दारु वान्तर्दध्यात् ।।४०।। प्रातर्दोहाय वत्सानपाकरोति ।।४१।। उपसर्जनप्रभृति समानमोद्वासनात् ।।४२।। गार्हपत्ये हवींषि श्रपयति । आहवनीये जुहोति ।।४३।। नाग्निभ्यो व्यावर्तेत । अविपरिहरन् कुर्यात् ।।४४।। शुल्बार्थे प्रदक्षिणँ शुल्बम् । रज्ज्वर्थे प्रदक्षिणा रज्जुः ।।४५।। प्रोक्षणमुत्पवनँ सँमार्जनमिति त्रिर्दर्भैः कुर्याद्वैहारिकाणि वैहारिकाणि ।।४६।। //३//

।। इति मानवसूत्रे प्राक्सोमे प्रथमोऽध्यायः ।।

KAUŚIKASŪTRA

Edited by
S. S. Bahulkar

INTRODUCTION

1. Background

A century has passed since Maurice Bloomfield published, for the first time, his critical edition of the Kauśikasūtra (=KauśS) in 1889[1]. The publication of this Sūtra was a landmark in the field of Vedic studies in general and the study of the Atharvaveda and its ancilliary literature in particular. The Sūtra is of prime importance as a tool for the interpretation of the hymns of the Atharvaveda, which are to be employed in various rites as laid down in the KauśS. It may be observed however that a very few scholars have paid serious attention to the study of the KauśS itself. The KauśS is perhaps the most obscure text among the Sūtra-literature. The ritualistic tradition—especially that of the genuinely Atharvanic rites—has no parallel in the ritualistic tradition of the first three Vedas. For more than eighty years after the publication of Bloomfield's edition, no exegetical text—either the Bhāṣya or the Paddhati on the KauśS—was accessible to scholars. Moreover, there is hardly any possibility of getting some help from the present-day Atharvavedins who are not much familiar with their tradition. For these reasons, the difficulties with this Sūtra have yet remained unsolved. During the last hundred years, a few scholars, such as Bloomfield[2], Caland[3], Haas[4], Weber[5] and Gonda[6] have

---

1. M. Bloomfield, *The Kauśikasūtra of the Atharvaveda*, *J. A. O. S.* XIV, 1890, Reprint, Motilal Banarasidass, Delhi, 1972.
2. M. Bloomfield, *Hymns of the Atharvaveda*, *SBE* XLII, Oxford, 1897.
3. W. Caland, *Altindisches Zauberritual*, Amsterdam, 1900.
4. E. Haas, *Die Heirathsgebrauche der alten Inder, nach den Gṛhyasūtra, Indische studien V.*
5. A. Weber, *Zwei Vedische Texte über Omina und Portenta*, Berlin, 1859.
6. J. Gonda, *Savayajñas*, Amsterdam, 1965.

translated some portions of the KauśS. Nevertheless, no complete and authentic translation of the KauśS has been done so far. C.R. Lanman observed in this connection : "As I have more than once said, no one ought to be so well able to give a trustworthy translation of a difficult text as the man who has made a good edition of it; and for this reason one must regret that Bloomfield did not give us—in the natural sequence of the sūtras—as good a version as he was at the time able to make, instead of the detached bits of interpretation which are scattered through the notes of SBE xlii[7]." Caland translated the Kaṇḍikās 7 to 52—the genuinely Atharvanic portion—in his *Altindisches Zauberritual.* However, he was not satisfied with his effort. Although Bloomfield has furnished valuable information in the form of cross-references to the identical verses in other Saṁhitās and excerpts from the exegetical literature on the KauśS, the source-material given in his edition was too little to understand the most obscure ritual as well the special characteristics of the domestic rites in the Atharvaveda-tradition. Before taking up a translation of the KauśS, it is essential to consult the exegetical material on this Sūtra, which was not easily available till recently.

In 1967, the Tilak Maharashtra Vidyapeeth, Pune launched a project of KauśS and entrusted the work to the editorial board consisting of five members, viz., Dr. H. R. Diwekar, Acharya V. P. Limaye, Dr. R. N. Dandekar, Dr. C. G. Kashikar and Dr. V. V. Bhide. The editorial board soon realized that in order to prepare a revised critical edition and translation of the Sūtra, it was necessary first to bring out critical editions of Dārila's Bhāṣya and Keśava's Paddhati on that Sūtra. The editorial board, therefore, worked upon those two treatises and brought out the critical editions of the same in 1972 and 1982 respectively, as the first and the second part of the research-project. After 1982, the work of preparing a critical edition was assigned to the Balamukunda Sanskrit Mahavidyalaya. The work of collecting MSS and other material and of the collation was started. Here is presented a specimen of the critical edition of the first Adhyāya of the KauśS for the criticism of scholars.

7. *Atharvaveda Saṁhitā,* English trans. by W. D. Whitney, *H. O. S.* Vol. VII, reprint, Motilal Banarasidass, Delhi, 1971, Vol. I, General Introduction, p. lxxvi.

2. MSS and other material

The present edition is based on nine MSS of the KauśS seven of which have been used for the first time. Besides, there is some other source-material : Dārila's Bhāṣya, Keśava's Paddhati and Sāyaṇa's commentary on the Atharvaveda in which the sūtras are cited. Moreover, other commentaries on the KauśS viz., the Daśakarmāṇi and the Ātharvaṇapaddhati, which were used by Bloomfield, have also been consulted. The Prayogadīpa of Devabhadra, the Prayogabhānu of Raviśaṅkara Nāgara and a Sthālīpākaprayoga by some unknown authority have also been taken into consideration. These Prayoga-texts were probably not available to Bloomfield. These texts throw light on the actual performance of the ritual and thereby provide more help for understanding the Sūtra.

i) Description of MSS

1) Bh_1 - No. 4 of 1866-68, Bhandarkar Oriental Research Institute (BORI), Pune.
2) Bh_2 - No. 150 of 1879-80, BORI, Pune; used by Bloomfield and designated as Bü.
3) Bh_3 - No. 5 of 1866-68, BORI, Pune.
4) Bh_4 - No. 9 of 1870-71, BORI, Pune (incomplete); used by Bloomfield and designated as P.
5) G - No. 4185, Gore collection, Vaidika Saṁśodhana Maṇḍala, Pune.
6) B_1 - No. 7596, Oriental Institute, Baroda.
7) B_2 - No. 397, Oriental Institute, Baroda.
8) V_1 - No. 40392, Sarasvati Bhavana Library, Sampūrṇānanda Saṁskṛta Viśvavidyālaya, Varanasi.
9) V_2 - No. 41219, Sarasvati Bhavana Library, Sampūrṇānanda Saṁskṛta Viśvavidyālaya, Varanasi.

While it is not possible to describe at length the characteristics of the MSS and their groupings, a brief comment may be made on those lines. Generally, the readings in Bh_1 and G are identical with each other and seem to be more close to what may be called the genuine text of the Sūtra. Other MSS except V_2 form a broad second group where they are at variance with the first group as well as with each other at certain places. V_2 is a modern copy of Saṁvat 1992 (i.e. 1946 A. D.), beautifully written but cannot be treated as authentic, for it has certain readings, unique to itself, some of which are identical with the emendations made by Bloomfield as mere conjectures.

ii) Other Material

1) D - Dārila's Bhāṣya, *Kauśikasūtradārilabhāṣya;* Tilak Maharashtra Vidyapeeth, Pune, 1972.
2) K - Keśava's Kauśikapaddhati; *Keśavakṛtā Kauśika-paddhatiḥ,* T. M.V, Pune, 1982.
3) S - Sāyaṇa's commentary on the Atharvaveda in *Atharvaveda with Sāyaṇa's commentry,* Vols. I - IV, Hoshiarpur, 1960-1964.
4) Bl. - Bloomfield's edition of Kauśikasūtra *J. A. O. S. XIV,* 1890.

other material, namely, the Paddhatis and Prayogas have been consulted but not mentioned in the present edition.

3. The Present Edition

The present editon may be claimed as a step forward in the study of the Kauśikasūtra. While collating the MSS, it was observed that the readings or emendations in Bloomfield's edition will have to be re-considered and corrected at certain places. Out of the MSS used for his and the present edition, the MSS having genuine readings will have to be selected and their grouping will have to be made. It is also expedient to re-consider the punctuation of the Sūtra Bloomfield has made; the sautra-mantras which are cited in the Sakalapāṭha and which could not be traced by Bloomfield may be traced in the newly available Vedic texts, particularly, the Paippalāda Saṁhitā in its Kashmirian and Orissan recensions. Bloomfield has supplied explanatory notes along with the variants in the foot-notes. Instead, it is thought advisable to give exegetical notes in the appendix. In his edition, Bloomfield has numbered the Kaṇḍikās irrespective of the Adhyāya-division, i.e. Kaṇḍikās 1-141 and has consequently adopted only two divisions, namely, Kaṇḍikās and sūtras. It is not proper to ignore the traditional Adhyāya-division, . Therefore, a threefold division of the text will be adopted, namely, Adhyāya, Kaṇḍikā and sūtra[8].

Below are given the tables showing the difference between Bloomfield's edition and the present one:

i) Revised readings and emendations

Bloomfield's edition	Revised edition
ब्राह्मणविधिः (1.4)	ब्राह्मणं विधिः (I.1.4)
दक्षिणप्रत्यगपवर्गं (1.16)	दक्षिणाप्रत्यगपवर्गं (I.1.17)
व्रतेन त्वं (1.34)	व्रतेन त्वां (I.1.37)
अधिशृत्य (2.31)	अधिश्रित्य (I.2.31)
दघातु (4.1)	दधाति (I.4.1)
अनुख्यः (4.2)	अनुक्षः (I.4.2)
जिगासि (4.2)	जिगाय (I.4.2)
प्रजावती (5.2)	प्रजापती (I.5.2)
पार्वणौ होमौ (5.4)	पार्वणहोमौ (I.5.4)
हव्यमूहिषे । अया नो (5.13)	हव्यमूहिष आ नो (I.5.13)
भक्ष्याणि (7.15)	भक्षाणि (I.7.15)
मित्येका तदेव (9.1)	मित्येका उत देवाः (I.9.1)
शंतातीयं शिवा नः (9.4)	शंतातीयं च यद्यन्तरिक्षे पुनर्मैत्विन्द्रियं शिवा नः (I.9.3)
सवितृप्रसूतः भवान् (9.9)	सवितृप्रसूतः कुरुतां भवान् (I.9.8)

ii) Division of sūtras

Bloomfield's edition	Revised edition
1.9	I.1.9, 10
1.19	I.1.21, 22
1.35	I.1.38, 39
3.9, 10	I.3.9
5.8, 9	I.5.8
9.1, 2	I.9.1

8. C. R. Lanman has noted the traditional division and has made a concordance of both the divisions. C. R. Lanman, *op. cit*, p. 1012.

iii) Punctuation-marks (daṇḍa) to denote the end of the sūtra

Bloomfield's edition	Revised edition
शान्तानामिति ॥19॥एतावाज्या-भागौ ॥20॥ (3.19, 20)	शान्तानाम् ॥8॥ इत्येतावाज्यभागौ ॥19॥ (I.3.18, 19)
बर्हिराज्यशेषेऽनक्ति पृथिव्यै ..... (6.5)	बर्हिराज्यशेषेऽनक्ति ॥5॥ पृथिव्यै ..... (I.6.5, 6)
दिवे त्वेत्यग्रम् ॥5॥ एवं त्रिः ॥6॥ (6.5, 6)	दिवे त्वेत्यग्रमेवं त्रिः ॥6॥ (I.6.6)
सपर्येण्या अन्ये देवाः । (6.26)	सपर्येण्या अन्ये । देवा (I.6.27)

4. Method of reference adopted in the present edition

Abbreviations

AVŚ Atharvrveda, Śaunakasaṁhitā

AVP/nxl Atharvrveda, Paippalādasaṁhitā (Kashmir recension)

The references to the mantras, given in brackets without mentioning the text are from AVŚ.

ACKNOWLEDGMENTS

I am grateful to Dr. C. G. Kashikar who made valuable suggestions and enlightened me on revising the text of the KauśS. I thank the authorities of the libraries, who kindly made the MSS available to me. I should also express my sense of gratitude towards Pt. Radhey Shyamaji Shastri who has constantly been encouraging me to pursue this project.

[कौशिकसूत्रम्]

[प्रथमोऽध्यायः ।।]

।। ॐ ।।

अथ विधिं वक्ष्यामः ।।१।। स पुनराम्नाय[1]प्रत्ययः ।।२।। आम्नायः पुनर्मन्त्राश्च ब्राह्मणानि च ।।३।। तद्यथा ब्राह्मणं[2] विधिरेवं कर्मलिङ्गा मन्त्राः ।।४।। तथान्यार्थाः ।।५।। तथा ब्राह्मणलिङ्गा मन्त्राः ।।६।। तदभावे संप्रदायः ।।७।। प्रमुक्तत्वाद् ब्राह्मणानाम् ।।८।। यज्ञं व्याख्यास्यामः[3] ।।९।। देवानां पितृणां च ।।१०।। प्राङ्मुख उपांशु करोति ।।११।। यज्ञोपवीती देवानाम् ।।१२।। प्राचीनावीती पितृणाम् ।।१३।। प्रागुदग्वा देवानाम् ।।१४।। दक्षिणा पितृणाम् ।।१५।। प्रागुदगपवर्गं देवानाम् ।।१६।। दक्षिणा[4]प्रत्यगपवर्गं पितृणाम् ।।१७।। सकृत्कर्म पितृणाम् ।।१८।। त्र्यवरार्ध्यं देवानाम् ।।१९।। यथादिष्टं वा ।।२०।। अभिदक्षिणमाचारो देवानाम्[5] ।।२१।। प्रसव्यं पितृणाम् ।।२२।। स्वाहाकारवषट्कारप्रदाना देवाः ।।२३।। स्वधाकारनमस्कारप्रदानाः पितरः ।।२४।। उपमूललूनं बर्हिः पितृणाम् ।।२५।। पर्वसु देवानाम् ।।२६।। प्र यच्छ[6] पर्शुम् (१२.३.३१) इति दर्भाहाराय दात्रं प्रयच्छति ।।२७।। ओषधीर्दान्तु पर्वन् (१२.३.३१) इत्युपरि पर्वणां लूत्वा तूष्णीमाहृत्योत्तरतोऽग्नेरुपसादयति ।।२८।। नाग्निं विपर्यावर्तेत ।।२९।। नान्तरा यज्ञाङ्गानि

---

1. Thus Bh_1, Bh_2 and G; Bh_3, Bh_4, B_1, B_2, V_1, V_2 आम्नायः
2. Thus Bh_1 and G; Bh_3, Bh_4, B_1, B_2, V_1, V_2, Bl. ब्राह्मणविधिः Bl. has not noted the variant.
3. Bl. treats यज्ञं....पितृणां च as one sūtra. Separation on the basis of D.
4. Thus all MSS except V_2 which has दक्षिण°; Bl. दक्षिण°
5. B_1 treats 21 and 22 as one sutra.
6. So all MSS except V_2 प्रयच्छ°

व्यवेयात् ।।३०।। **दक्षिणं जानु**[7] **प्रभुज्य जुहोति** ।।३१।। **या पूर्वा पौर्णमासी**[8] **सानुमतिर्योत्तरा सा राका** ।।३२।। **या पूर्वामावास्या सा सिनीवाली योत्तरा सा कुहूः** ।।३३।। **अद्योपवसथ इत्युपवत्स्यद्-भक्त**[9]**मश्नाति** ।।३४।। **मधुलवणमांसमाष**[10]**वर्जम्** ।।३५।। ममाग्ने वर्चः[11] (५.३.१) **इति समिध**[12] **आधाय व्रतमुपैति** ।।३६।। व्रतेन त्वां[13] व्रतपते (७.७४.४) **इति वा** ।।३७।। **ब्रह्मचारी व्रती**[14] ।।३८।। **अधः शयीत** ।।३९।। **प्रातर्हुतेऽग्नौ** कर्मणे वां वेषाय वां[15] सुकृताय वाम् **इति पाणी प्रक्षाल्यापरेणाग्नेर्दर्भानास्तीर्य तेषूत्तरमानडुहं रोहितं चर्म**[16] **प्राग्ग्रीव**[17]**मुत्तरलोम**[18] **प्रस्तीर्य पवित्रे कुरुते** ।।४०।। **दर्भावप्रछिन्न**[19]**प्रान्तौ**[20] **प्रक्षाल्यानुलोममनुमार्ष्टि** विष्णोर्मनसा पूते स्थः **इति** ।।४१।। *।।१।।*

त्वं भूमिमत्येष्योजसा त्वं वेद्यां सीदसि चारुरध्वरे ।
त्वां पवित्रमृषयो भरन्तस्त्वं पुनीहि दुरितान्यस्मत् ।।

(१९.३३.३) **इति पवित्रे अन्तर्धाय हविर्निर्वपति** देवस्य त्वा सवितुः प्रसवेऽश्विनोर्बाहुभ्यां पूष्णो हस्ताभ्यामग्नये[1-] जुष्टं निर्वपामि **इति** ।।१।। **एवम्** अग्नीषोमाभ्याम् **इति** ।।२।। इन्द्राग्निभ्याम् **इत्यमावास्यायाम्** ।।३।। **नित्यं पूर्वमाग्ने**[1]**यम्**[2] ।।४।। **निरुप्तं पवित्राभ्यां प्रोक्षति** अमुष्मै त्वा जुष्टम् **इति यथादेवतम्** ।।५।। **उलूखलमुसलं**[3] **शूर्पं प्रक्षालितं चर्मण्याधाय व्रीहीनुलूखल**[4] **ओप्या-**

---

7. Bh_1 दक्षिणजानु; V_1 दक्षिणं जानुं
8. Bh_1 पूर्णमासी
9. Bh_2 °वस्यद्°; B_1 °वश्यद्°; V_1 °वत्स्येद्°; D °वसथ्य; but reads correctly as °वत्स्येद्° in the gloss.
10. B_1 °मासमारव°
11. Bh_3 Bh_4 B_2 वर्च्चं
12. Bh_3 °समिधमाधाय
13. Thus all MSS except B_1 and Bl. which have °त्वं. The variant त्वां occurs in AVŚ Saṁhitā itself.
14. Sūtra. separated on the basis of D(text)
15. Bh_1 repeats वेषाय वां
16. Bh_3, Bh_4, B_2 चर्म्म
17. Bh_1, G, B_1 लोमोपस्तीर्य; D लोम पस्तीर्य
18. G प्राग्रीव
19. V_2 °वप्रच्छिन्न°
20. Bh_3 °प्रांक्तौ; Bh_3 °प्रान्तो
1-1. V_1 repeats wrongly the portion °ये जुष्ट ... पूर्वमाग्ने°
2. Bh_1, G °माग्नियं; Bh_3 °माग्नय°
3. B_1 उलूषल°
4. B_1 °नुलूषल

वघ्नंस्त्रिर्हविष्कृता[5] वाचं विसृजति[6] हविष्कृदा[7] द्रवेहि इति ।।६।। अपहत्य सुफलीकृता[8]न्कृत्वा त्रिः प्रक्षाल्य तण्डुलान् अग्ने चरुर्यज्ञियस्त्वाध्यरुक्षत् (११.१.१६) इति चरुमधिदधाति।।७।। शुद्धाः पूताः (११.१.१६) इत्युदकमासिञ्चति ।।८।। ब्रह्मणा शुद्धाः (११.१.१८) इति तण्डुलान् ।।९।। परि त्वाग्ने पुरं वयम् (७. ७१.१) इति त्रिः पर्यग्नि करोति ।।१०।। नेक्षणेन त्रिः प्र[9]दक्षिणमुदायौति ।।११।। अत्त ऊर्ध्वं यथाकामम् ।।१२।। उत्तरतोऽग्नेरुपसादयतीध्मम् ।।१३।। उत्तरं बर्हिः ।।१४।। अग्नये त्वा जुष्टं प्रोक्षामि इतीध्मम् ।।१५।। पृथिव्यै इति बर्हिः ।।१६।। दर्भमुष्टिमभ्युक्ष्य पश्चादग्नेः प्रागग्रं निदधाति ऊर्णम्रदं प्रथस्व स्वासस्थं देवेभ्यः इति ।।१७।। दर्भाणामपादाय ऋषीणां[10] प्रस्तरोऽसि (१६. २.६) इति दक्षिणतोऽग्नेर्ब्रह्मासनं निदधाति ।।१८।। पुरस्तादग्नेरास्तीर्य तेषां मूलान्यपरेषां प्रान्तैरवछादय[11]न्परिसर्पति दक्षिणेनाग्निमा[12]पश्चार्द्धात् ।।१९।। परि स्तृणीहि (७.९९. १) इति संप्रेष्यति ।।२०।। देवस्य त्वा सवितुः प्रसवेऽश्विनोर्बाहुभ्यां पूष्णो हस्ताभ्यां प्रसूतः प्रशिषा परिस्तृणामि इति ।।२१।। एवमुत्तरतोऽयुजो धातून् कुर्वन् ।।२२।। यत्र समागछन्ति[13] तद्दक्षिणोत्तरं करोति ।।२३।। स्तीर्णं प्रोक्षति हविषां त्वा जुष्टं प्रोक्षामि इति ।।२४।। नानभ्युक्षितं संस्तीर्णमुपयोगं लभेत ।।२५।। नैध्मोऽभ्याधानम् ।।२६।। नानुत्पूतं हविः ।।२७।। नाप्रोक्षितं यज्ञाङ्गम् ।।२८।। तस्मिन्प्रक्षालितोपवातानि निदधाति ।।२९ ।। स्रुवमा[14]ज्यधानीं च ।।३०।। विलीनपूतमाज्यं गृहीत्वाधिश्रित्य[15] पर्यग्नि कृत्वोदगुद्वास्य पश्चादग्नेरुपसाद्योदगग्राभ्यां पवित्राभ्यामुत्पुनाति ।।३१।। विष्णोर्मनसा पूतमसि ।।३२।। देवस्त्वा सवितोत्पुनातु ।।३३।। अछिद्रेण[16] त्वा पवित्रेण शतधारेण सहस्रधारेण[17]

---

5. Bh_1 G हविःकृता 6. Bh_4 विसृजते
7. Bh_1 हविःकृदा
8. V_1 सुफलीकृतां 9. D (text) त्रिष्प्र°
10. Bh_4 °मपादायऽऋषीणां
11. So all MSS including V_2 which elsewhere has °च्छ°
12. V_2 दक्षिणेणाग्निना
13. So emended by Bl.; all MSS and D(text) °गछति; V_2 °गच्छति
14. V_1 स्रुव आज्य°
15. So all MSS except V_1 and Bl. °धिशृत्य
16. So all MSS except V_2 अच्छिद्रेण
17. Bh_3, B_2 सहस्रा°

सुप्वो[18]त्पुनामि **इति तृतीयम्** ।।३४।। **तूष्णीं चतुर्थम्** ।।३५।। **शृतं हविरभिघारयति** मध्वा समञ्जन्घृतवत्कराथ **इति** ।।३६।। **अभिघार्योदञ्चमुद्वा[19]सयति** उद्वासयाग्ने:[20] शृतमकर्म[21] हव्यमा सीद पृष्ठममृतस्य धाम (पै. ५.१६.३) **इति** ।। ३७ ।। **पश्चादाज्यस्य निधायालंकृत्य समानेनोत्पुनाति** ।।३८।। अदारसृत् (१.२०.१) **इत्यवेक्षते** ।।३९।। उत्तिष्ठत (७.७२.१-३) **इत्यैन्द्रम्** ।।४०।। अग्निर्भूम्याम् (१२.१.१९-२१) **इति तिसृभिरुपसमादधाति** अस्मै क्षत्राणि (७.७८.२) एतमिध्मम् (१०.६.३५) **इति वा** ।।४१।। ।।२।।

युनज्मि त्वा ब्रह्मणा दैव्येन हव्यायास्मै वोढवे जातवेदः ।
इन्धानास्त्वा सुप्रजसः सुवीरा ज्योग्जीवेम बलिहृतो वयं ते

इति[1] ।।१।। **दक्षिणतो जाङ्मायन[2]मुदपात्रमुपसाद्याभिमन्त्रयते**

तथोदपात्रं धारय यथाग्रे ब्रह्मणस्पतिः ।
सत्यधर्मा अदीधरद्देवस्य सवितुः सवे **इति** ।।२।।

अथोदकमासिञ्चति

इहेत देवीरमृतं वसाना हिरण्यवर्णा अनवद्यरूपाः ।
आपः समुद्रो वरुणश्च[3] राजा संपातभागान् हविषो जुषन्ताम् ।।
इन्द्रप्रशिष्टा वरुणप्रसूता आपः[4] समुद्राद्दिवमुद्वहन्तु ।
इन्द्रप्रशिष्टा वरुणप्रसूता दिवस्पृथिव्याः श्रियमावहन्तु

इति ।।३।। ऋतं त्वा सत्येन परिषिञ्चामि जातवेदः[5] **इति सह हविर्भिः**[6] **पर्युक्ष्य जीवाभिराचम्योपोत्थाय**[7] **वेदप्रपद्भिः प्रपद्यत** ओं प्रपद्ये भूः प्रपद्ये भुवः प्रपद्ये स्वः प्रपद्ये जन[8]त्प्रपद्ये **इति** ।।४।। **प्रपद्य**

---

18. So emended by Bl.; all MSS except V_2 read सुपो°; V_2 सुप्वो°
19. Bh_1, Bh_2, Bh_3, Bh_4, G, B_1, B_2 °दन्व उ°; V_1, V_2 °दन्व मु°
20. Bh_2 and V_2 °सयाग्ने
21. Bh_4 शृतकर्म
1. Bh_1, B_1, V_1 तव इति; G तव इति, corrected to तवेति
2. Bh_3, B_2 जाङ्मयन; G seems to read जाङ्मायन corrected to जाङ्म°
3. Bh_2 and B_1 वरुणस्य
4. So Bh_1, Bh_3, G, B_2; Bh_2 and V_1 अपं, Bl. अपः
5. Bh_1 जातवेदस
6. Bh_1 सहविर्भिः; G originally सहविर्भिः, corrected to सहहविर्भिः; D(text) सहविर्भिः and ह added in the margin.
7. Bh_2, Bh_4, G, B_1, V_2 पोछाय
8. Bh_1 जन; Bh_2, B_1 जनः; V_1 जनं

पश्चात्स्तीर्णस्य दर्भानास्तीर्य अहे दैधिषव्योदतस्तिष्ठान्यस्य सदने सीद योऽस्मत्पाकतरः **इति ब्रह्मासन**[9]**मन्वीक्षते** ।।५।। निरस्तः पराग्वसुः सह पाप्मना निरस्तः सोऽस्तु[10] योऽस्मान्द्वेष्टि यं च वयं द्विष्मः **इति दक्षिणा तृणं निरस्यति** ।।६।। **तदन्वालभ्य जपति** इदमहमर्वाग्वसोः सदने सीदाम्यृतस्य सदने सीदामि सत्यस्य सदने सीदामीष्टस्य सदने सीदामि [11]-पूर्तस्य सदने सीदामि-[11] मामृषदेव बर्हिः स्वासस्थं त्वाध्यासदेयमूर्ण-म्रदमनभिशोकम्।।७।। विमृग्वरीम् (१२.१.२९) **इत्युपविश्या**[12]**सनीयं ब्रह्मजपं**[13] **जपति बृहस्पतिर्ब्रह्मा ब्रह्मसदन आसिष्यत**[14] **बृहस्पते**[15] यज्ञं गोपाय यदुदुद्वत[16] उन्निवतः[17] शकेयम् **इति** ।।८।। **दर्भैः स्रुवं निर्मृज्य** निष्टप्तं रक्षो निष्टप्ता अरातयः प्रत्युष्टं रक्षः प्रत्युष्टा अरातयः **इति प्रतप्य**[18] **मूले स्रुवं गृहीत्वा जपति**

विष्णोर्हस्तोऽसि दक्षिणः पूष्णा दत्तो बृहस्पतेः[19] ।
तं त्वाहं स्रुवमाददे देवानां हव्यवाहनम् ।।
अयं स्रुवो विदधाति होमाञ्छताक्षर[20]छन्दसा जागतेन ।
सर्वा यज्ञस्य समनक्ति विष्ठा[21] बार्हस्पत्येष्टिः शर्मणा दैव्येन ।।
इति ।।९।।

ओं भूः शं भूत्यै त्वा गृह्णे भूतये **इति प्रथमं ग्रहं गृह्णाति** ।।१०।। ओं भुवः शं पुष्ट्यै त्वा गृह्णे पुष्टये **इति द्वितीयम्** ।।११।। **ओं स्वः शं त्वा** गृह्णे सहस्रपोषाय **इति तृतीयम्** ।।१२।। **ओं** जनच्छं[22] त्वा

---

9. Bh_1 ब्रह्मासन°; corrected to आत्मा° in the margin
10. V_1 सो अस्तु
11-11. Bh_3 omits
12. D(text) उपविशति
13. B_1 ब्रह्मजपं, corrected to आत्म°
14. So emended by Bl.; MSS आशिष्यते; V_2 has आशिष्यते, corrected to आसि°
15. Bh_3 बृहस्पतेर्यज्ञं
16. So emended by Bl.; Bh_1 पदुद्यत; Bh_3 यदुवृत; Bh_2, Bh_4, B_1 य उदुद्वत; V_1 V_2 यदुद्वत
17. So emended by Bl.; Bh_1 उन्ममत्तः, Bh_3, Bh_4, B_2, उन्नमतः, B_1 उन्निमतः corrected to उन्नमतः; V_1 उन्नियतः, V_2 only has उन्निवतः
18. Bl. puts the punctuation-mark प्रतप्य; Bh_1 and G put it after जपति. D(text) reads the sūtra contineously as ... प्रतप्य मूले गृहीत्वा जपति विष्णोर्हस्तोसीति
19. Bh_2 and B_1 बृहस्पते
20. Bh_1 and G put *avagraha* between छताक्षर and छन्दसा. Bh_2 छताक्षर, corrected to °क्षरः; V_2 छताक्षरः
21. Bh_1, Bh_2, Bh_4, B_1, V_1 विष्टा
22. So Bl.; MSS and D(text) जनछं

गृह्णेऽपरिमितपोषाय **इति चतुर्थम्** ।।१३।। **राजकर्माभिचारिकेषु** अमुष्य त्वा प्राणाय गृह्णेऽपानाय व्यानाय समानायोदानाय **इति पञ्चमम्** ।।१४।। अग्नावग्निः, हृदा पूतम् (४.३९.९-१०), पुरस्ताद्युक्तः (५.२९.१), यज्ञस्य चक्षुः (२.३५.५) **इति जुहोति**[23] ।।१५।। **पश्चादग्नेर्मध्यदेशे समानत्र**[24] **पुरस्ताद्धोमान्** ।।१६।। **दक्षिणेनाग्निमुदपात्र**[25] **आज्याहुतीनां संपातानानयति** ।।१७।। **पुरस्ताद्धोम आज्यभागः**[26] **संस्थितहोमः समृद्धिः शान्तानाम्** ।।१८।। **इत्येता**[27]-**वाज्यभागौ** ।।१९।। //३//

वृष्णे बृहते स्वर्विदे अग्नये शुल्कं[1] हरामि त्विषीमते ।
स न स्थिरान्बलवतः कृणोतु ज्योक्च नो जीवातवे दधाति[2] ।।
(cf. पै १९.५२.६)

अग्नये स्वाहा **इत्युत्तरपूर्वार्ध आग्नेयमाज्यभागं जुहोति** ।।१।। **दक्षिणपूर्वार्धे सोमाय**

त्वं सोम दिव्यो नृचक्षाः सुगाँ[3] अस्मभ्यं पथो अनुक्षः[4] ।
अभि नो गोत्रं विदुष इव नेषोऽछा[5] नो वाचमुशतीं जिगाय[6]।।
(पै १.५१.३)

सोमाय स्वाहा **इति** ।।२।। **मध्येहविः** ।।३।। **उपस्तीर्याज्यं संहताभ्यामङ्गुलिभ्यां द्विर्हविषोऽवद्यति मध्यात्पूर्वार्धाच्च** ।।४।। **अवत्तमभिघार्य**

---

23. D(text) omits this word, however reads it in the gloss.
24. Bh_1, G समानात्र
25. B_1 पात्रमाज्या, corrected to पात्र आज्या; Bh_2 and D(text) पात्रमाज्या
26. Bh_1, G पुरस्ताद्धोमाज्यभागसंस्थितहोम समृद्धि।। शांता; D(text) पुरस्ताद्धोमाज्यभागसंस्थितहोमः समृधिः
27. Bl. puts a punctuation-mark after शान्तानामिति to separate the sūtra D(text) has इति after शान्तानाम् and also before आज्यभागौ. The separation of the sūtras here can probably be supported by Dārila's gloss: इति ।। शांतानुकर्षणार्थः emended as इतिः शांतानुकर्षणार्थः

1. Bh_1, Bh_2 शुक्लं, B_1 शुक्तं, corrected to शुक्रं in the margin
2. So all MSS except V_2 which reads दघातु. Bl. emends it as दधातु. The verse at AVP. 19.52.6 reads बलिरुचः and दधातु
3. Bh_1, G सुगमस्मभ्यं; B_1 सुगं
4. Bh_1, Bh_2, Bh_3, B_2, V_1 अनुक्षः B_2 and V_2 अनुक्षः corrected to अनुख्यः 5. B_1 नेशो; V_2 नेषोच्छा
6. So Bh_1 and G; Bh_2, B_1 जिगासि corrected to जिगाय; The verse occurs at AVP with variants where it reads जिगासि

द्विर्हविः प्रत्यभिघारयति ।।५।। यतो यतोऽवद्यति तदनुपूर्वम् ।।६।। एवं सर्वाण्यवदानानि ।।७।। अन्यत्र सौविष्टकृतात्[7] ।।८।। उदेनमुत्तरं[8]- नय (६.५.१) इति पुरस्ताद्धोमसंहतां पूर्वाम्[9] ।।९।। एवं पूर्वांपूर्वां संहतां जुहोति[10] ।।१०।। स्वाहान्ताभिः प्रत्यृचं होमाः ।।११।। यामुत्तरां-[8] मग्नेराज्यभागस्य जुहोति रक्षोदेवत्या सा यां दक्षिणतः सोमस्य पितृदेवत्या सा ।।१२।। तस्मादन्तरा होतव्या[11] देवलोक एव[12] हूयन्ते ।।१३।। यां हुत्वा पूर्वामपरां जुहोति सापक्रामन्ती[13] स पापीयान्यजमानो भवति ।।१४।। यां परांपरां[14] संहतां जुहोति साभिक्रामन्ती[15] स वसीयान्य[16]जमानो भवति ।।१५।। यामनग्नौ जुहोति सान्धा तया चक्षुर्यजमानस्य मीयते सोऽन्धंभावुको यजमानो[17] भवति ।।१६।। यां धूमो जुहोति सा तमसि हूयते सोऽरोचको यजमानो भवति ।।१७।। यां धूमे ज्योतिष्मति[18] जुहोति तया ब्रह्मवर्चसी[19] भवति तस्माज्ज्योतिष्मति[18] होतव्यम् ।।१८।। एवम् अस्मै क्षत्रम् (६.५४.२), अग्नीषोमौ इत्य[20]ग्नीषोमीयस्य ।।१९।। ।।४।।

अग्नीषोमा सवेदसा[1] सहूती[2] वनतं गिरः ।
स देवत्रा बभूवथुः ।।
युवमेतानि दिवि रोचनान्यग्निश्च सोम सक्रतू अधत्तम् ।
युवं सिन्धूँरभिशस्तेरवद्यादग्नीषोमावमुञ्चतं गृभीतान् ।।
अग्नीषोमा य आहुतिं[3] यो वां दाशाद्धविष्कृतिम्[4] ।
स[5] प्रजया सुवीर्यं विश्वमायुर्व्यश्नवत्[6] ।।

---

7. D(text) सौविष्टकृतत्वात्
8-8. V_1 omits the portion from (उदेनमुत्त)रं.....to यामुत्त(रामग्ने)
9. Bh_3 पूर्वं
10. This sūtra is wanting in D(text), but the gloss points to it.
11. Bh_1, G तस्मादन्तराऽहोतव्या
12. Bh_3, Bh_4, B_2, V_1 D(text) देवलोकमेव
13. Bh_4, B_2,V_1 क्रामंति
14. Bh_3 यां परां संहतां; B_1 परां परं
15. Bh_4, B_2, V_1 क्रामंति
16. So emended by Bl. MSS वशीयान्
17. B_1 जजमानो
18. Bh_1, V_1, V_2, D(text) ज्योतिष्मती
19. B_2 ब्रह्मवर्च्चसी
20. Bh_3 omits अग्नीषोमाविति
1. D(text) सवेदसमिति
2. B_2 सहुती 3. B_1 आहुतीं
4. B_1 हविःकृतिं 5. Bh_4 सः
6. B_1 has accent-marks for these verses; the accentuation (especially that of the real circumflex) resembles that occuring in the MS - Ch used by Bloomfield. See his note on the same portion.

इन्द्राग्नी रोचना दिवः परि वाजेषु भूषथः ।
तद्वां चेति प्र वीर्यम् ।।
श्नथद्वृत्रमुत सनोति वाजमिन्द्रा यो अग्नी सहुरी सपर्यात् ।
इरज्यन्ता वसव्यस्य भूरेः सहस्तमा[7] सहसा वाजयन्ता[8] ।।
इन्द्राग्नी अस्मान्रक्षतां यौ प्रजानां प्रजापती[9] ।
स प्रजया सुवीर्यं विश्वमायुर्व्यश्नवत् ।। (पै १६.३७.१)
गोमद्धिरण्यवद्वसु यद्वामश्वावदीमहे ।
इन्द्राग्नी तद्वनेमहि ।। स्वाहा **इति** ।।२।।

ऐन्द्राग्नस्य हविषोऽमावास्यायाम् ।।३।। **प्राक्स्विष्टकृतः पार्वणहोमौ**[10] **समृद्धिहोमाः काम्यहोमाश्च**[11] ।।४।। पूर्णा पश्चात् (७.८०.१) **इति पौर्णमास्याम्** ।।५।। यत्ते देवा अकृण्वन्भागधेयम् (७.७९.१) **इत्यमावास्यायाम्** ।।६।। आकूत्यै त्वा स्वाहा । कामाय त्वा स्वाहा । समृधे[12] त्वा स्वाहा । आकूत्यै त्वा कामाय त्वा समृधे त्वा स्वाहा ।
ऋचा स्तोमं समर्धय गायत्रेण रथन्तरम् ।
बृहद्गायत्रवर्तनि[13] ।। स्वाहा[14] ।।७।।

पृथिव्यामग्नये समनमन् (४.३९.१-८) **इति संनतिभिश्च** प्रजापते न त्वदेतान्यन्यः (७.८०.३) **इति च**[15] ।।८।। **उपस्तीर्याज्यं सर्वेषामुत्तरतः सकृत्सकृदवदाय द्विरवत्तमभिघारयति** ।।९।। **न हवींषि** ।।१०।।

आ देवानामपि पन्थामगन्म यच्छक्नवाम तदनुप्रवोढुम् ।
अग्निर्विद्वान्स यजात्स इद्धोता सोऽध्वरान्स ऋतून्कल्पयाति ।।
(१९.५९.३; cf. पै १९.४७.६)

---

7. Bh_3, B_2 सहस्र
8. Bh_2, B_2, V_1 वाजयंतां
9. So emended on the basis of the variant at AVŚ 10.1..21 and AVP 16.37.1ab; MSS and Bl. प्रजावती
10. So Bh_1, Bh_2, G, V_1, V_2, rest and Bl. पार्वणौ; D(text) प्राक्स्विष्टकृतौ पार्वणहोमौ and put a punctuation-mark.
11. Bh_4, B_1, B_2 काम्याश्च
12. V_2 समृद्धे
13. B_1 वर्छनि corrected to वर्तनि
14. Bh_1, Bh_4, G, B_1 have इति after स्वाहा
15. Bl. divides the sūtra after संनतिभिश्च; D(text) treats it as one sūtra.

अग्नये स्विष्टकृते[16] स्वाहा **इत्युत्तरपूर्वार्धेऽवयुतं हुत्वा सर्वप्रायश्चित्तीयान्होमाञ्जुहोति** ।।११।। स्वाहेष्टेभ्यः स्वाहा[17] । वषडनिष्टेभ्यः स्वाहा[18] । भेषजं स्विष्ट्यै स्वाहा । निष्कृतिर्दुरिष्ट्यै स्वाहा । दैवीभ्यस्तनूभ्यः स्वाहा ।

अयाश्चाग्नेऽस्यनभिशस्तिश्च[19] सत्यमित्त्वमया असि[20] ।

अयासा मनसा कृतोऽयास्य[21] हव्यमूहिष[22] आ नो[23] धेहि भेषजम् ।।

स्वाहा **इति।** ओं स्वाहा भूः स्वाहा भुवः स्वाहा स्वः स्वाहों भूर्भुवः स्वः स्वाहा **इति** ।।१२।। ।।५।।

यन्मे स्कन्नं मनसो जातवेदो यद्वास्कन्दद्धविषो यत्रयत्र ।

उत्प्रुषो विप्रुषः सं जुहोमि सत्याः सन्तु यजमानस्य कामाः ।।

स्वाहा **इति** ।।१।। यन्मे स्कन्नं, यदस्मृति (७.१०६.१) **इति च स्कन्नास्मृतिहोमौ** ।।२।। **यदद्य त्वा प्रयति** (७.९७) **इति संस्थितहोमाः**[1] ।।३।। मनसस्पते (७.९७.८) **इत्युत्तमं चतुर्गृहीतेन** ।।४।। **बर्हिराज्यशेषे**[2]**ऽनक्ति**[3] ।।५।। पृथिव्यै त्वा **इति मूलम्** अन्तरिक्षाय त्वा **इति मध्यं** दिवे त्वा **इत्यग्रमेवं त्रिः** ।।६।। सं बर्हिरक्तम् (७.९८) **इत्यनुप्रहरति**[4] **यथादेवतम्** ।।७।। **स्रुवमग्नौ धारयति** ।।८।। **यदाज्यधान्यां तत्संस्रावयति**

संस्रावभागास्तविषा[5] बृहन्तः प्रस्तरेष्ठा[6] बर्हिषदश्च देवाः ।

---

16. B_1 स्विष्टकृतये
17. This word is wanting in Bh_2 Bh_3, Bh_4, B_1
18. This word is wanting in Bh_4 B_1
19. Bh_1 G, V_1 श्चाग्नेः स्यनभिशस्तिश्च; Bh_3, B_2 शस्तीश्च
20. Bh_1 त्वमयाऽअसि
21. Bh_1, Bh_2, Bh_3, G, B_2 यास्मं; V_1 यास्म; Bh_4, B_1 यास्मां
22. V_1 मूहिषं; all other MSS have मूहिष; Bl. reads मूहिषे and gives a vertical stroke (daṇḍa) after that to denote the end of the hemistich.
23. So all MSS; Bl. emends it as अया नो

1. D(text) ओमः
2. D(text) and S on AVŚ 7.97 बर्हिराज्यशेषेणा
3. The sūtra is divided on the basis of D(text). Bl. has the sūtra running upto त्वेत्यग्रम्
4. Bh_1, G have a punctuation-mark after अनुप्रहरति AVŚ on 7.98 also has the sūtra upto अनुप्रहरति.
5. Bh_1, G भागाः हविषा; Bh_3, B_2 स्तहविषा; V_1 भागाः स्तविषा
6. Bh_2, B_1 प्रस्तरेष्टा; V_1 प्रस्तरेष्या

इमं यज्ञमभि विश्वे गृणन्तः स्वाहा देवा अमृता मादयन्ताम् ॥
(cf. पै २०.३४.२) **इति** ॥९॥

स्रुवोऽसि घृतादनिशितः[7] सपत्नक्षयणो दिवि षीद । अन्तरिक्षे सीद पृथिव्यां सीदोत्तरोऽहं भूयासमधरे मत्सपत्नाः **इति स्रुवं प्राग्दण्डं निदधाति** ॥१०॥

वि मुञ्चामि ब्रह्मणा जातवेदसमग्निं होतारमजरं रथस्पृतम्[8] ।
सर्वा देवानां जनिमानि विद्वान्यथाभागं वहतु हव्यमग्निः ॥
(पै १३.१०.१)

अग्नये स्वाहा **इति समिधमादधाति** ॥११॥ एधोऽसि (७.८९.४a) **इति द्वितीयां** समिदसि (७.८९.४b) **इति तृतीयाम्** ॥१२॥ तेजोऽसि (७.८९.४c) **इति मुखं विमार्ष्टि** ॥१३॥ **दक्षिणेनाग्निं त्रीन्विष्णुक्रमान्क्रमते** विष्णोः क्रमोऽसि (१०.५.२५-२७) **इति दक्षिणेन पादेनानुसंहरति सव्यम्** ॥१४॥ सूर्यस्यावृतम् (१०.५.३७) **इत्यभि-दक्षिणमावर्तते** ॥१५॥ अगन्म स्वः (१६.९.३,४) **इत्यादित्यमीक्षते** ॥१६॥

इन्द्रस्य वचसा वयं मित्रस्य वरुणस्य च[9] ।
ब्रह्मणा स्थापितं पात्रं पुनरुत्थापयामसि ॥

इत्यपरेणाग्निमुदपात्रं परिहृत्योत्तरेणाग्निम् आपो हि ष्ठा मयोभुवः (१.५) इति **मार्जयित्वा**[10] **बर्हिषि पत्न्याञ्जलौ**[11] **निनयति** समुद्रं वः प्र हिणोमि (१०.५.२३-२४) **इति** इदं जनासः (१.३२) **इति वा** ॥१७॥ वीरपत्न्यहं भूयासम् **इति मुखं विमार्ष्टि** ॥१८॥ व्रतानि व्रतपतये (**कौसू** ५.६.१६) **इति समिधमादधाति** ॥१९॥ सत्यं त्वर्तेन[12] **इति परिषिच्योदञ्चि**[13] **हविरुच्छिष्टान्युद्वासयति** ॥२०॥

---

7. Bh_1 दनीषतः; Bh_3, B_2, G दनिषीतः; Bh_4, V_1 दनिशीतः D probably observed the irregular division of the mantra : क्वचिन्मन्त्रस्य भागपाठः प्रमादात् (! भागः पाठप्रमादात्)
8. So emended by Bl. MSS रथस्मृतं
9. The first hemistich is found in AVŚ 6.85.2 ab = AVP. 19.6.2ab.
10. Bh_1 मार्जइत्वा
11. Bh_1 पत्न्यां अंजलौ; Bh_3, Bh_4, B_2 पत्न्यंजलौ; D(text) पत्न्या अंजलौ. Acc. to Bl. this is a case of a double sandhi.
12. Bh_1, G add परिषिञ्चामि जातवेद after त्वर्तेन
13. Bh_3 षिच्योदंन्नि; B_1 षिच्योदंति

पूर्णपात्रं दक्षिणा ।।२०।। नादक्षिणं हविः कुर्वीत यः कुरुते कृत्यामात्मनः कुरुत इति ब्राह्मणम् ।।२१।। अन्वाहार्यं ब्राह्मणान्भोजयति ।।२३।। यद्वै यज्ञस्यानन्वितं भवति तदन्वाहार्येणान्वाह्रियते ।।२५।। एतदन्वाहार्यस्यान्वाहार्यत्वम् ।।२६।। ईड्या वा अन्ये देवाः सपर्येण्या [14]-अन्ये[15] । देवा ईड्या देवा[16] ब्राह्मणाः सपर्येण्याः ।।२७।। यज्ञेनैवेड्यान्प्रीणात्यन्वाहार्येण सपर्येण्यान्[-14] ।।२८।। तेऽस्योभे प्रीता यज्ञे भवन्तीति ।।२९।। इमौ दर्शपूर्णमासौ व्याख्यातौ ।।३०।। दर्शपूर्णमासाभ्यां पाकयज्ञाः ।।३१।। अथाप्यपरो हवनयोगो भवति ।।३२।। कुम्भीपाकादेव व्युद्धारं जुहुयात् ।।३३।। अधिश्रयणपर्यग्निकरणाभिघारणोद्वासनालंकरणोत्पवनैः संस्कृत्य ।।३४।। अथापि[17] श्लोकौ भवतः ।

आज्यभागान्तं प्राक्तन्त्रमूर्ध्वं स्विष्टकृता सह ।
हवींषि यज्ञ आवापो यथा तन्त्रस्य तन्तवः ।।
पाकयज्ञान्स[18]मासाद्यै[19]काज्यानेकबर्हिषः ।
एक[20]स्विष्टकृतः कुर्यान्नानापि सति दैवतेति[21] ।।३५।।

एतेनैवामावास्यो व्याख्यातः।।३६।। ऐन्द्राग्नोऽत्र द्वितीयो भवति।।३७।। तयोर्व्यतिक्रमे त्वमग्ने व्रतपा असि (१९.५९) कामस्तदग्रे (१९.५३) इति शान्ताः ।।३८।। //६//

अश्नात्यनादेशे स्थालीपाकः ।।१।। पुष्टिकर्मसु सारूपवत्से ।।२।। आज्यं जुहोति।।३।। समिधमादधाति।।४।। आवपति व्रीहियवतिलान् ।।५।। भक्षयति क्षीरौदनपुरोडाश[1]रसान् ।।६।। मन्थौदनौ प्रयछति[2] ।।७।। पूर्वं त्रिषप्तीयम् ।।८।। उदकचोदनायामुदपात्रं प्रतीयात् ।।९।। पुरस्तादुत्तरतः संभारमाहरति ।।१०।। गोरनभि-

---

14-14. This portion is wanting in Bh_3

15. Bl. gives a punctuation-mark between अन्ये देवा and ईड्या देवा and thus divides the sūtra in two parts.

16. G has some word between देवा and ब्राह्मणा, which is not clear.

17. D(text) अत्रापि

18. B_2 यज्ञान्त्स

19. Bh_3 द्येकाज्या

20. B_1, B_2 एकः

21. So emended by Bl., MSS देवतेति (with a double sandhi, see the note by Bl.)

1. V_2 has प्रयछति, as other MSS do; elsewhere it has च्छ,

2. Bh_3 पुरोलाश

प्रापा[3]द्वनस्पतीनाम् ॥११॥ सूर्योदयनत:[4] ॥१२॥ पुरस्तादुत्तरतोऽरण्ये कर्मणां प्रयोग: ॥१३॥ उत्तरत उदकान्ते प्रयुज्य कर्माण्यपां सूक्तैराप्लुत्य प्रदक्षिणमावृत्य अप उपस्पृश्यानवेक्षमाणा[5] ग्राममुदाव्रजन्ति ॥१४॥ आश्यबन्ध्याप्लवनयानभक्षाणि[6] संपातवन्ति ॥१५॥ सर्वाण्यभिमन्त्र्याणि[7] ॥१६॥ स्त्रीव्याधितावाप्लुतावसिक्तौ शिरस्त: प्रक्रम्या प्रपदात्प्रमार्ष्टि ॥१७॥ पूर्वं प्रपाद्य प्रयछति[8]॥१८॥ त्रयोदश्यादयस्तिस्रो दधिमधुनि वासयित्वा[9] बध्नाति ॥१९॥ आशयति ॥२०॥ अन्वारब्धायाभिमन्त्रणहोमा: ॥२१॥ पश्चादग्नेश्चर्मणि हविषां संस्कार: ॥२२॥ आनडुह:[10] शकृत्पिण्ड: ॥२३॥ जीवघात्यं चर्म ॥२४॥ अकर्णोऽश्मा ॥२५॥ आप्लवनावसेचनानामाचामयति च ॥२६॥ सम्पातवतामश्नाति न्यङ्क्ते वा ॥२७॥ अभ्याधेयानां धूमं नियछति[11] ॥२८॥ शुचिना कर्मप्रयोग: ॥२९॥ ॥७॥

पुरस्ताद्धोमवत्सु निशाकर्मसु पूर्वाह्णे यज्ञोपवीती[1] शालानिवेशनं समूहयत्युपवत्स्यद्भक्त[2]मशित्वा स्नातोऽहतबसन: प्रयुङ्क्ते ॥१॥ स्वस्त्ययनेषु च[3] ॥२॥ इज्यानां[4] दिश्यान्बलीन्हरति ॥३॥ प्रतिदिशमुपतिष्ठते ॥४॥ सर्वत्राधिकरणं कर्तुर्दक्षिणा ॥५॥ त्रिरुदकंक्रिया ॥६॥ अनन्तराणि[5] समानानि युक्तानि[6] ॥७॥ शान्तं सम्भारम् ॥८॥ अधिकृतस्य सर्वम् ॥९॥ विशये[7] यथान्तरम्[8] ॥१०॥ प्र यछ[9] पर्शुम्[10] (१२.३.३१) इति दर्भलवनं प्रयछति[11] ॥११॥

---

3. So Bh_4, G, B_1, B_2 and D(text); Bh_1, Bh_3, V_1, V_2 मनभिप्रायाद्
4. Bh_1, G सूर्योदयेनत:
5. B_1, B_2 वेक्ष्यमाणा; D(text) पेक्षमाणा but वेक्षमाणा in the gloss.
6. So all MSS, D(text), K(text) except V_2 which has भक्ष्याणि; B_1, भक्ष्याणि on the basis of his MSS K and Bu.
7. Bh_1, D(text and gloss) मंत्राणि
8. V_2 प्रयच्छति
9. Bh_1, Bh_3, B_1 वासइत्वा
10. Bh_1, Bh_4, G, B_2 अनडुहशकृत् D(text) आनदुहशकृत्
11. V_2 नियच्छति

1. Bh_1, G यज्ञोपवीति
2. B_1 °त्युपवश्यद्°
3. Bh_4वे (ज्यानां); wanting in D (text)
4. D (text and gloss to the next sūtra) ईह्यानां
5. D (text) अंतराणि
6. Wanting in D (text)
7. So emended by Bl. MSS विषये
8. Bh_1, G, B_2, V_2 यथोत्तरं 9. V_2 यच्छ
10. V_2 परशु° 11. V_2 प्रयच्छति

अरातीयोः (१०.६.१) इति तक्षति ॥१२॥ यत्त्वा शिक्वः (१०.६.३) इति प्रक्षालयति ॥१३॥ यद्यत्कृष्णः (१२.३.१३) इति मन्त्रोक्तम्॥१४॥ पलाशोदुम्बरजम्बुकाम्पीलस्रग्वङ्घशिरीषस्रक्त्यवरणबिल्वजङ्गिडकुटकगलावलवेतसशिम्बलसिपुनस्यन्दनारणिकाश्मयोक्ततुन्युपूतुदारवः[12] शान्ताः ॥१५॥ चितिप्रायश्चित्तिशमीशमका सवंशाशाम्यवाकातलाशापलाशवाशाशिंशपाशिम्बलसिपुनदर्भापामार्गाकृतिलोष्टवल्मीकवपादूर्वाप्रान्तव्रीहियवाः[12] शान्ताः ॥१६॥ प्रमन्दोशीरशलल्युपधानशकधूमा जरन्तः[13] ॥१७॥ सीस[14]नदीसीसे अयोरजाँसि कृकलासशिरः सीसानि ॥१८॥ दधि घृतं मधूदकमिति रसाः॥१९॥ व्रीहियवगोधूमोपवाकतिलप्रियङ्गुश्यामाका[12] इति मिश्रधान्यानि ॥२०॥ ग्रहणमाग्रहणात् ॥२१॥ यथार्थमुदर्कान्योजयेत् ॥२२॥ इहैव ध्रुवाम् (३.१२) एह यातु (६.७३) यमो मृत्युः (६.९३) सत्यं बृहत् (१२.१) इत्यनुवाको वास्तोष्पतीयानि ॥२३॥ दिव्यो गन्धर्वः (२.२) इमं मे अग्ने (६.१११) यौ ते माता (८.६) इति मातृनामानि ॥२४॥ स्तुवानम् (१.७) इदं हविः (१.८) निस्सालाम् (२.१४) अरायक्षयणम् (२.१८.३) शं नो देवी पृश्निपर्णी (२.-२५) आ पश्यति (४.२०) तान्त्सत्यौजाः (४.३६) त्वया पूर्वम् (४.३७) पुरस्ताद्युक्तः (५.२९) रक्षोहणम् (८.३-४) इत्यनुवाकश्चातनानि ॥२५॥ ॥८॥

अम्बयो यन्ति (१.४) शंभुमयोभू[1] (१.५,६) हिरण्यवर्णाः (१.३३) निस्सालाम् (२.१४) ये अग्नयः (३.२१.१-७) ब्रह्म जज्ञानम् (४.१.१) इत्येका उत देवाः[2] (४.१३) मृगारसूक्ता[3]न्युत्तमं

---

12. MSS have various corrupt readings, similar to those in the MSS collated by Bl. The text in Bl. is accepted here.

13. So in Bh_2, V_2 and Bl.; remaining MSS and D (text) चरंतः

14. Bh_1, Bh_3, G, B_2, V_1 सीसं

1. So all MSS. The reading may be corrected to शंयुमयोभू.

2. Bl. °मित्येका तदेव

3. Bl. divides the sūtra after मृगारसूक्तानि

वर्जयित्वा (४.२३-२९) अप नः शोशुचदघम् (४.३३) पुनन्तु मा (६.१९) सस्रुषीः (६.२३) हिमवतः प्र स्रवन्ति (६.२४) वायोः पूतः पवित्रेण (६.५१) शं च नो मयश्च नः (६.५७.३) अनड्डुद्भ्यस्त्वं प्रथमम् (६.५९) मह्यमापः (६.६१) वैश्वानरो रश्मिभिः (६.६२) यमो मृत्युः (६.९३) विश्वजित् (६.१०७) संज्ञानं नः (७.५२) यद्यन्तरिक्षे (७.६६) पुनर्मैत्विन्द्रियम् (७.६७) शिवा नः (७.६८.३) शं नो वातो वातु (७.६९) अग्निं ब्रूमो वनस्पतीन् (११.६) **इति** ।।१।। पृथिव्यै श्रोत्राय (६.१०) **इति त्रिः प्रत्यासिञ्चति** ।।२।। अम्बयो यन्ति (१.४) शंभुमयोभू[1] (१.५,६) हिरण्यवर्णाः (१.३३) **शंतातीयं** [4]-**च** (४.१३) यद्यन्तरिक्षे (७.६६) पुनर्मैत्विन्द्रियम्-[4] (७.६७) शिवा नः (७.६८.३) शं नो वातो वातु (७.६९) अग्निं ब्रूमो वनस्पतीन् (११.६) **इति** ।।३।। पृथिव्यै श्रोत्राय (६.१०) **इति त्रिः प्रत्यासिञ्चति** ।।४।। **इति शान्तियुक्तानि** ।।५।। **उभयतः सावित्र्युभयतः** शं नो देवी (१.६) ।।६।। **अहतवासाः कंसे शान्त्युदकं करोति** ।।७।। अतिसृष्टो अपां वृषभः (१६.१) **इत्यपोऽतिसृज्य** सर्वा इमा आप ओषधयः **इति पृष्ट्वा**[5] सर्वाः **इत्याख्यात**[6] ओं बृहस्पति[7]प्रसूतः[8] करवाणि **इत्यनुज्ञाप्य** ओं सवितृप्रसूतः कुरुतां[9] भवान् **इत्यनुज्ञातः कुर्वीत** ।।८।। **पूर्वया कुर्वीतेति गार्ग्यपार्थश्रवसभागालिकाङ्कायनोपरिबभ्रवकौशिकजाटिकायनकौरुपथयः** ।।९।। **अन्यतरया कुर्वीतेति युवा कौशिको युवा कौशिकः** ।।१०।। ।।९।।

।। [10]इति कौशिकसूत्रे प्रथमोऽध्यायः समाप्तः[10] ।।

4-4. Curiously enough, this portion is wanting in Bl. All MSS have unanimous reading as given above.

5. Bh_2, Bh_3, B_1, B_2 सृष्ट्वा

6. So Bh_4 and Bl.; remaining MSS आख्याता

7. Bh_2, Bh_4, B_1, B_2 बृहस्पतिः

8. Bh_3 प्रसूत

9. So all MSS and D (text); the word is wanting in Bl. The word कुरुतां was omitted in Bl. probably due to an oversight. The विसर्ग in सवितृप्रसूतः is retained, though it is followed by भ in the subsequent word.

10-10. MSS have different colophons at the end of the Adhyāya.